Germany since 1945

STUDIES IN CONTEMPORARY HISTORY

Series Editors: T. G. Fraser and J. O. Springhall

PUBLISHED

THE ARAB–ISRAELI CONFLICT, THIRD EDITION   *T. G. Fraser*

AMERICA AND THE WORLD SINCE 1945 *T. G. Fraser and Donette Murray*

THE ULSTER QUESTION SINCE 1945, SECOND EDITION
James Loughlin

GERMANY SINCE 1945 *Pól O'Dochartaigh*

THE RISE AND FALL OF THE SOVIET EMPIRE,
SECOND EDITION
Raymond Pearson

THE CIVIL RIGHTS MOVEMENT: Struggle and Resistance,
SECOND EDITION
William T. Martin Riches

THE UNITED NATIONS AND INTERNATIONAL POLITICS
Stephen Ryan

JAPAN SINCE 1945
Dennis B. Smith

DECOLONIZATION SINCE 1945
John Springhall

Studies in Contemporary History
Series Standing Order
ISBN 0–333–71706–6 hardcover
ISBN 0–333–69351–5 paperback
(*outside North America only*)

You can receive future titles in this series as they are published by placing a standing order. Please contact your bookseller or, in the case of difficulty, write to us at the address below with your name and address, the title of the series and the ISBN quoted above.

Customer Services Department, Macmillan Distribution Ltd
Houndmills, Basingstoke, Hampshire RG21 6XS, England

GERMANY SINCE 1945

PÓL O'DOCHARTAIGH

First published 2004 by
PALGRAVE MACMILLAN
Houndmills, Basingstoke, Hampshire RG21 6XS and
175 Fifth Avenue, New York, N.Y. 10010
Companies and representatives throughout the world

PALGRAVE MACMILLAN is the global academic imprint of the Palgrave Macmillan division of St. Martin's Press, LLC and of Palgrave Macmillan Ltd. Macmillan® is a registered trademark in the United States, United Kingdom and other countries. Palgrave is a registered trademark in the European Union and other countries.

ISBN-13: 978-978-0-333-96471-2 hardback
ISBN-13: 978-0-333-96472-9 paperback
ISBN-10: 0-333-96471-3 hardback
ISBN-10: 0-333-96472-1 paperback

This book is printed on paper suitable for recycling and made from fully managed and sustained forest sources. Logging, pulping and manufacturing processes are expected to conform to the environmental regulations of the country of origin.

Library of Congress Cataloging-in-Publication Data

O'Dochartaigh, Pól.
    Germany since 1945 / Pól O'Dochartaigh.
        p. cm. – (Studies in contemporary history)
    Includes bibliographical references and index.
    ISBN 0-333-96471-3—ISBN 0-333-96472-1 (pbk.)
        1. Germany—History—1945–1990. 2. Germany—History—
Unification, 1990. 3. Germany (East)—History. 4. Cold war. 5. German
reunification question (1949–1990) 6. Germany—History—1990–
I. Title. II. Studies in contemporary history (Palgrave (Firm))

DD258.3.O36 2003
943.087—dc21

                                                                    2003046955

A catalogue record for this book is available from the British Library.

Printed in Great Britain by the MPG Books Group, Bodmin and King's Lynn

For two mentors who have become friends,
Dr Colin Walker of Belfast
and
Professor Ian Wallace of Carlisle and Bath

CONTENTS

Contents

Contents

Contents

Contents

SERIES EDITORS' PREFACE

There are those, politicians among them, who feel that historians should not teach or write about contemporary events and people – many of whom are still living – because of the difficulty of treating such matters with historical perspective, and that it is right to draw some distinction between the study of history and the study of current affairs. Proponents of this view seem to be unaware of the concept of contemporary history to which this series is devoted, that the history of the recent past can and should be written with a degree of objectivity. As memories of the Second World War recede, it is surely time to place in perspective the postwar history that has shaped all our lives, whether we were born in the 1940s or the 1970s.

Many countries – Britain, the United States and Germany among them – allow access to their public records under a thirty-year rule, opening up much of the postwar period to archival research. For more recent events, diaries, memoirs, and the investigations of newspapers and television, confirm the view of the famous historian Sir Lewis Namier that all secrets are in print provided you know where to look for them. Contemporary historians also have the opportunity, denied to historians of earlier periods, of interviewing participants in the events they are analysing. The problem facing the contemporary historian is, if anything, the embarrassment of riches.

In any case, the nature and extent of world changes since the late 1980s have clearly signalled the need for concise discussion of major themes in post-1945 history. For many of us the difficult thing to grasp is how dramatically the world has changed over recent years: the end of the Cold War and of Soviet hegemony over eastern Europe; the collapse of the Soviet Union and Russian communism; the unification of Germany; the pace of integration in the European Union; the disintegration of Yugoslavia; political and economic turbulence in South-East Asia; communist China's reconciliation with consumer capitalism; the faltering economic progress of Japan. Writing in a structured and cogent way about these seismic changes is what makes contemporary history so challenging, and we hope that the end result will convey some of this excitement and interest to our readers.

The general objective of this series is to offer concise and up-to-date treatments of postwar themes considered of historical and political significance, and to stimulate critical thought about the theoretical assumptions and conceptual apparatus underlying interpretation of the topics under discussion. The series should bring some of the central themes and problems confronting students and teachers of recent history, politics and international affairs into sharper focus than the textbook writer alone could provide. The blend required to write contemporary history that is both readable and easily understood but also accurate and scholarly is not easy to achieve, but we hope that this series will prove worthwhile for both students and teachers interested in world affairs since 1945.

University of Ulster at Coleraine T. G. FRASER

J. O. SPRINGHALL

ACKNOWLEDGEMENTS

I am grateful to my colleagues in both the School of Languages and Literature and the School of History and International Relations at the University of Ulster for their support in the writing of this book. I am particularly indebted to my colleague in German Studies, Dr Ian Connor, for his insights and comments at various stages. My thanks also to the Faculty of Arts Research Committee under the directorship of Dr John Gillespie for granting me a period of study leave to complete this book, to the series editors for suggesting this book when I had a different plan, and to my students of GDR history and of German area studies for their sometimes insightful and stimulating questions.

For their continued love and support I also wish to thank, as always, Geraldine Cuskelly and my parents, Elizabeth and John Doherty.

LIST OF ABBREVIATIONS

AFL-CIO	American Federation of Labor and Congress of Industrial Organisations
Apo	Opposition outside parliament
BDL	Bank of German States
Benelux	Belgium, Netherlands and Luxemburg
BHE	League of Expellees
BND	'Federal News Service' (West German Secret Service)
BRD	Federal Republic of Germany
BVG	Federal Constitutional Court
BVP	Bavarian People's Party
CDU	Christian Democratic Union
Comecon	Council for Mutual Economic Aid
CPSU	Communist Party of the Soviet Union
CSCE	Conference on Security and Co-operation in Europe
CSU	Christian Social Union
DA	Democratic Awakening
DBD	Democratic Farmers' Party
DEFA	East German Film Production Company
DGB	(West) German Federation of Trade Unions
DKP	German Communist Party
DNVP	German National People's Party
DP	German Party
DRP	German Reich Party
DSU	German Social Union
DVU	German People's Union
EDC	European Defence Community

EEC	European Economic Community
EKD	Protestant Church in Germany
ERM	(European) Exchange Rate Mechanism
EU	European Union
FDJ	Free German Youth
FDP	Free Democratic Party
FRG	Federal Republic of Germany
FU	Free University Berlin
GAZ	Green Action for the Future
GDP	Gross Domestic Product
GDR	German Democratic Republic
GNP	Gross National Product
GSG9	Elite West German Military Unit
IM	Informal collaborator (with the Stasi)
IRA	Irish Republican Army
JCS	Joint Chiefs of Staff
KFOR	Kosovo Force
KoKo	Commercial Co-ordination (in the GDR)
KPD	Communist Party of Germany
LDPD	Liberal Democratic Party of Germany
LPG	Agricultural collective
NATO	North Atlantic Treaty Organisation
NDPD	National Democratic Party of Germany (GDR)
NÖSPL	New Economic System of Planning and Leadership
NPD	National Democratic Party of Germany (FRG)
OAPEC	Organisation of Arab Petroleum Exporting Countries
ÖSS	Economic System of Socialism
PDS	Party of Democratic Socialism
PR	Proportional representation
RAF	Red Army Faction
SALT	Strategic Arms Limitation Treaty
SDI	Strategic Defense Initiative ('Star Wars')
SDS	Socialist German Student Union
SED	Socialist Unity Party of Germany

SFOR	Stabilisation force (in Bosnia–Herzegovina)
SHB	Social Democratic University Union
SPD	Social Democratic Party of Germany
Stasi	State Security Service (of the GDR)
TUC	Trades Union Congress (Britain)
UK	United Kingdom
UN	United Nations
VAT	Value added tax (Purchase Tax)
VDS	Union of German Student Unions
WEU	West European Union

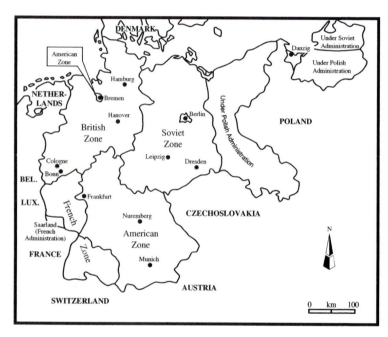

Map 1 *Germany under occupation after 1945*

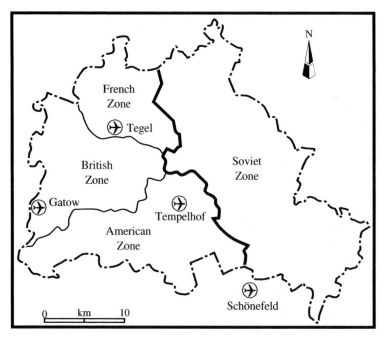

Map 2 *Berlin: the four sectors*

Map 3 *Reunified Germany after 1990*

INTRODUCTION: GERMANY BEFORE 1945

Before the twentieth century was even half over Germany had led Europe and the world into two wars of mass destruction in which over seventy million people died. By 1945 its neighbours were not inclined to trust a country that had visited such a degree of death and destruction on them. The reconstruction of Europe was a mammoth undertaking, as was also the rebuilding and recivilising of Germany, especially since some of its neighbours would have preferred to dismantle rather than reconstruct it. Most of all, however, there was a determination that such wars should never again emanate from German soil. If this were to happen, then a range of issues would have to be addressed.

Germany in 1945 was still a relatively young country. Only in 1871 was it united for the first time after centuries of existence as a loose grouping of kingdoms, principalities, dukedoms and city states. Prussia was dominant, a state that had its origins in the territory of Brandenburg around Berlin but which on unification stretched from Memel in the far north-east (in today's Lithuania) to the Rhineland and the French border in the south-west. In addition, united Germany included Alsace-Lorraine and stretched from Schleswig-Holstein in the north to Bavaria in the south, though the great German power of the previous centuries, Austria, had been excluded from the moves towards unification by defeat in a war with Prussia in 1866. In January 1871 in Versailles near Paris, after the French had been roundly defeated in war, the Prussian king became the first emperor, or Kaiser, of the new Germany, as Wilhelm I. German unity came from war.

Yet Prussia, and therefore the new Germany, was more militarist than democratic. Created on territory taken from Slav peoples over centuries of colonisation by Germans, Prussia was a state that had very strong cultural and social ties with eastern Europe and which was in some ways removed from western European values. Its leadership was largely in the hands of princes and dukes who held land and had traditionally provided military support for the king, a breed of marcher lords almost. One of them, Otto von Bismarck, engineered German unity and then its colonial expansion into Africa and the Far East. Prussia had accepted the Protestant reformation and provided refuge for many French Protestants in the eighteenth century, but at a time when western Europe was moving towards broad male suffrage and liberal democracy, Germany was not firmly rooted in western democratic ideals: many conservatives saw a specifically German path in history, a *Sonderweg*, as it has come to be called. Right up until 1918 this attitude was rooted in the idea that Germany must continually expand its territory, subjecting neighbouring peoples on the way, while tolerating only a limited form of democracy with a class-based suffrage at home.

After defeat in the First World War Germany lost territory to France, Belgium, Denmark, Poland and Lithuania. The Kaiser abdicated at the end of the war and a republic was created, but there was no real change in political attitudes. Though democratic elections were held in the new Weimar Republic, named after the small Thuringian town in which the constitution was promulgated, many parties played the democratic game in order merely to subvert it. Economic recessions in 1923 and 1929 also destabilised the system, compounded by resentment at the punitive reparations demanded of Germany and the charge that Germany was solely to blame for World War I. Many militarists propagated the myth that Germany's soldiers had been 'stabbed in the back' by politicians at home while remaining undefeated on the battlefield. Weimar was a democracy with few democrats, where many people retained their pre-1918 convictions. Its political system was also inherently unstable, with few votes needed in order to gain representation in parliament and no single party ever able to dominate, so that the composition of government coalitions changed regularly.

It was a combination of these factors that created the conditions that led to the Nazi rise to power. Germany sank into barbarism in 1933, and the nature of that barbarity became clearer and more horrific with each passing year of the 1930s and early 1940s. The mass murder of some six million Jews in what has come to be known as the Holocaust stands out as the most horrific single example in history of systematically organised mass killing. The racist ideology that lay behind that killing was a twisted pseudo-scientific set of theories that had their roots in European anti-Semitism, but the same theories were also used to justify killing millions of supposedly 'inferior' Poles, Russians and other so-called 'non-Aryans', too. By 1945 some 55 million people had died in the conflict, of whom 20 million alone were Soviet citizens. By 1945 Germany was a pariah and the German people were branded as uncivilised, for there had been only minimal resistance to Hitler from within the country, even if some Germans in exile fought and lost their lives fighting Nazism.

The task facing the Allies and the Germans in 1945 was to create a political system and foster a set of attitudes in Germany that would ensure that this could never happen again. Nazism, militarism and racism would have to be eradicated, to be replaced by a democracy that would be stable and lead to no more wars. Democratisation should lead to a Germany that would co-operate with rather than fight its neighbours and that would share Europe instead of always coveting its neighbours' territory. That was the challenge.

3

1

DEFEAT, OCCUPATION AND DIVISION, 1945–9

Whither Germany?

In May 1945, when Hitler's armies had finally been defeated, there was no obvious future for Germany, just a terrible legacy. The country was devastated, with a scarcity of food, fuel and housing and millions of refugees scattered throughout the country. Normal life had broken down and millions had died. The victorious Allies had worked out an agreement on the occupation of Germany, but there was little certainty about what would come after this. The Germans were a defeated people, not a liberated one, and the Allies were agreed that Germans should be made to pay for the horrendous crimes that had been committed by them and in their name. They agreed that 'democracy' should be established in Germany, but there was no single concept of 'democracy'. Various leaders talked of breaking Germany up into a number of smaller states, but they could not agree how this should be done. 1945 was a beginning not just for Germans, but for the Allies as well. The 'Anti-Hitler Coalition' of the war years now found itself facing the much harder task of trying to agree on what they were *for*, rather than simply what they were *against*. It was no easy task; indeed, some might regard it as an impossible task, though such an assertion may be to pander too much to the benefit of hindsight.

The Allies had agreed in 1944 in the so-called London Protocols of the European Advisory Commission to divide

4

Germany into zones of occupation, while also dividing Berlin into sectors. Austria, which had been incorporated into Germany in 1938, was immediately separated and occupied separately, its independence being restored in 1955. Germany was divided under the First London Protocol, on 12 September 1944, into three zones of occupation, which were allocated to the Soviet Union (in the east), the USA (in the south) and Britain (in the north and west). The Second Protocol, of 14 November 1944, regulated the terms of Three-Power control. On the same date a French Zone in the south-west was agreed, to be carved from parts of the US and British zones, though France did not sign up to the Protocols until 1 May 1945. Berlin, located geographically entirely within the Soviet Zone, was divided into four sectors, with the Soviets taking the East (including the central government district), while the other Allies were in the West. Some of the lines on the map, which initially delineated areas of control during the Allied Occupation of Germany, later came to demarcate a more lasting division of Germany into two mutually hostile states.

This future was not obvious in 1945. The Berlin Declaration of 5 June 1945 stated that the Allies would now take over 'supreme authority with respect to Germany'. The terms of the Occupation had previously been decided, but most of the political decisions were made at the Potsdam Conference, held from 17 July to 2 August 1945 in the castle of Sanssouci in Potsdam, near Berlin. It was attended by Churchill, Truman and Stalin, but not by any French leader.

The conference decided on a range of measures for Germany, including what became known as the five Ds: Demilitarisation, Denazification, Democratisation, Disarmament and Decentralisation. Despite the last of these, there would be central administrations for finance, transport, foreign trade and industry. Germany was to be treated as an economic unit and its industry would be controlled. Whereas its armaments industries were to be eliminated, its agriculture and non-military industries would be promoted.

It was decided that German living standards should remain below those of its neighbours. Germany would also pay reparations, with the Soviet Union, as the country most devastated by the war, to receive the most, including some from the western zones. Nearly one-quarter of German territory, including such famous cities as Königsberg and Breslau as well as the 'Free City' of Danzig, was given over to Polish or Soviet 'administration', because Stalin wanted to compensate the Poles for territory taken from them under the Hitler–Stalin Pact of 1939. The Oder–Neisse Line, named after the two rivers along which it runs, became the new Polish–German frontier, though its legality was disputed by West Germany until 1990. Most Germans in Poland who had not already fled the advancing Red Army, as well as the German minorities in Czechoslovakia and Hungary, were forcibly expelled to Germany.

The unified Allied Kommandatura in Berlin had begun operating on 11 July 1945. The Allied Control Council for the whole of Germany began functioning formally on 30 August 1945. The principle of unanimity was to prevail on matters that related to Germany as a whole. Germany was to be treated as a single economic unit, 'a principle which clashed with the supremacy of each zonal commander within his own sphere' (Dennis, 2000, p. 4). On 7 August 1945, France had agreed to the Potsdam Conference decisions 'with reservations', in particular in relation to the planned central administrations, and the creation of these was vetoed by France in the autumn of 1945.

Nevertheless, essentially unified structures for the administration of Germany had been put in place. The Potsdam Conference and the establishment of these structures appeared to show that the alliance between the Western powers and the Soviet Union had survived the defeat of Hitler despite all of the differences of opinion over the type of Germany that should be created. Despite this, no one at the time was under any illusions about the difficulties that lay ahead.

Democratisation

If Nazism was to be successfully eradicated from German life, then the establishment of democratic political parties was of paramount importance. As early as 11 June 1945, the first political party in postwar Germany was founded, the Communist Party (KPD) in Berlin. It was followed on 15 June by the Social Democratic Party (SPD) in Berlin, the Christian Democratic Union in Cologne (17 June) and Berlin (26 June), the Liberal Democratic Party in Berlin on 5 July, the Christian Social Union in Bavaria on 13 October and the Free Democratic Party in Bavaria on 30 November. These parties came to dominate political life in all parts of Germany.

The Communist Party, which had been the third-strongest party in the 1930s and was banned by Hitler in 1933, had maintained an underground existence in Germany throughout the Nazi period, in addition to functioning in both Soviet and Western exile as a focus for anti-Nazi activity. The declaration of 11 June was made by two of its most prominent Moscow exiles, Walter Ulbricht and Anton Ackermann. In it the party called for the democratisation of Germany in terms that were more bourgeois than communist: it specifically referred to the bourgeois revolution of 1848 in Germany rather than the Bolshevik revolution of 1917 in Russia as the way forward for Germany at this time. The party wanted land reform, a democratic civil service and a new education system. It spoke of a specific German path to socialism, expressly rejecting Sovietisation. The declaration can be seen as a clear appeal to a new middle ground in German politics.

By contrast, the Social Democrats, who had been the largest party in Weimar Germany, overtaken by the Nazis only in 1932 and also banned by Hitler in 1933, spoke openly of the need to nationalise key industries, the banks and the land, and clearly espoused an anti-capitalist programme. Their leader in the Western zones, Kurt

Schumacher, attempted to broaden the base of the party beyond the industrial working class towards the self-employed and middle classes. He also vehemently defended the interests of Germany and the cause of equal treatment for Germans, taking the moral right to do this from his party's opposition to Hitler: SPD members, including himself, were in Nazi concentration camps when the Americans, British and Russians were still courting Hitler's Germany (Nicholls, 1997, pp. 37–8). Schumacher's organisational skills and stout defence of Germany led to a remarkable flow of new members for the party.

The founding of two essentially working-class parties led to much debate about the need for working-class unity. Many rank-and-file members of both parties had always favoured co-operation or even unification of the two parties, and in the final days of the Nazi period they joined with each other and with other anti-Nazi individuals to create so-called 'antifa' (i.e. antifascist) groups to take over the civil administration from the Nazis. This was in part a response to events in the early 1930s, when Social Democrats and Communists had sometimes been more intent on fighting each other than on fighting the Nazis.

Despite this, the leaders and some of the ordinary members of the two parties were filled with mutual distrust. Aside from the historical differences that dated back to the 1920s and 1930s, the Communists had accepted the Allies' plans for postwar Germany, whereas the Social Democrats, as we have seen, opposed them. Initially, the Berlin leadership of the SPD under Otto Grotewohl advocated unity with the KPD, but this was rejected both by the western SPD and by the Communist Party. However, within six months the increase in membership and support for the SPD in the Soviet Zone, which threatened to overshadow the KPD, led to the latter moving towards a position of support for unity by late 1945. The Soviets also supported this, and pressure was applied on SPD members. Eventually, in April 1946, the SPD and KPD in the Soviet Zone were amalgamated as the

SED (Socialist Unity Party of Germany). The official leaders were Wilhelm Pieck for the Communists and Otto Grotewohl for the Social Democrats, but power was effectively concentrated in Pieck's hands, and within a couple of years Social Democrats were being purged from the unified party. In the West, the SPD became the dominant party of the left, with the KPD reduced to the status of a splinter group.

Liberalism was re-established in Germany in 1945 by various diverse groups with a range of names, including the Liberal Democratic Party in Berlin, the German People's Party in the south-west, and the Free Democratic Party in Bavaria. These parties were heterogeneous groupings, containing left–liberals, national liberals, and even secular conservatives. In 1948 the various groups in the western zones united under the name Free Democratic Party (FDP), while in the Soviet Zone the name Liberal Democratic Party of Germany (LDPD) was retained.

Conservatism in pre-1933 Germany had been divided into many factions as well as by religion: the Centre Party had been Catholic, the Bavarian People's Party (BVP) a separatist Catholic party, the German National People's Party (DNVP) a largely Protestant conservative party. Active opposition to the Nazis in conservative circles had been limited: both major churches had welcomed the Nazi assumption of power in 1933, and only with time did some of the clergy begin to oppose. After 1945 the Centre Party tried to re-establish itself, but without success. A new 'Bavarian Party' enjoyed some initial success in Bavaria but declined throughout the 1950s and eventually all but disappeared.

Instead, the forces of Christian conservatism in all four zones of occupation were realigned under the banner of Christian Democracy. In 1945 Christian Democratic parties were established throughout Germany, especially in Berlin, Frankfurt and Cologne. The name taken by the Berlin grouping, the Christian Democratic Union (CDU), was eventually adopted as the name for all of Germany except

Bavaria, where a more conservative and anti-centralist (though not separatist) group, the Christian Social Union (CSU), has maintained a separate party organisation. It carries the banner of Christian Democracy in Bavaria in all elections, including federal ones, while the CDU fights elections in the rest of Germany.

The CDU was thus an attempt at overcoming confessional differences in the name of adherence to a common western, Christian cultural heritage that had been subsumed by the evil of Nazism in Germany. Politically, the party covered a spectrum from Christian socialism through liberal—conservative reformism to conservative nationalism. The group founded in Berlin in 1945 spoke of Christian Socialism, and the 'Ahlen Programme' of 1947 moderated this critique of capitalism only slightly. By 1949, however, the influence of the dominant figure in the CDU in the western zones, the former mayor of Cologne, Konrad Adenauer, led to the adoption of the Düsseldorf Principles. These were based on the principle of a 'social market economy', advocated by the economist and later West German Minister for the Economy, Ludwig Erhard. He sought to combine basic free market economic principles with a social 'safety net' for the less privileged in society. This is discussed further below.

Other parties at this time were essentially splinter groups. The German Party (DP) started as a separatist party in the Hanover region, and with the establishment of the state of Lower Saxony it allied itself to the CDU, gaining election to the first West German parliament in 1949 and participating in government throughout the 1950s. In the Soviet Zone in 1948 a Farmers' Party (DBD) was established, as well as a National Democratic Party (NDPD), which sought to recruit former Nazis to the cause of socialism. This was in part an attempt to dilute the influence of the CDU and LDPD, which were resisting attempts to impose SED control. The battle for separate policies was finally lost in 1949 when all parties in the East were integrated into the SED-led National Front, which put up single lists of candidates for election.

Political life was thus re-established in two very different ways in the eastern and western parts of Germany, despite the creation of ostensibly similar party structures. In the West a multi-party democracy was created with parties of the left, right and centre and elections based on real choice. In the East, the same parties were initially created, but the two big parties of the left were forcibly amalgamated as early as 1946, and the other parties were forced to toe the Soviet line. The contrast is a clear indication of the division that was rapidly being created in Germany after 1945.

Denazification

At Potsdam a method of dealing with Nazi war criminals had essentially been agreed between the Allies. The Nuremberg Trials, deliberately held in what was regarded as the symbolic capital of Nazism, the scene of Hitler's annual mass rally, were a way of dealing with some of the leadership of the Nazi movement. Many, such as Hitler, Goebbels and Himmler, had escaped justice by committing suicide, but others, such as Goering, Hess and Field Marshals Keitel and Jodl remained to face the court. Some 22 people faced trial, of whom three were acquitted (against the vote of the Soviet judge) and twelve were sentenced to death, the others receiving varying terms in prison. Goering escaped the death penalty by committing suicide in his cell, while Martin Bormann was tried and sentenced in his absence. The other ten death sentences were carried out after the end of the trials, on 1 October 1946.

The Nuremberg Trials were an extremely symbolic event, but they were only the beginning of the problem of addressing the legacy of Nazi rule, at the end of which the party had had some 8 million members, with another 4 million members of associated organisations. The Nazi Party had governed the country for twelve years, and its pernicious ideology had permeated the very core of German society.

The Allies' common aim was to re-establish democracy, though they had differing interpretations of the word. Nevertheless, they were agreed that establishing a democratic system meant eliminating both Nazi ideology and those who had played a significant role in the Nazi movement. 'Denazification' was the name given to this process.

The process was not without its problems. In the US Zone denazification was taken so seriously that a number of directives were issued, initially disqualifying members of a range of Nazi organisations from holding administrative posts after 1945. Thousands of people were arrested in all zones and placed in internment camps. By September 1945 some 66,000 people had been interned in the American Zone alone, while by the end of 1946 a quarter of a million people had been interned throughout Germany.

The US deputy military governor General Lucius D. Clay launched an ambitious questionnaire by means of which individuals could be put into one of five categories: (1) major offenders, (2) offenders, (3) lesser offenders, (4) fellow travellers, and (5) exonerated. By March 1946, 1.3 million questionnaires had been returned. In October 1946 this categorisation became mandatory for the whole of Germany. Yet the sheer weight of numbers made it almost impossible to deal with every single case. Up to 1950 more than 6 million people were investigated in the three western zones, of whom more than 5 million were either amnestied or exonerated (Glees, 1996, p. 33). Nevertheless, more than a million people were put into the other four categories and punished, though only 1667 were classed as 'major offenders'.

In this period only 486 death penalties were carried out, across all four zones, while many thousands more people were imprisoned, usually for relatively short periods: almost all were amnestied by 1951. Yet the feeling remained that the process was unjust. Many of those punished had played a very minor role during the Nazi years. By contrast, the steel baron Gustav Krupp, who had bankrolled the Nazi Party and much of Hitler's war effort, escaped prosecution by being declared senile, though he lived for another four years. Others in middle-ranking roles also escaped punishment because, as has been shown in recent years, they were deemed useful to the various occupying powers. Easier cases were often dealt with first, so that those who were most culpable were dealt with later when more leniency had begun to be applied.

Some felt that the process amounted to little more than 'victors' justice', and complained that the Allies, who had dropped atomic bombs on Hiroshima and Nagasaki, blanket bombed Dresden or massacred civilians in the way Stalin had, had no moral authority in the matter. Some had problems coming to terms with the Nazi legacy and their own role in it. Others wished simply to forget those twelve years and move on. Alexander Mitscherlich wrote years later of the Germans' 'inability to mourn'. Still others abused the process to denounce neighbours with whom they had disagreements. Many who had been exonerated by the system used their certificates to gain employment while those not yet investigated remained under suspicion, causing more resentment – it thus seemed that individuals were being 'cleansed', rather than society as a whole. These certificates were known as 'Persil certificates', because Persil 'makes browns white again', according to an advertisement at the time. Brown was the Nazi colour, white symbolises innocence.

In the Soviet Zone, denazification was not initially carried out in a uniform way. Thus, in some southern states, minor Nazis were allowed to remain in post provided they subjected themselves to political and ideological indoctrination, while in the northern states of Brandenburg and Mecklenburg all Nazis were liable to dismissal. The Soviets, like their western counterparts, came to use a degree of pragmatism in their dismissal policies. Whereas almost all teachers, lawyers and public administrators who had been Nazi Party members were removed from office, a large number of doctors and engineers were allowed to remain in post, though many chose to flee to the West.

Denazification in the Soviet Zone was ended in April 1948 by order of the Soviet Military Administration. By this time some 450,000 people had been dismissed. The process there may be seen, together with the heroisation of communist resistance to the Nazis, as part of a determined effort to create the antifascist myth that was essential to the GDR's self-legitimacy when it came into being in 1949. By contrast, in the West, it came to be seen as an intolerable and unjust burden that dragged on for far too long. In the western zones no new cases for denazification were taken on after 1 January 1949. In 1950 the West Germans effectively declared the process of denazification over, though the prosecution of individual war crimes would continue. The statute of limitations was later lifted, and it does not now apply in any way to war crimes. Nevertheless, of almost 104,000 people investigated for war crimes between 1945 and 1992, only 6 per cent were convicted (Glees, 1996, p. 31).

Denazification was founded in the belief that the ideology of Nazism must be swept aside if Germany was to become a democratic society. Initially, members of organisations were targeted on the basis that those organisations were criminal. Later, individuals were investigated since, it was felt, many Nazi Party members were probably less culpable than some who had remained outside the party. The injustices of the process have been outlined here. It might also be noted that all sides found some Germans who could be useful to them in the postwar period, especially as tensions between the Eastern and Western Allies increased, and helped them to avoid investigation and punishment. Ultimately, the incomplete nature of the task was its biggest failing. Pragmatism ruled the day, since all sides needed experienced Germans who would co-operate in the running of the country. Some, such as the British General Sir Brian Robertson, felt that putting large numbers of ex-Nazis out of work could lead to security problems, whereas retaining them could generate loyalty. Whether the process helped or retarded the process of coming to terms with the legacy of Nazism is still the subject of dispute.

Stalinisation in the East

We have already seen how political life was re-established in Germany, and how, despite the existence of a range of parties in the Soviet Zone, most were forced to toe the Soviet line by 1948 at the latest. In particular, the merger of the Social Democratic and Communist Parties in 1946 drove a wedge between the political left in the East and West. The western SPD, led by the fiercely anti-communist Kurt Schumacher, fundamentally rejected this amalgamation. In the one place where a free vote on the subject was allowed among SPD members, the western sectors of Berlin, a 72 per cent turnout showed an overwhelming majority (87 per cent) opposed to immediate unification with the Communists, though a large majority (73 per cent) favoured co-operation between the parties

The popularity of the SED was tested in state elections that were held throughout the Soviet Zone in September 1946. Despite polling 48 per cent of the vote, it failed to achieve an outright majority in any single state. In still-united Berlin its performance was disastrous, polling just 19 per cent, far behind the SPD on 49 per cent and even behind the CDU on 22 per cent. Even in the Soviet Sector of Berlin the SED managed just 30 per cent. 'The party's poor performance was attributable not only to its own policies but also to its close identification with the Soviet Union' (Dennis, 2000, p. 27).

The SED in 1947 seemed at times to be lacking a clear sense of direction. Some of the first political measures after May 1945, despite being seen by some historians since then as communist, were not necessarily Marxist in their thrust. Many Germans supported the idea of expropriating Nazis, war criminals and those who had prospered under the Nazi regime. The Soviets went further, regarding, for example, the whole class of large landowners (Junkers) as a mainstay of Nazism and using this excuse to expropriate all farms larger than 100 hectares (around 250 acres) as early as September 1945. Most of the land was redistributed in small parcels, but frequently these proved too small to be viable, and farmers were dependent on the state for the machinery needed to work the farms. Many simply left the land untilled. In the 1950s these farms were more or less forcibly collectivised.

In October 1945 the Soviet Military Administration ordered the confiscation of the property of the German state, the armed forces and the Nazi Party. In addition, enterprises belonging to Nazis and war criminals were expropriated without compensation after a referendum in Saxony in March 1946 – some 78 per cent voted in favour of this measure (Fulbrook, 1991, p. 155). This mandate was used to justify similar measures in all states in the Soviet Zone without recourse to further votes. It was the first of many moves towards redistributing wealth in the Soviet Zone, most of which ultimately led to greater state control.

Such measures were initially popular, though it is probable that the popularity was due to a desire to punish Nazis rather than support communism. Soviet-owned companies were created from much of the expropriated property, while nationalised industries became an ever more important element in the economic life of the Soviet Zone: by mid-1948, nationalised and Soviet-owned companies together accounted for some 61 per cent of the Zone's GDP. By then, the economic life of the Soviet Zone was being co-ordinated by the 'German Economic Commission', which had been created in June 1947 and restructured in March 1948. Essentially, the foundations of a planned economy were being laid in the Soviet Zone in this period, though it would be some years before it was fully implemented. Such a planned economy involved state ownership of all large factories, mines and banks, strict regulation of foreign trade, price fixing, and centrally devised economic plans for the production of goods. These plans usually ran for five to seven years. Thus the economic thrust was in the direction of the Soviet economic system and directly opposed to the kind of market economics that existed in the USA or the UK.

Since the last days of the war the Soviets had been subverting attempts to build a strong economy in the Soviet Zone by insisting on large-scale reparations payments. Whole factories were dismantled and transported to the Soviet Union to help rebuild the shattered Soviet economy, reparations payments were made from what remained of current production, and the Germans had to contribute to the costs of the occupation. Soviet policy passed through three phases in respect of reparations. From March 1945 until summer 1946, factories that produced consumer goods and arms were dismantled and taken away, while trained teams searched for treasures to confiscate. However, many factories were not reassembled when they reached Russia, so that in the second phase, Soviet-owned companies in the Zone (discussed above) were created instead. After dismantling stopped completely in the summer of 1948, the Soviets concentrated on obtaining a large portion of industrial output, much of it from engineering firms. The damage inflicted on the economy of the Soviet Zone is estimated at over 30 per cent of the zone's 1944 industrial capacity (Dennis, 2000, pp. 41–2).

If the uncertainty about SED policies that existed in 1945–6 was replaced by a clear move towards planned economic structures, so too the pluralist politics both of the zone and of the SED were gradually replaced by a uniform Marxist–Leninist position. Some in the party had favoured a Soviet model, while others such as Anton Ackermann espoused a specifically German path to socialism. Many ex-SPD members retained their belief in social democracy rather than Marxism, and there were also 'ultra-leftists', those who had been in various smaller communist and Trotskyist parties before 1933.

The Stalinisation of the party began in late 1946 and continued through to the adoption of a Bolshevik model in January 1949. Some oppositionists had been interned as early as 1945 together with Nazi war criminals, and many SPD and even KPD members now found themselves placed in internment camps, some of which, such as Buchenwald and Sachsenhausen, had been Nazi concentration camps. Approximately 150,000 Germans were interned between 1945 and 1950, of whom almost 43,000 died and nearly 13,000 were sent to the Soviet Union, many of them because of political opposition to the Soviets rather than support for Nazism. In 1947 Stalin reacted to the independent communist line being pursued by Tito in Yugoslavia by stamping his authority on other communist parties. In June 1948 Otto Grotewohl described the SED as a 'Marxist–Leninist party' (Staritz, 1996, p. 26). In July 1948 a series of purges and expulsions was launched that continued well into the 1950s. In September 1948 Ackermann was forced to retract his calls for a separate German path to socialism. Finally, the ideological transformation was completed at the First Party Conference of the SED in January 1949. Protests from the CDU and the Liberals were brushed aside, with some of their leaders removed by the Soviets. Ultimately, these parties were forced to toe the SED line as part of the 'National Front', the mechanism by which seats were distributed among parties and presented as a single list to electors. Naturally, the SED and its allies dominated this list. By the spring of 1949 the SED was ready to become the governing party in a new state.

Capitalism in the West

It is one of the great ironies of post-1945 Germany that just as the Communists initially spoke of creating a bourgeois democracy and market economy but went on to oversee the creation of communism and a planned economy in the East, so the Christian Democrats initially talked of Christian Socialism and large-scale public ownership of industry but went on to lead the way in establishing bourgeois democracy and a capitalist market economy.

Anti-capitalism was common in the early years, even in the ranks of the Christian Democrats. The 'Ahlen Programme', an economic and social programme formulated by the CDU in the British Zone in February 1947, stated that the capitalist economic system had not met the national and social needs of the German people (Bedürftig, 1998, p. 13). This manifesto was opposed to monopolies while favouring the breaking up of large concerns, nationalisation of the mines and the involvement of employees in management decisions. Despite this agenda, it was clear that very little of this programme was likely to be implemented.

To some extent the Ahlen Programme was an attempt to pre-empt the policies of the Social Democrats. The pre-1933 SPD had been an essentially Marxist party that favoured collective and state ownership of the most important industries, though not the kind of state control of all of society envisaged by the Communists. The party's leader after 1945, Kurt Schumacher, despite being a vehement opponent of the course of Sovietisation in the East and of the amalgamation of the SPD and KPD, nevertheless favoured a strong degree of socialisation and nationalisation. This appeared to be popular in the early period after 1945. The combined Social Democratic and Communist vote was between 46 per cent and 60 per cent in all of the central and northern states in state elections held in the western zones in 1946–7, while many CDU voters also supported the nationalisation of key industries. Just as Ackermann in the Soviet Zone spoke of a German path to socialism, so many westerners also favoured a strongly socialist, though not Soviet, Germany.

This was never likely to happen. The Western Allies disagreed among themselves about precisely the kind of

Germany that should be created, but they were unanimous on one issue at least: Germany should not become socialist. When a clause was inserted into the constitution of the state of Hessen proposing passing the property of Nazis and war criminals into state ownership, the American Deputy Military Governor, General Clay, insisted on a referendum. The 72 per cent vote in favour of the proposal was simply overruled by General Clay, who refused permission for the clause to be put into operation. Similarly, when the parliament of North Rhine-Westphalia voted in August 1948 to nationalise the coal industry, the British Government, though it had taken some of the important German industries into state ownership in 1946 and had just nationalised the British coal industry, simply refused to accept the proposal. The USA was the main driving force behind opposition to such proposals.

The Western Allies were ideologically opposed to empowering the working class in Germany, for the most part through fear of Soviet expansion. Thus antifascist committees which had sprung up all over Germany in 1945 in the vacuum created by the end of Nazism were not recognised in the western zones. Later attempts by the newly created SED to organise on an all-German basis were thwarted with the quite legitimate counter-demand that the SPD be allowed to do the same. Some attempts were made to break up the banks and larger industries, but they were half-hearted: the great chemical combine I. G. Farben, for example, was not broken up into four smaller companies until 1953.

Aside from ideology, the most important difference between the Soviet Zone and the western zones was in the attitude of the occupying powers to the question of reparations. Ultimately it was this that laid the foundations for prosperity in the West, leaving the East to play economic catch-up for the next forty years, and arguably, right up to the present day. At a conference in Quebec in September 1944 the Allies had decided not to require reparations payments on the scale which had been demanded from

Germany after World War I. Other measures were preferred. At the Yalta Conference in February 1945 it had been agreed that the German arms industry would be destroyed, that the Ruhr industrial area and the Saarland would be placed under international control, and that reparations payments could be made in kind as industrial output increased. The details were then laid down at Potsdam, with the Soviet Union due to obtain 10 per cent of reparations from the western zones because of the low industrial output in its zone.

Initially all of the Allies began dismantling factories. We have seen that the dismantling was extensive in the Soviet Zone in the first three or four years. The Morgenthau Plan, which foresaw the deindustrialisation and dismemberment of Germany, had found some resonance in the provisions of the Potsdam Agreement. The Joint Chiefs of Staff Document known as JCS 1067 was largely based on Morgenthau's plans, though it was interpreted with varying degrees of latitude. Nevertheless, 'its most consistent theme was punishment' (Glees, 1996, p. 41).

Yet dismantling German industry made no real sense. Europe was in ruins, the Germans had the capacity to contribute to the reconstruction of Europe, and yet they were to be prevented from working. As early as 1946 the USA and Great Britain seemed to change their minds about reparations. The British feared social discontent brought on by mass unemployment and the shortages of food that existed: by March 1946 it was clear that there was not even enough food to sustain the daily ration of 1550 calories, which was below the League of Nations minimum of 2400 calories. Germans were being fed by food from abroad, while the British, who had won the war, had to put up with food shortages at home. The situation was exacerbated by the fact that the western zones were also trying to accommodate some 8 million to 10 million refugees and expellees from the German territories in the East that had been given to Poland, and from the Sudetenland districts of Czechoslovakia. The presence of these uprooted Germans with their different regional cultures often led to friction with the native inhabitants of the western zones, friction that was exacerbated by the economic shortages.

Despite their differences on how best to organise food distribution in their respective zones, the American, British and French authorities quickly came to the conclusion that continuing to punish Germany could harm other European countries as well. By May 1946 the British Foreign Minister, Ernest Bevin, was presenting the Soviet Union as a greater threat than Germany and suggesting to cabinet colleagues that they might have to choose a separate western German state in order to reduce communist influence.

That a new, more lenient policy towards Germany was being adopted was made public in Stuttgart on 6 September 1946 by the US Secretary of State, James Byrnes. Two days previously the US and British authorities had agreed to amalgamate their zones with effect from 1 January 1947 to form a Bizone, which was to function as a single economic unit. Harry Truman's policy on stemming the advance of communism (discussed below) was reinforced in June 1947 by the announcement of the programme of Marshall Aid, as the European Recovery Programme became known. The US now wished to help European nations recover from the devastation of World War II and was prepared to send financial and economic support to help them do so. Germany was one of those nations, but the Soviets refused to allow the countries under its influence to accept this aid, so that in Germany only the three western zones benefited. Thus, at the very time when eastern Germany was still financing reparations to its Soviet occupiers, the western zones were being subsidised by their occupying powers. In contrast to the 30 per cent of industrial output that was lost by the Soviet Zone after the war, it is estimated that the western zones lost only 8 per cent of their output.

The political institutions that were being created in the western zones will be discussed below. Economically there was a move away from almost all forms of socialisation and nationalisation. The CDU's Ahlen Programme of 1947 was replaced in 1949 by the Düsseldorf Guidelines, in which no further reference was made to socialism. In March 1948 Ludwig Erhard, an economics professor, was appointed director of the economics administration in the Bizone. Erhard was essentially a neo-liberal economist who believed firmly in the free market, but with two important modifications to the principle of *laissez-faire* economics. First, he believed that the state should have a regulatory function that should prevent the creation of cartels and ensure competition. Secondly, he believed that the market economy needed an important social element in order to be able to intervene in support of the sick and infirm. Thus, a social net should be established through an element of redistributive taxation. The economy thus created came to be known as the 'social market economy', and, together with the Marshall Plan, it was the cornerstone of West Germany's economic success in the 1950s. It was also a fundamentally different system from that which was created in the Soviet Zone.

The Cold War

It is impossible to consider events in Germany in the period 1945–9 without reference to the global political situation as it developed in those years. It was not only Germany, but Europe as a whole, and to some extent the world, which became divided into two bitterly hostile camps during those years. Former allies almost went to war with each other over what they saw as principles of democracy, freedom and security. Germany, as the state in the centre of Europe and therefore in the front line of conflict, was the only European country to suffer political division as a result. Winston Churchill's speech on 5 March 1946 in Fulton, Missouri, in which he claimed that an iron curtain from Stettin in the Baltic to Trieste on the Adriatic separated the free West from the communist East, ironically located all of Germany in the free West. By 1947 it was becoming clear that this 'curtain' also divided Germany, with the Soviet Zone definitely on the 'unfree' side.

The Cold War was a military and economic stand-off between the liberal democracies of the West under US leadership and the 'People's Democracies' or communist states of the East under Soviet leadership. Sometimes it degenerated into actual military conflict on a regional scale, such as in Korea in the early 1950s or in Vietnam in the 1960s and 1970s. Nevertheless, the 'War' was fought largely on the ideological, espionage and economic fronts.

The Cold War had its origins in the ideological differences that had existed between the Soviet Union and the Western powers since the successful Bolshevik revolution in Russia in 1917. Then, Western powers had intervened to try to overthrow the Soviet government before it could take control of the whole country, but without success. In the 1920s and 1930s the Bolsheviks had consolidated their power, with Stalin emerging as the most powerful man. The principles of economic control which the Bolsheviks espoused were anathema to Western governments, in particular the stifling of free enterprise in favour of state control of the means of production. In addition, the one-party state, in which dissent was not tolerated, stood in contrast to the multiparty democracies that existed in the West. Communists would argue, however, that capitalism's main ideological objection to communism is based on a rejection of egalitarian principles being applied to the economic sphere. Capitalism for the most part advocates equality of opportunity rather than the redistribution of wealth to achieve economic equality.

Nevertheless, the two sides had made common cause against the threat of Nazism, despite Stalin's pact with Hitler in 1939. After Hitler's defeat each side became afraid of the influence of the other. Soviet troops had liberated most of the countries of eastern Europe, while American and British troops had liberated most of the countries of western Europe. At Yalta in February 1945, Churchill, Roosevelt and Stalin did not formally divide Europe up into 'spheres of influence', though Churchill and Stalin had informally mooted this idea in 1944. Rather, Churchill and Roosevelt agreed that the Soviet Union should have 'friendly' neighbours in eastern Europe. They saw Russia's security concerns as legitimate: in 1941 it had been invaded by Germany for the second time in less than thirty years, and the devastation and destruction of this war had left some 20–25 million Soviet citizens dead. Whereas Churchill and Roosevelt felt that liberal democratic governments could guarantee 'friendly' policies, Stalin, mindful of the hostility his country had faced from its neighbours in the inter-war period, 'was willing to trust himself only to communist-led governments' (Young, 1996, p. 13). Communists took control in Poland, Romania and Bulgaria by 1946, Hungary by 1947 and Czechoslovakia in February 1948.

Similarly, the Western Allies had ensured that liberal democratic governments were re-established in Belgium, Denmark, Luxemburg, the Netherlands and Norway. France and Italy had coalition governments in which the Communists participated, at least until their removal from both in May 1947. The hard political reality in Europe was that numerically far superior Soviet forces could not be removed by any kind of western threat. By the same token, the Soviets were wary of the US strength that had been demonstrated in the summer of 1945 by the dropping of atomic bombs on Japan. Though the Soviets had not yet developed their own bomb, many in the West saw their numerically superior forces as a threat. In particular, it was felt that if war flared up as a result of any kind of misunderstanding, at a time when diplomatic contacts were poor, then these forces might easily overrun western Europe.

Other battles between communist and capitalist forces were also being fought at this time. In Greece a civil war was raging between the royalist government and the communist resistance, with British intervention on behalf of the government and limited Soviet support for the resistance. In Yugoslavia, where the communist resistance had played a greater role than Soviet forces in defeating the German occupying armies, the communist government under Tito was pursuing a decidedly independent line in foreign policy, something which made Stalin nervous. Western pressure had forced Soviet troops out of northern Iran, which the Soviet Union had occupied at the end of the war, but there were fears that the Soviets might pressurise Turkey into conceding territory. In the Far East, the communist forces of Mao Zedong were marching to victory in the Chinese civil war, which ended in 1949.

Whether Stalin had expansionist plans or merely wanted a buffer zone for defence purposes is still the subject of disagreement. The US diplomat George Kennan, who was in Moscow until 1947, wrote an influential paper in 1946 in which he described the Soviet Union as expansionist. This coloured US attitudes to the Soviets. The Truman Doctrine, espoused by US President Harry Truman in March 1947, was a response to such fears. It stated that the USA would 'assist free peoples to work out their own destinies in their own way' (quoted in Young, 1996, p. 15). The Marshall Plan, announced in June 1947, was the concrete economic form given to the Truman Doctrine. A conference of the foreign ministers of the four victorious Allies in London in November and December 1947 produced no agreement, after which US policy changed significantly towards support for a separate West German state. NATO, the North Atlantic Treaty Organisation, which was established in Washington in April 1949, was the military response to the perceived Soviet threat. The creation of Cominform, an agency designed to co-ordinate international communist activity, and the establishment of a military alliance, the Warsaw Pact, were Stalin's direct responses to these moves.

Germany and the Germans were caught in the middle of this ideological divide. The development of the four zones of occupation towards the formation of two states in 1949 must be seen firmly in the context of these global events.

Steps in Opposite Directions

It is generally accepted now that in 1945 the Soviets did not set out to divide Germany. The Potsdam Agreement clearly stipulated that Germany must be treated as a single economic unit, even if some of the other decisions, such as giving the military commander in each zone absolute authority, seemed to run counter to this. The primary concerns in 1945 were economic, with the denazification of the country seen as essential to the rebuilding process. That Germany did not remain united was due to a number of factors. The external ones have been considered. As regards the internal factors it is clear that 'both sides had either forced or tolerated structural decisions in their zones which reduced at an early stage the chances of post-War Germany developing in a uniform manner' (Staritz, 1996, p. 22).

For a start the Allies could not agree on precise political plans for postwar Germany. The French still dreamed of dividing up the country into a number of small states to re-create something like the type of Germany that had existed before 1871. France's expansionist plans were illustrated by its attitude to the Saarland, which it forced into economic union with France. In 1947, it created a separate Saar citizenship and even banned political parties from using the word 'German' in the state elections. The Soviets' primary interest appeared to be in dismantling their zone. All were agreed that the state of Prussia, so dominant that it stretched from Lithuania in the east to France in the west and covered two-thirds of Germany's territory, should be broken up and new states created. And, of course, approximately one-quarter of German territory was ceded to Poland and Russia. What might become of the rest was, in 1945, anyone's guess.

It was in April 1946 that the British Foreign Office decided that the West German states 'would have to be strengthened and made able to resist any communist-dominated central government; and that if it were to come to a division of Germany, the Soviet Union would have to be made to look responsible' (Fulbrook, 1991, p. 161). For reasons already outlined, the Americans also came to support German economic recovery. The French, by contrast, still maintained a somewhat aloof, separatist attitude in their zone.

It is against this backdrop that the merging of the British and American zones to create the Bizone on 1 January 1947 must be seen. The British had other economic reasons, too, for the economic burden was becoming so great that the UK was borrowing American dollars to feed the Germans while some food was still being rationed back home. Though the merger was primarily driven by economics, it soon became clear that the Bizone was the nucleus of a new political entity. A single economic policy was pursued under Ludwig Erhard from March 1947, and the Marshall Plan came into operation in June 1947. The Economic Council that was created was a putative political forum for the whole territory of the Bizone.

Still attempts were made to retain all-German political institutions. In June 1947 a conference of the minister presidents of the German states was held in Munich. The host, Bavaria's Hans Ehard, fully expected that the SED representatives from the Soviet Zone would not attend (Thränhardt, 1996, p. 59). The representatives from the French Zone had been forbidden to discuss political questions, while the SED delegates were determined to discuss German unity. The conference opted not to discuss politics, or even make a declaration in favour of unity, whereupon the delegates from the Soviet Zone departed. Ehard commented that 'this incident means division [of Germany]' (quoted in Thränhardt, 1996, p. 60).

Ehard's comment is debatable. It is true that the attitude of the Western politicians at the meeting was typical of the vehemently anti-communist attitude among many western Germans at the time. It is also true that the SED's insistence on discussing unity or nothing was symptomatic of a determination to drive the political agenda throughout Germany where the opportunity arose. Each side was inflexible. Each side had also obtained a large mandate from its electorate in state elections held throughout Germany in 1946 and 1947.

Throughout 1947 and into 1948 steps were taken in both the Soviet Zone and the western zones that led directly to the creation of separate governments. In the Bizone, an Economic Council was created, made up of 52 members chosen by the state parliaments. It had the power to pass economic laws and also to ensure that they were carried out: it was thus, in effect, the nucleus of a separate government. Though the SPD and the CDU/CSU had twenty seats each, most of the smaller parties were sympathetic to the CDU, so that the SPD failed to get its nominees appointed to run any of the five administrative offices that had been set up. As a result it went into opposition, remaining there for another twenty years as the CDU reaped the electoral benefits of the economic upturn that followed. The Soviet response to the creation of the Bizone was the creation of the German Economic Commission on 14 June 1947. It was intended to co-ordinate economic policy in the Soviet Zone and, though it might similarly be seen as the nucleus of a new government, the Soviets played down its significance by emphasising that it was under the control of the Soviet Military Administration.

Following on the failed London meeting of November and December 1947, a Six-Power Conference was held in London in February–March 1948, with a further meeting in May–June. The USA, Great Britain, France and the Benelux countries accepted the concept of a West German state as the basis for the development of their policies *vis-à-vis* Germany. The new state would only slowly acquire economic control of its resources. In December 1948 the same six states agreed the 'Ruhr Statute', which came into force in

April 1949. Rather than accede to French demands for a separation of the Ruhr from Germany, the six states set up an international authority which would control the production of coal, iron and steel and set quotas for export and for German use. Some 80 to 90 per cent of West Germany's production of these materials was thereby placed under international control.

In the East, the SED leadership was pressing Stalin to authorise the creation of a separate state there, but even as late as March 1948 Stalin was still unsure, perhaps partly because he knew that the French were still unenthusiastic about Western developments (Dennis, 2000, p. 44). On 3 April 1948 the Marshall Plan came into force in the three western zones. In July 1948 the rules were laid down for the establishment of a Parliamentary Council which would have the task of creating a constitution for the West German state: the Council was set up in September 1948. Eventually, in December of that year, Stalin authorised provisional steps towards the creation of an East German parliamentary body, but he refused to admit the Soviet Zone as a member of Cominform. Arguably, he still held out hopes of a settlement based on something other than partition. After all, the 'German People's Congress for Unity and a Just Peace', which had been formed in 1947, was still active. It was SED-sponsored and largely an eastern affair, but nearly 500 of its 2200 delegates came from the West, most of them Communists. Though Stalin's precise intentions were often unclear, one thing is certain: he made sure that in all cases the West took the first open steps towards separation. He did not want to be seen to initiate the division of Germany.

The Berlin Blockade

On 1 March 1948 the Western Allies created the new 'Bank of German States' (BDL) in the western zones. It was also clear that if the Marshall Plan was to be successful in Germany, then it would be necessary to eliminate the massive cash surplus that had been built up during the war, only some of which had been spent in the restrictive economic conditions of the postwar period. Thus, it was decided to introduce a new currency to replace the 'Reichsmark', and simultaneously to lift price restrictions on most goods.

On 20 June 1948, a Sunday, the new 'Deutschmark' was introduced in the three western zones. Citizens were allowed to convert the first 60 old Marks into 40 Deutschmarks. Beyond this, old Marks were converted into Deutschmarks at a rate of 100 to 6.5. Pensions, salaries and rents were converted at the rate of 1:1. Essentially, those who owned factories and property profited from the conversion, while others saw their savings all but wiped out overnight. Nevertheless, the strength of the new currency meant that the black market disappeared within a few weeks.

The Soviets reacted to the introduction of the new currency and devaluation of the old by introducing a new currency of their own on 23 June, created initially by attaching stickers to the old notes. The Soviets feared that the old currency, now worth only a fraction of its value in the West, would flood their Zone and cause massive inflation and devaluation. On the same day they also instructed the acting mayor of Berlin, Ferdinand Friedensburg, to introduce their currency in all four sectors of the city. Berlin was supposed to be governed as a single unit, and it lay geographically entirely within the Soviet Zone. The Soviets argued that it was economically part of their Zone, despite its special status.

The Western Allies rejected this argument. They saw it as a thinly disguised attempt by the Soviets to integrate West Berlin into the Soviet Zone and ultimately to force the Western Allies out of Berlin completely. Within hours they forbade the introduction of the new Eastern currency in their sectors of Berlin and instead introduced the Deutschmark there. The Soviets in turn saw this as an attempt to integrate West Berlin into the western zones. One day later the Soviets responded by launching the so-called Berlin Blockade. From 24 June 1948, access by road and rail from the western zones to West Berlin was blocked by the Soviet military. A few days later the waterways were also cut off, along with energy supplies to West Berlin. There remained only the air as a supply route to West Berlin. It is almost certain that the Soviets thought this would force the Western Allies out.

In response, on the initiative of the US Military Governor, General Clay, a massive operation was launched to supply West Berlin with food and fuel. Over the next eleven months foodstuffs, medicines, coal and building materials were brought from the western zones to the 2.5 million inhabitants of West Berlin. 'Operation Vittles', as this airlift became known, was funded by emergency taxes and contributions introduced in the British and US zones in October 1948. Thousands of flights were flown, and a number of accidents cost air crews their lives. The people of West Berlin had to survive on reduced rations throughout. Despite this, a Soviet offer to provide all West Berliners with ration cards was taken up by only 5 per cent of the population. On 12 May 1949, the Soviets finally abandoned the Blockade. West Berlin's position as part of the West German economy was effectively assured, despite its special political status (see Chapter 2).

As an attempt to force the integration of West Berlin into the Soviet Zone the Berlin Blockade was a singular failure. The Western Allies were resolute in their determination to defend the city. West Berliners also had no desire to live under the Soviets. It was during the Blockade that a new Berlin saying came into existence: 'Better to be occupied by the Americans than liberated by the Soviets.' In the end, the Blockade served only to reinforce West Berlin's position as a Western enclave in the Soviet Zone and, later, the GDR.

1949: Two States

While the conflict over Berlin continued, the 'Parliamentary Council' met from September 1948 and drew up a constitution for the new West German state. As in the earlier Economic Council, the SPD and CDU/CSU were equally represented, but most of the smaller parties tended towards the CDU. A liberal democracy was established, but the constitution was called 'the Basic Law', because it was felt that a full 'constitution' should be reserved for a future, unified German state. It came into force on 23 May 1949, and with it the 'Federal Republic of Germany' was created, the French Zone having joined the Bizone to create a Trizone on 8 April 1949.

In the Soviet Zone the key decisions regarding the creation of a new state were made at the Third German People's Congress, which met in Berlin on 29 and 30 May 1949. The Congress had been elected two weeks previously as a single list of delegates from all parties, the list receiving a 66 per cent 'yes' vote. Elections in West Germany were held on 14 August 1949, and the CDU and SPD each obtained around 30 per cent of the vote, with the CDU somewhat unexpectedly just ahead. As before, most of the smaller parties favoured the CDU, so that on 15 September 1949 the CDU candidate, Konrad Adenauer, was elected Federal Chancellor by a majority of just one vote, his own. Three days previously West Germany had elected its first President, the Free Democrat Theodor Heuss.

On 4 October 1949 the SED Party Leadership decided to constitute a 'Provisional Government of the German Democratic Republic', and on 7 October 1949 the GDR was proclaimed. On 11 October, Wilhelm Pieck was elected first President of the GDR, and on 15 October Otto Grotewohl was confirmed as Minister President by the Provisional Parliament.

Germany was now divided *de facto* into two political entities, each claiming to support the unity of Germany, but

belonging to mutually hostile ideological camps in a politically divided world. Each state was backed by its respective
occupying powers, and other states wasted no time in according their preferred German state diplomatic recognition. The division of Germany, though difficult to grasp for
many at the time, did not look as if it would be easily
overcome.

Conclusion

Was the division of Germany inevitable? The answer to that
question is, arguably, 'No'. Certainly, the Cold War was
inevitable, since the Alliance against Hitler was always an
alliance of opposites against a common enemy. However,
once Hitler's armies were defeated, two quite different world
views came into competition for domination in Europe, and
neither wanted to appear weak in the face of the other. It
was Germany's misfortune to be caught in the middle of this
conflict.

Nevertheless, the question might be asked whether, if
German politicians had insisted that the unity of their country was the most important single issue, then a way to keep
the country united might not have been found. The Austrian example is sometimes quoted in support of this theory.
In a replica of the situation in Germany, Austria was divided
into four zones of occupation with a capital divided into four
sectors but lying in the Soviet Zone. Yet Austria gained
independence as a unified, multi-party liberal democracy
in 1955, on condition that it commit itself to permanent
military neutrality. Of course, Austria is small, and there
the Soviet Zone was probably not economically viable on
its own. But its position in the centre of Europe could hardly
have been more important strategically.

The argument is used that the Soviets wanted a buffer
zone for defence purposes. This is undoubtedly true. Yet
what is sometimes forgotten is that they had this buffer

zone without eastern Germany. Russia could have felt, and possibly did feel, secure behind Poland and Czechoslovakia. That is one reason why uncertainty remains as to the nature of Stalin's plans. Of course, there is little reason to doubt that, had the opportunity arisen, Stalin would have welcomed a united Soviet Germany as an ally. But there is limited evidence that this was his actual aim.

By the same token, there is no reason to doubt that the Western Allies would have welcomed a united, capitalist Germany as an ally. Yet such a solution could only be predicated on a Soviet climbdown and retreat from its position as a victorious power. This was no more likely than a Western climbdown enabling a communist Germany to be put in place. In the stand-off that postwar European politics came to be and which was most potently symbolised by the Berlin Blockade, neither side was prepared for concessions unless they were forced. Each side gained victories in this battle; the overcoming of the Berlin Blockade and the defeat of the communist guerrillas in Greece were Western victories, while the elimination of the bourgeois parties from government in Hungary and Czechoslovakia are seen as Communist victories.

In Germany, we have seen that both the Western Allies and the Soviets quickly started fashioning the areas they controlled after their own image. More importantly, they found Germans in their area who willingly co-operated in this process. When SED leader Ulbricht and the other German Communists spoke of German unity, they defined that unity on their own pro-Soviet terms, though they spoke of neutrality. When CDU leader Konrad Adenauer spoke of German unity, it was a pro-Western, capitalist Germany that he desired. Ultimately, both chose to settle for half a cake baked to their own preferred recipe. The respective recipes had been supplied by the occupying forces.

In the final analysis it should not be forgotten that ultimately the division of Germany was the legacy of an occupation that was the culmination of a war ignited by German racism, German expansionism and German tanks and guns. The primary responsibility for the division of Germany lies not in the events of 1945–9, but in the behaviour of the German people after 1933.

2

ECONOMIC SUCCESS WHILE CEMENTING DIVISION, 1949–61

Introduction

Anyone who may have thought in 1949 that the division of Germany would be a temporary measure was to become severely disillusioned during the 1950s. Simply put, the two German states rapidly grew apart, politically, economically, socially and culturally. Hundreds of thousands of Germans voted with their feet for one or other of the two states, with East Germany suffering a net loss of over 2 million people. By the summer of 1961 the division of Germany was set in stone, quite literally, through the building of the Berlin Wall.

There was one point on which everyone seemed to agree. Throughout the 1950s both sides argued that they wanted German unity, and the initiatives launched in this respect are far too numerous to be recounted individually here. Yet the measures taken on a daily basis by the respective governments always prioritised other considerations. The initiatives themselves were invariably couched in terms that were obviously unacceptable to the other side. Ultimately, the only issue on which unity was achieved was the creation of an all-German team for the Olympic Games in 1956, 1960 and 1964.

Each state had to deal with the legacy of Nazism, refugees from the territories in the East that Germany had lost, reparations payments and the Cold War. Each state found its place in opposing military and economic blocks. The leaders on both sides attempted to create a new, successful economy to legitimise the political choices that were made, and each became a leading economy in its respective half of Europe. Yet West Germany was the more open, less restrictive and, above all, more economically successful of the two, with the result that it also had to absorb a net influx of more than 2 million GDR citizens by 1961. As it turned out, these were a welcome source of labour in an expanding economy. Since many of them were well educated and skilled, they were also a severe loss to the GDR.

The leadership in each state also faced dissent and opposition to its policies. There were many in both states who felt that political measures in the international arena should only be taken as long as they did not work against German unity. The SPD in West Germany, especially in the early 1950s, opposed Chancellor Konrad Adenauer's pro-Western policies. And the policy of rearmament pursued in both states had many critics. Nevertheless, the CDU leadership in the West and the SED leadership in the East achieved total domination of political life in this period. The 1950s consolidated a political division of Germany that was to remain in place for almost two generations.

Expellees and Refugees

On 1 April 1947 some ten million refugees and expellees were counted in Germany. These were Germans who had left or been expelled from territories in the east such as East Prussia, Pomerania and Silesia, which now came under Polish or Russian control. Some, like the 2.3 million Sudeten Germans, were expelled because they had come to be seen in the wake of Hitler's expansionism as a potential fifth column by which Germany might again claim territory from its neighbours.

Initially, the largest number of refugees had been in the Soviet Zone (3.9 million), followed by the British Zone

(3.2 million), while the US Zone had 2.9 million refugees, primarily from the Sudetenland in Czechoslovakia. However, as the 1950s progressed a large number of GDR residents left the former Soviet Zone to settle in the West – how many of these had themselves been expelled from the eastern territories is unclear. According to official West German statistics 2.74 million refugees left the GDR in the period 1949–61. This does not take into account the numbers of people the GDR claimed returned from the West, anything between 24,000 in the quiet year of 1952 to 77,000 in 1954, one year after the record emigration figure from East to West (Baumann et al., 2001, p. 125 and p. 162). A net gain of 2 million people for the West is a reasonable estimate.

The problem of integrating these refugees was massive, but very unevenly divided across the federal states. The rural states of Schleswig-Holstein and Lower Saxony in the north had the largest concentrations of refugees, but it was in the industrial heartland that manpower would be required in the longer term (Kettenacker, 1997, p. 85). Several decisions were made to relocate refugees to areas where their numbers were lower, especially in the French Zone. In addition, a 'Federal Equalisation of Burdens Law' was passed in West Germany in 1952 with the intention of redistributing taxes towards those states with greater burdens.

The difficulties which many of the expellees faced, and above all the prospect that they might never be able to return to their homes, led directly to the creation of a political party to represent their interests. The 'League of Expellees' (BHE) was created in January 1950 in Kiel and won 23 per cent of the vote in Schleswig-Holstein in July of the same year, followed by less spectacular successes in some other states. As the 'All-German Block/League of Expellees' it won 5.9 per cent at the federal election of 1953 and entered the CDU-led coalition government.

The party had a very clearly right-wing agenda from the beginning. Its leader was a former SS officer, Waldemar

Kraft, and it repeatedly called into question the borders that had been created in 1945 by the victorious Allies. Of course, in doing this it could be said to be merely following official West German policy. Right up until 1990 the West German position was that in the absence of a formal peace treaty Germany in its 1937 borders continued to exist *de jure*, if not *de facto*. In 1955 the BHE split as a result of the Saar controversy (see below), with its leaders joining the CDU. In the national election in 1957 the party fell below the 5 per cent barrier, thus winning no seats, and it disappeared from political life. Most of its leaders had by then found a political home in the CDU, though some re-emerged in the neo-Nazi NPD in the 1960s.

The integration of the refugees and expellees, both socially and politically, was one of the great achievements in 1950s West Germany. Yet the challenge that such massive numbers created was not without its benefits. In some ways the constant stream of refugees from the east may be seen as a source of cheap labour for the new, emerging West German economy (Fulbrook, 1991, p. 184).

A New Economy in the West

West German economic success in the 1950s was built on the 'social market economy', the principles of which were largely formulated by Ludwig Erhard. As Director of the Economic Administration in the Bizone he introduced these principles in June 1948, and maintained them as Economics Minister from 1949 to 1963, when he replaced Adenauer as Chancellor. Erhard presided over the implementation of what the French historian Alfred Grosser has called the 'Doctrine of Prosperity' (Grosser, 1974, p. 272).

Erhard's aim was to create a maximum of prosperity based around capitalist, free market economic principles, but with a social safety net for the weaker individuals and families in society: a 'social market economy' rather than simply a free market economy. Whereas the classical liberal economists of the nineteenth century argued for as little state intervention as possible, Erhard now argued for only as much state intervention as necessary. It was a subtle shift of emphasis.

Of course, any kind of market economics cannot be entirely free of state intervention. In West Germany a number of laws were passed which helped create a wider sense of ownership of the economy by limiting some of the freedoms that employers in other countries took for granted. One such example was the 'Works Constitution Law', passed in 1952, by which there had to be a works council in every company with more than 20 employees, with employees occupying one-third of the seats. Similarly, the 1951 law on parity of representation on the boards of companies in the coal mining industry is another example of state intervention in industry.

The Marshall Plan played a significant role in the last years of the occupation, but the economic position of the new Federal Republic in 1949 and 1950 was not good. In January 1950 more than 2 million people were unemployed, representing 13.3 per cent of the workforce, while in West Berlin unemployment lay at 30 per cent. In late 1949, Marshall Aid accounted for 37 per cent of West Germany's imports. Yet by 1952 this figure had dropped to just 3 per cent. The main reason was an economic boom caused by the Korean War, which started in June 1950.

As in Japan, which benefited enormously from its proximity to the conflict, so too, in Germany, industry benefited from contracts to supply goods, especially machine tools, steel and vehicles for the Western Allies. Unemployment sank rapidly during the war years (1950–3) and continued to decline throughout the decade, dropping below one million in April 1955 and reaching just 1.3 per cent by 1960. Co-operation with its neighbours in Western Europe provided West Germany with a wider context for this economic growth (this is discussed further below). In addition, the need for reconstruction after the destruction of the war years meant that, like Japan, West Germany equipped itself with modern machinery and technologies which quickly surpassed the capacity of the technology used in, for example, Britain.

West Germans also equipped themselves with modern consumer goods in this period. Televisions, cars, refrigerators and washing machines became the symbols of prosperity. The percentages owning these items steadily increased, with 63 per cent of households owning a fridge by 1962, while 42 per cent had a television, 38 per cent a car and 36 per cent a washing machine. West Germany became, by the standards of its neighbours, a wealthy society that effectively enjoyed full employment.

Erhard's control of the economy continued throughout this period, and his commitment to the principles of the social market economy remained. In 1957 the CDU formally dispensed with its socialist-sounding 'Ahlen Programme', which had in any case already been revised in 1949. In that year it also renamed the Bank of German States the 'Bundesbank', thus creating an institution which remains a powerful economic force to this day, and which has widely been perceived as one of the most successful German institutions.

The 'economic miracle', as it has sometimes been called, was not particularly miraculous. Erhard himself disliked the term. Rather, the West German economic recovery benefited from sound economic planning, favourable external circumstances such as the Korean War and European co-operation, and a constant supply of new labour from the GDR, estimated by some as having been worth DM 2.6 billion per year (Kramer, 1991, p. 103). The average annual rate of economic growth in the period 1950–61 was 8.3 per cent (Baumann et al., 2001). Erhard's declared aim, also the title of a book by him, was 'Prosperity for All'. By the end of the 1950s it seemed that this was precisely what he had achieved, so much so that the author and political commentator Heinrich Böll found many West Germans to be just a little too smug and self-satisfied.

A New Economy in the East

The economy that was created in the GDR could not have been more different from the Western model. It entailed central planning, continued payment of reparations to the Soviet Union (until 1953), compulsory nationalisation measures, collectivisation of agriculture, and the continued rationing of some foodstuffs until the late 1950s. Though material wealth increased for East Germans in the 1950s, the rate of increase was much slower than in West Germany. Whereas in 1950 East Germany's GDP was 20 per cent that of West Germany, by 1960 its GDP was only 12 per cent of West Germany's (its population was 37 per cent that of West Germany in 1950 and 31 per cent in 1960).

The basic premise behind the communist planned economy was that full employment and an increase in material wealth for all could be achieved through central planning, coupled with state and collective rather than private ownership of the means of production. Agriculture was therefore collectivised into large farms: at first, in the early 1950s, on a semi-voluntary basis, but later, in 1959–60, on a compulsory basis, so that by 1960 virtually all East German agricultural land was in collective ownership. Productivity in these agricultural collectives (LPG) was higher than in most other East European countries, and they were also more effective than small farms in the West, though they could not match the production of large Western farms.

Similarly, industry was progressively nationalised throughout the 1950s, with only a very few small factories remaining in private ownership. The first five-year economic plan began on 1 January 1951. The plan emphasised basic industries 'in order to increase the supply of fuel and power, steel and iron to the chemical and investment goods industries' (Dennis, 1988, p. 129). Although production targets were met, it was at the expense of the kinds of consumer goods that West Germans were increasingly able to purchase. This policy was reversed somewhat after the June 1953 uprising (see below), a change that was helped by the end of reparations payments to the Soviets in that year. A second five-year plan was instituted in 1956, but it was discarded in 1959 in favour of a seven-year plan, and 1959 saw a massive 12 per cent increase in productivity, a rate that matched West Germany's best year of growth in that decade (1955).

Yet the overall growth in economic output and ownership of consumer goods remained modest by West German standards. Most of the GDR's trade was with Eastern European countries rather than the expanding capitalist economies of the West and much of the trade was with the Soviet Union on terms that were unfavourable to the GDR. The glowing reports that filled the pages of the SED's daily newspaper, *Neues Deutschland*, could not mask the disparity between East and West. Though the number of GDR households with a television was comparable to that in the West by 1962 (31 per cent), many fewer households owned a car (5 per cent), a washing machine (12 per cent) or a refrigerator (11 per cent) (Niehuss and Lindner, 1998, p. 431). Ulbricht's and the SED's claim in 1958 that the GDR would overtake West German consumption of foodstuffs and consumer goods by 1961 was pie in the sky.

It was in no small part for economic reasons that many East Germans chose to vote with their feet by leaving for West Germany. The gain to the West German economy that this represented has already been discussed. The loss to the GDR economy cannot be over-estimated. Many of those leaving were skilled workers and professional people. Often they had been trained or received a free education in the GDR, only to go west and sell their skills to the highest bidder. Though political repression also played a role in forcing this emigration, it is noticeable that in periods of economic repression emigration increased dramatically. Perhaps the most significant such event in the entire history of the GDR occurred in June 1953.

17 June 1953

The initial phase of agricultural collectivisation in 1950 was one factor in the increase in the number of people leaving for the West that year. In total, 198,000 left, nearly 70,000 more than in 1949. In the mid-1950s hopes of liberalisation after the death of Stalin were dashed internally by the SED leadership and externally by events such as the crushing of the Hungarian rising in 1956, and this also raised the number of people leaving: the annual average in the period 1955–7 was 265,000. Numbers dropped after this, but began to rise again in 1960 when forced collectivisation began and rumours about the possible building of a wall became current. However, the year 1953 saw the largest number of emigrants from the GDR. In that year, 331,000 people left for the West.

In 1952 the SED leader, Ulbricht, had proclaimed the building of socialism, and this was a signal for increased production norms in heavy industry while wages remained the same or were reduced, and prices were also increased. It also came at a time of increased paranoia in the SED, which arrested thousands of supposed spies, enemy agents and saboteurs. The result was an upsurge in the numbers of citizens fleeing the country. After Stalin's death in March 1953, the Soviet Communist Party (CPSU) leadership recommended that the SED leaders ease their policies. A GDR delegation, which included Ulbricht and Grotewohl, flew to Moscow in late May to receive the Soviet proposals. The CPSU leadership encouraged the SED to be more conciliatory towards farmers, small businesses and consumers but without entirely abandoning the drive towards socialism. Yet there was no prospect of real political liberalisation, nor was there any mention of the hated production norms.

An SED communiqué issued on 11 June promised most of the measures suggested by the Soviets. For many it was an astonishing admission by the party that it had got some things wrong, but for some die-hard SED members it was a betrayal.

Then, on 13 June, the party leadership reaffirmed its previously announced intention to increase production norms by 10 per cent on 30 June. Because many workers already relied on bonus payments for overfulfilment of norms in order to supplement low wages, this could have meant for some 'a cut in real wages of between 25 per cent and 30 per cent' (Dennis, 2000, p. 62). There was widespread discontent among the workers, and the concessions made on 11 June to other groups but not them served to reinforce their anger.

Throughout May and the first half of June there had been lightning strikes in various towns and cities. There was also unrest in the countryside. Then, on 16 June, incensed by an article in the Trade Union paper confirming the norms, workers on the massive construction project on Stalinallee in East Berlin downed tools. This action triggered the first widescale revolt against Communist rule in any of the states of the Soviet Bloc. In Berlin workers marched through the streets to the House of the Council of Ministers and demanded a lowering of the work norms and that Ulbricht and Grotewohl address them. After demanding the resignation of the government, the workers called a strike for the next day.

By 9a.m. on 17 June around 25,000 protesters had gathered in Stalinallee. They demanded the withdrawal of the work norms, a reduction in the cost of living, the resignation of the government and free elections. In towns and cities across the country people came out in support, alerted to the previous day's events in Berlin by Western radio. Halle was the district most affected, followed by Berlin itself. By midday on 17 June it was clear that the GDR authorities could not control the situation, partly because its police and paramilitary forces could not be relied on. At 12.30p.m. the Soviet military commander in Berlin ordered his troops onto the streets, and the Soviet Military Administration imposed a state of emergency at 1p.m. Riots and fighting ensued in which a number of people were killed and injured on both sides and cars were overturned and burned. By the evening of 17 June, order had essentially been restored, though sporadic strikes and protests continued up to 21 June. Strikes in Jena and Schkopau in July were quickly crushed (Dennis, 2000, pp. 65–71).

The SED leadership immediately branded the workers Western *agents provocateurs*, a simplistic and false claim, even if Western agencies were indeed active in East Berlin and some West Berliners joined the protests. Though there were attempts in the aftermath to moderate the raising of the work norms, Ulbricht and his clique quickly re-established control. Some figures within the SED who had been opposed to him, such as Rudolf Herrnstadt, editor of the party newspaper, and Wilhelm Zaisser, head of the security service, were removed from the Politburo in July after a failed attempt to remove Ulbricht. Ultimately, Ulbricht's leadership survived the death of Stalin, the June uprising and the changes in leadership in the Soviet Union in 1953.

The extent to which the party itself was out of touch with its own workers is illustrated by the story of the writers Kurt Barthel and Bertolt Brecht. Barthel, as secretary of the Writers' Union, distributed leaflets after 17 June arguing that the people had lost the confidence of the party and would have to work hard to win it back. In reply, Brecht asked in a sarcastic poem whether in this case it might not be easier if the government simply dissolved the people and elected another (Dennis, 2000, pp. 71–2).

Consolidating Power in the East

Once in power, the SED never had any intention of relinquishing control of the GDR government. We have seen that other political parties were forced into the so-called 'National Front', which presented a single list of candidates for election to the parliament, known as the 'People's Chamber'. Young people were organised in the 'Free

German Youth', a communist-led group which promoted support for the state and was also used as a vehicle for combatting the influence of the churches on young people. In 1954 the SED decided to introduce the *Jugendweihe*, a kind of atheist confirmation which directly challenged Christian confirmation. By 1958, 44 per cent of young people were already taking communist 'confirmation'. By the 1970s it was almost universal, resisted only in a few committed Christian families.

Voting was compulsory, and a vote of 'yes' for the single list could be given simply by folding the ballot paper, whereas a 'no' vote required the voter to go into a polling booth to mark the paper, an act which was recorded by SED observers. Those who voted 'no' could be harassed or arrested, or could lose their jobs. Under such circumstances the vote in the November 1958 election was not untypical: officially, 98.89 per cent of voters went to the polls and 99.87 per cent of them voted 'yes'. Electoral opposition was non-existent.

If the masses voted either by striking, as in 1953, or by leaving throughout the 1950s, there was also ongoing internal party opposition. It is in the nature of Stalinism to be paranoid, always looking for the enemy within. In the early 1950s large numbers of people were expelled from the SED and many were arrested. Some were ex-Social Democrats, some were accused of being 'Titoists' in the wake of Yugoslavia's split with Moscow, others were accused of being 'Trotskyists', a time-honoured Stalinist accusation, while others, especially after the Slanský Trial in Czechoslovakia in November 1952, were accused of being Zionists (see below). Most of those accused at this time were not high-ranking party members, and some, such as ex-foreign minister Georg Dertinger of the CDU, were members of other parties (O'Doherty, 1997, pp. 27–45).

In the mid- and later 1950s opposition crystallised among some more senior SED members. The removal of Herrnstadt and Zaisser in 1953 is one example of Ulbricht's successful resistance to such challenges. In 1956, in the wake of the 20th Party Congress of the Soviet Communist Party, at which Khrushchev tried to shake off the legacy of Stalinism, some of the most prominent scholars in East Germany (indeed Germany as a whole), including the philosophers Ernst Bloch in Leipzig and Wolfgang Harich in Berlin and the scientist Robert Havemann in Berlin, began to formulate alternative policies, such as promoting a specifically German path to socialism. Harich was sentenced to ten years in prison in 1957, a fate also suffered by the publisher Walter Janka. Bloch was faced with campaigns against his writings and finally stayed in the West after the building of the Berlin Wall in 1961. Havemann, who had been sacked as head of a science institute by the West Berlin Senate (government) in 1950 because of protests against US nuclear policy, was sacked as professor at the Humboldt University in East Berlin in 1964 for his continued criticism of the leadership.

Inner-party opposition also returned after 1956. Karl Schirdewan, the secretary of the SED Central Committee, who had survived Nazi concentration camps, and Fred Oelssner, a member of the Council of Ministers who had spent the war years in Moscow, were among the leading opponents of Ulbricht in the Politburo. They favoured a revisionist form of socialism which was to be more open and accountable and more oriented towards Germany rather than the Soviet Union. Though they claimed to have been encouraged by elements in the Soviet leadership, the World Conference of Communist Parties in November 1957 condemned revisionism, and Ulbricht moved against them soon after. In 1958 Schirdewan was removed from the Politburo and Central Committee for 'factionalism' and given a minor administrative post in Potsdam. Oelssner was similarly removed in 1958 and given an academic job in Berlin (Dennis, 2000, pp. 80–5).

Ultimately, Ulbricht was ready to brook no opposition. He survived the major upheavals in the Soviet Union in the 1950s and remained in power with the support of the Soviets. One aspect of the GDR system which allowed him to do this, and which contrasted sharply with the West German political system, was 'democratic centralism'.

Federalism versus Centralism

The GDR's political system was built on the concept of democratic centralism. Essentially, this meant that power must be concentrated in one place. Officially this was the Council of Ministers, chosen by the parliament, but effectively it was the Politburo of the SED, of which Ulbricht was General Secretary (renamed First Secretary in 1954). All major decisions in political, social and economic life either emanated from or had to be approved by the Politburo.

Ensuring that this happened meant emaciating other potential centres of power. Other political parties had been brought into line in the late 1940s, but the five federal states in the GDR remained as potential sources of alternative power, and Saxony, Thuringia and Mecklenburg had long traditions of autonomy within a highly regionalised German system. In 1952 the states were abolished and replaced by fourteen districts, based around some of the main cities and towns, such as Leipzig, Dresden, Rostock and Potsdam. East Berlin, still technically under four-power control, was treated in many ways as a fifteenth district. These new units would never be strong enough to be a focus for serious opposition. As a logical step, the upper house of parliament, the 'States' Chamber', was abolished in 1958.

By contrast, West Germany pursued a federalist structure from the very beginning, with a distribution of power between the states and the central government. Each of the states had its own parliament and government, and some responsibilities, such as education and culture, lay entirely with the states. Other areas were split, including taxation, while foreign affairs and defence remained in the hands of the central government. Though the central parliament made the major decisions on policy, administration was largely in the hands of the states (Kettenacker, 1997, pp. 106–11). The central parliament had a two-tier structure, with the Bundestag, directly elected by citizens, using proportional representation, the main lawmaking body. The Bundesrat was created as the house in which the state *governments* were represented (unlike the US Senate, where senators are directly elected by the citizens of each state), and it had a delaying power over most legislation, but a veto only on taxation matters directly affecting the states. This system was applied to the whole of Germany after 1990 and, though the trend now is increasingly towards the centre, this division of responsibilities was seen in the 1950s as an important guarantor against the concentration of too much power in one place.

In the wake of the postwar Allied decision to dismantle Prussia, the Federal Republic in 1950 consisted of eleven states, with West Berlin a twelfth, affiliated state which was not a full part of West Germany. Some states, such as Bavaria and Schleswig-Holstein, had a long tradition. Others, such as Lower Saxony and North Rhine-Westphalia, had been cobbled together by the occupying powers. In 1952 three south-western states amalgamated to form 'Baden-Württemberg', reducing the number of states to nine. In 1957 the Saarland was admitted as the tenth state (eleventh if West Berlin is included). (On reunification in 1990 the five East German states were restored, so that the total is now sixteen.) The states are massively unequal in size. In 1955 North Rhine-Westphalia with 14.5 million people had more than one-quarter of West Germany's population, while the city state of Bremen, with around 600,000 inhabitants, had just 1 per cent of the total.

Defending Democracy

West German federalism was just one aspect of a comprehensive attempt to break with the Nazi past and with the mistakes made in the Weimar period that allowed Hitler to come to power. Other measures included the abolition of popular plebiscites and the election of the President by a parliamentary convention rather than by popular vote. In addition, the President would be a figurehead with no powers other than formally appointing the Chancellor on the recommendation of the Bundestag, and of appointing ministers on the nomination of the Chancellor.

The Bundestag was to be subject to two important provisions which, it was felt, would stabilise democracy and help defend it against extremist minority groups. One was that the Chancellor could only be removed by a so-called 'constructive vote of no confidence', by which a majority of the members of the Bundestag were required to agree on a named successor. The second was the introduction of a 5 per cent clause for elections. The principle of proportional representation was carried over from the Weimar period, but, from 1953, with a provision by which a party which obtained less than 5 per cent of the vote would only be represented in parliament if it won one constituency (half the seats in parliament were for directly elected constituencies, half for party lists to establish the PR principle). In 1957 the 'one seat' requirement was raised to three. The result was that from 1961 until 1983 only three parties were ever represented in the Bundestag.

Stabilising democracy on a parliamentary level also meant combatting anti-parliamentary elements outside parliament. In September 1950 the government decided that membership of a range of organisations, eleven of them communist, including the Free German Youth (FDJ), and two neo-Nazi, including the Socialist Reich Party (SRP), was incompatible with working for the state. In 1952 the SRP, which had won seats in state elections in Lower Saxony and Bremen in 1951, was banned by the Federal Constitutional Court. Other extremely conservative nationalist parties such as the German Party (DP), and neo-Nazis such as the German Reich Party (DRP), also won seats at this time. In 1953 the League of

German Youth (BDJ), a neo-Nazi organisation, was also banned, while officers of the FDJ were arrested. In January 1953 the US High Commissioner released the results of an opinion poll which, in US eyes, confirmed that Nazism was a bigger problem than communism in the Federal Republic. Nevertheless, in 1954 a number of communist functionaries were arrested and sentenced to jail for 'treasonous activities', and in November of that year the legal process of banning the Communist Party began. It was completed with a judgement against the party by the Federal Constitutional Court in August 1956, which led to a new wave of arrests. In a measure that for communists was reminiscent of March 1933 under Hitler, all communists were stripped of their seats in West German elected bodies as a consequence of the judgement.

Neo-Nazis remained organised in various groups, often disguised as 'old soldiers'. They generally adopted a hardline stance towards the GDR, and some were fundamentally opposed to even the West German constitution and the pro-Western stance of the Federal Republic. Some ex-Nazis remained in prominent positions in the Federal Republic. A Bundestag report in 1952, for example, stated that the re-employment of four ex-Nazis in the Foreign Ministry could damage confidence abroad in West Germany. In the late 1950s cases began to emerge of leading Nazis high in government. Theodor Oberländer, a member of Adenauer's own CDU, was forced to resign as Minister for Refugees in 1960 following a claim that he had actively participated in a massacre of Jews in the Ukrainian city of Lvov in 1941. In the same year an accusation was made in the GDR against the Secretary of State in the Chancellor's Office, Hans Globke, that not only had he written a Nazi commentary on the 1935 Nuremberg Race Laws, but he had helped to formulate the laws themselves. The West German judiciary ceased its investigation for lack of evidence in 1961, whereas the GDR's Supreme Court found him guilty in 1963 of 'intellectual mass murder'. He resigned in 1963 at the same time as Adenauer.

The 1950s saw the building of a stable Western democracy in the Federal Republic. That democracy had its blemishes: in keeping with the spirit of Cold War times it was a cold house for communists. In a decision reminiscent of similar actions in the GDR, the Bundestag decided in July 1953 to offer compensation to victims of Nazi persecution, but to exclude those who opposed the 'democratic order'. Neo-Nazi organisations kept resurfacing and they enjoyed minor electoral success on a regional level, such as in Bremen, Lower Saxony and Rhineland-Palatinate in 1959. The institutions of West German democracy still employed a large number of individuals who had enjoyed successful careers in the Nazi period. Despite this, there was one area in which Adenauer was determined throughout his period in office to make amends for Germany's recent past.

Israel and Reparations

In July 1949 in Heidelberg the US High Commissioner John J. McCloy had made it clear that he regarded Germany's future treatment of the Jews as the touchstone by which its progress towards democracy would be measured. In his government statement in September 1949, Adenauer had sounded rather lame on the question of German guilt towards the Jews, which brought a sound rebuke in the Bundestag the following day from SPD leader, Kurt Schumacher. Nevertheless, as early as November 1949 Adenauer offered Israel reparations payments.

Negotiations were carried on in secret for some eighteen months beginning in early 1951. Israel had gained independence only in 1948 and had immediately had to defend its borders against its Arab neighbours. It was economically poor and also faced a surge in immigration in 1949–50. It desperately needed financial assistance to pay for the integration of the new arrivals. Eventually, and despite an attempt by an 'Organisation of Jewish Partisans' to assassinate Adenauer in March 1952, agreement was reached in September 1952 on payments totalling DM3 billion to Israel, in the form of goods, and over a period of twelve years up to 1964. The agreement was extremely controversial in Israel, while in Germany Adenauer had to rely on the support of the SPD in the Bundestag because of massive defections and abstentions in his own party. The amount of reparations paid throughout the 1950s was continually revised upwards.

In addition, secret negotiations between the West German Defence Minister, Franz-Josef Strauss, and the General Secretary in the Israeli Defence Ministry, Shimon Peres, led to West Germany supplying DM300 million-worth of weapons in spring 1958 free of charge. The controversy in Israel over the deal, which was denied by Adenauer, had caused Ben Gurion to resign on 30 December, though he re-formed his government one week later. When, in July 1959, the Israeli parliament approved the sale of Uzi submachine-guns to West Germany, the tensions that had been created caused the resignation of Ben Gurion. This time, he was unable to form a new government immediately and elections were held later that year, which he won.

In the midst of these controversies, West Germany refused to accord Israel diplomatic recognition. Adenauer claimed that the time was not right (such a move would certainly have been controversial in Israel, too), but it seems also that Adenauer was afraid that such a move could lead to the Arab states recognising the GDR, something he desperately wanted to avoid (see the Hallstein Doctrine, below). Also, in the winter of 1959–60 there was a concentration of the type of anti-Semitic incidents that had never been completely absent from West German life, including the painting of swastikas on synagogues and Jewish graves. The GDR gleefully exploited these incidents together with the Oberländer and Globke affairs for propaganda purposes.

Nevertheless, Adenauer's Germany had taken the first steps towards making reparation to the Jewish State for Nazism's crimes against the Jews. In March 1960 in New York, Ben Gurion and Adenauer contrived to 'accidentally' meet. The two men appeared to understand and respect each other, and Ben Gurion secured a commitment for further economic support for Israel. Ben Gurion, it seems, trusted Adenauer. Certainly, West Germany's actions in this respect gained international recognition (Deutschkron, 1991, pp. 106–18).

All of this stands in stark contrast to the GDR's attitude. There, though the state attempted to make individual reparation to citizens who had suffered under Nazism, it also introduced an evil distinction between 'victims of fascism' and 'fighters against fascism', with the latter obtaining greater benefits from the state. In addition there was a distinctly anti-Semitic feel to the purges and show trials of the early 1950s, with Paul Merker, a non-Jewish communist who had consistently supported the establishment of the Jewish state, being singled out for particular persecution. The state refused to pay any reparations to Israel, or to recognise Israel's existence, throughout its own forty years to 1990. Instead, the GDR became one of the most prominent supporters of the Arab and later Palestinian cause (Herf, 1997, pp. 106–61).

The Cold War and Military Alliances

Thus far, with the exception of relations with Israel, we have looked at developments inside the two German states after their foundation in 1949. Events in the wider world, such as the Korean War or the Hungarian uprising, have only been hinted at. It is time now to turn to these.

The two German states created in 1949 were already to some extent members of opposing military and economic blocs. Throughout the 1950s their membership of mutually hostile alliances was reinforced, thus deepening the rift between them. Though the military and economic alliances are linked, we shall consider first the military issue.

As early as 1950 West Germany began to re-arm. Differing signals came from the Western Allies as to the terms under which this should happen. The USA appeared to want a strong West Germany, whereas France was still afraid of Germany and preferred instead the idea of a joint military force in which West Germany could participate – under French leadership, of course. In November, Adenauer supported the French Premier, Pleven, who had called for a unified army, though he rejected the notion that West Germany should forgo its own army. These plans met with strong resistance in the West German population, and a series of demonstrations were held, though the authorities also banned many others. The Federal Minister of the Interior, Gustav Heinemann (CDU), a Protestant minister who had opposed the Nazis, resigned over the issue. In the late 1950s he joined the SPD.

On 26 May 1952 the Foreign Ministers of the USA, Britain, France and West Germany signed the Bonn Treaty formally ending the occupation of West Germany. On the following day, in Paris, the foreign ministers of France, Italy, West Germany and the Benelux countries signed the treaty establishing the European Defence Community (EDC). The treaty envisaged co-operation at all levels to defend Western Europe against 'aggression' from outside. In order to come into force both treaties had first to be approved by the parliaments of all the signatory states. The greatest opposition to both treaties emerged in France, however, and they were defeated in the parliament there in August 1954.

In July 1952 the East German special police, who had been armed with Soviet weapons since January, were effectively turned into an army and renamed the 'Paramilitary Police in Barracks'. It was formally turned into the National People's Army in March 1956, at which point it also became part of the Warsaw Pact military alliance, led by the Soviet Union, which the GDR had joined at its inception on 14 May 1955. In September 1955 the GDR signed a mutual friendship treaty with the Soviet Union, committing its long-term future to the Eastern Bloc.

Meanwhile, West Germany had been no less keen to integrate itself into the Western Alliance. The rejection of the EDC Treaty was but a minor hiccup. In October 1954 four new treaties were signed in Paris. The first ended the occupation statute in West Germany, the second created the 'West European Union', with France, Britain, Italy, West Germany and the Benelux countries as members. The third treaty admitted West Germany to Nato, the Western military alliance that had been created in April 1949, and the fourth regulated the position of the Saar. The French parliament approved the treaties in December 1954, the Bundestag in February 1955. They came into force on 5 May 1955. It was no accident that the GDR's membership of the Warsaw Pact followed just a few days later. Similarly, the GDR's friendship treaty with the Soviets had been preceded by a West German trade and friendship agreement with the USA, signed in October 1954.

By the mid-1950s each state was firmly in the opposite military bloc. Throughout this period Adenauer pursued a single-minded policy of Western integration. The SED and the Soviets were always careful to let the West make the first moves. As in the period up to 1949, the Soviets were keen not to be seen as the initiators of division.

West European Economic Integration

As early as 1950 the GDR had joined the Council for Mutual Economic Aid, or Comecon, as it came to be called by the West. This was a Communist equivalent to the later (West) European Economic Community. It was led by the Soviet Union, and the aim was to increase trade between member states. Already in 1950, 61 per cent of the GDR's trade was with other socialist countries, while only 28 per cent was with West Germany. Trade terms between the Soviet Union and its satellite states were rarely favourable to anyone other than the Soviet Union itself. The GDR was thus caught in something of a bind. Initially, its trade with Eastern Europe increased at the expense of West Germany, but in later years it succeeded in opening new markets in other Western countries.

West Germany found itself engaging in economic co-operation with its Western neighbours, especially France, from an early stage. France had long coveted the coal-rich Saar and Ruhr areas, and in May 1950 the French Foreign Minister, Robert Schuman, suggested integrating the French and German coal and steel industries while also allowing other European countries to participate in the project. The Schuman Plan, as it became known, led to the signing in April 1951 by France, Germany, Italy and the Benelux countries of the treaty establishing the European Coal and Steel Community (ECSC). The treaty took effect in July 1952.

The ECSC was, in effect, the forerunner of the European Economic Community (EEC), which came into existence on 1 January 1958 following the signing of the Treaty of Rome by the same six states in March 1957. The aim of both organisations was to create a common market by eliminating customs duties between member states and harmonising both customs duties for other states and also price, cartel and trade policies. The ECSC aimed to do this in the named areas, the EEC sought to do this in all areas, and it finally absorbed the ECSC in 1968.

West Germany's integration into Western agencies did not stop there. It also joined both the Organisation for European Economic Co-operation and the European Payment Union in 1950, became an associate member of the Council of Europe in 1950, joined the General Agreement on Tariffs and Trade in 1951 and the International Monetary Fund in 1952. And, of course, West Germany continued to benefit from the Marshall Plan into the 1950s. In 1960, French President Charles de Gaulle, who had built up a good relationship with Adenauer since their first meeting in

1958, even suggested a formal political union of France and West Germany. Adenauer rejected this idea.

Thus West Germany became thoroughly integrated, both economically and militarily, into the Western world. One commentator has argued that 'by including West Germany in these developments rather than applying punitive isolation it was a brilliant contrast to the fiasco of the post-first world war years' (Alcock, 1998, p. 245). This is true, but it is also true that West Germany, no less than Japan in the Far East, was seen as a necessary bulwark against possible Communist attempts at expansion. And in the midst of all this cooperation, there was one fly in the ointment which was not finally removed until 1957.

The Saar

France had always had ambitions in respect of the Saar. After the First World War, not content with recapturing the two German-speaking provinces of Alsace and Lorraine, it had forced the Saar region, rich in coal deposits, into economic union with France under a League of Nations mandate for fifteen years. When the mandate expired in 1935 the population of the Saar voted overwhelmingly to return to Germany.

In 1945 France had again made the Saar a special territory, which enjoyed customs and currency union with France from early 1948. By 1949 it was 'in the process of becoming a French satellite state' (Williamson, 2001, p. 39). The Saar Convention of March 1950 confirmed the autonomy of the region, while making France also responsible for the diplomatic representation of the territory. This caused massive protests in Germany. France even wanted to admit West Germany to the Council of Europe only if the Saar was also admitted separately, which Adenauer rejected.

In 1952 France appointed an ambassador to the Saar, which amounted to diplomatic recognition, and also proposed a Europeanisation of the region. Adenauer's government reacted by insisting that the Saar was German. All German political parties in the Saar remained banned, and for the state elections there in 1952 Bonn called on voters to spoil their ballot papers, which 24 per cent did. The ongoing negative effect on Franco-German relations led to the negotiation of the Saar Statute, signed in Paris in October 1954, which confirmed the customs and currency union with France but placed a WEU Commissioner in charge of defence and foreign policy. Effectively, this amounted to a Europeanisation of the region, but the population would be given a vote. When it voted in October 1955, 68 per cent rejected the Saar Statute on a 97 per cent turnout.

New elections called two months later, to which pro-German parties were admitted for the first time, saw these parties win 64 per cent of the vote. When the Saarland parliament voted on 31 January 1956 for unification with West Germany, France capitulated and opened new negotiations with Bonn. The Saarland became a state of West Germany on 1 January 1957, with economic union following in July 1959. Unification of the whole of Germany remained elusive.

Questions of Unification

In the light of the policy decisions made in the areas of economics and foreign policy throughout the 1950s by both German states and by the Allies, it is difficult to see calls for unity as anything other than humbug. Undoubtedly, there were many on both sides who genuinely wanted unification. It is difficult to argue that anyone set out with the express intention of dividing Germany (though this had been the preferred French option in 1945, not into two states but into several small ones). Yet the lasting impression that remains is that those who were prepared to compromise military and economic alliances in favour of German unity were a minority in the corridors of power in both states.

When the GDR formally recognised the Oder–Neisse border in 1950 there were rumblings of discontent even in the ranks of the SED. West Germany refused point blank to acknowledge the new border. Yet this was simply giving legal recognition to decisions made at Potsdam. For all practical purposes unification would now mean the unification of the remaining three-quarters of pre-1938 German territory.

The Western position was, fundamentally, that free and fair elections should be held in the whole of Germany. A free, elected German government would then be able to negotiate a peace treaty with the Allies, and also negotiate membership of whatever military and economic alliances it chose. Adenauer had little doubt that a non-communist government would be returned and that its political orientation would be towards the West and membership of Nato.

For the Soviets and the SED this was unacceptable. The Soviet Union had just lost 20 million people in a war against Germany and it was not prepared to contemplate a united Germany as part of a military alliance directed against it. For the German communists (and also for many Social Democrats) this thought was also completely unacceptable. The Soviets thus offered free elections in Germany as a whole in return for a commitment to neutrality. This was unacceptable to Adenauer, whose most famous dictum on the subject was that he would rather be wholly in control of half of Germany than half in control of the whole of Germany.

Perhaps the most significant communication on the subject was the Stalin Note of March 1952. Stalin attempted several times during the negotiations on the EDC to offer free elections in return for military neutrality. In March 1952 a concrete offer was addressed to the US government: free elections in return for a guarantee of military neutrality and recognition of the borders created in 1945. The American answer insisted on the right of a united Germany to join military alliances, and also pointed out that the borders created in 1945 had not been finally agreed. In the light of these two irreconcilable positions, German unification was a non-starter.

It seems that fear was the dominant emotion in both East and West. Some historians have wondered whether Stalin was bluffing. The likelihood is that he was not. 'As far as the USSR was concerned, western integration of the Federal Republic appeared extremely threatening, and [was] to be averted if at all possible' (Fulbrook, 1991, p. 178). Stalin was not merely afraid of a unified Germany allied to the West. He also saw Western integration of the Federal Republic as a threat and appears to have been prepared to sacrifice communist rule in East Germany to prevent this. A neutral, unified Germany he saw as no threat.

By the same token, many in the West saw Stalin's offer as a ploy, a subterfuge that would create conditions in which the Communists could take power in Germany, and they were not prepared to risk this happening. In rejecting Stalin's note, the US echoed the feelings of Adenauer and most of his government.

Allied conferences on the possibility of German unity were held on several occasions. In Berlin in January and February 1954, the foreign ministers of the Soviet Union, the USA, Britain and France reached agreement on Korea and Indochina but not on Germany. The four heads of government and their foreign ministers met in Geneva in July 1955, where despite much smiling no agreement was reached. In November 1955, the foreign ministers again met in Geneva, without success. The two-part conference of foreign ministers in Geneva in summer 1959 also ended with no breakthrough, though at a meeting in Camp David in September 1959 the Soviet leader Nikita Khrushchev and US President Dwight D. Eisenhower agreed to maintain contact on the issue.

From the mid-1950s Adenauer's government claimed to be the sole legitimate government in Germany and therefore to speak for all Germans. The legitimacy of the SED government in the GDR, which the West still officially referred to as the 'Zone' or 'Middle Germany' ('East Germany' being the territory lost to Poland), was explicitly denied. In 1955 West Germany formulated a policy known as the Hallstein

Doctrine, named after the state secretary in the Foreign Office who devised the policy. West Germany would refuse to have diplomatic relations with any state that recognised the GDR diplomatically. There was to be only one exception, the Soviet Union. The aim was to prevent international recognition of the division of Germany. The policy was effective for about ten years, and it was supported by economic subsidies to some Third World countries that might otherwise have recognised the GDR. The first victim of the policy was Yugoslavia, with which West Germany broke off diplomatic relations when it recognised the GDR in 1957. Cuba followed in 1963, but by the late 1960s a new atmosphere prevailed. This is discussed in the next chapter.

Some things began to change in the late 1950s. In 1958, Adenauer tentatively suggested the Austrian model of demilitarised neutrality for the territory of the GDR in a unified Germany (though not for West Germany). It was a sign that Adenauer was beginning to grasp the reality of division, but the proposal was simply ignored by the Soviets.

The 1959 Geneva Conference had taken place in the wake of Khrushchev's Berlin Ultimatum of November 1958, which in turn had been in part a response to the Bundestag's decision in March 1958 to approve the acquisition of atomic weapons for the West German army. The Cold War became decidedly heated in the course of 1958, and the conference of 1959 was a response to this. The division of Germany was set to last, but the problem of Berlin remained: a divided city with the Western, capitalist part located more than 100 miles inside at times hostile GDR territory. Berlin was to be the focus of the Cold War struggle from 1958 until the summer of 1961.

The Berlin Wall

Ever since 1945 Berlin had been in a curious position. The city administration had split in 1948, but technically the whole city was still under four-power control. As if to reinforce the point, Soviet troops would regularly drive through the streets of West Berlin, while US, British and French troops would make forays into East Berlin. When the two states were founded in 1949, Berlin's position became even more curious. Strictly speaking, it was part of neither state, a situation that was maintained at the insistence of the Allies, who were reluctant to give up their rights in the city.

Practically, however, East Berlin became integrated into the GDR, though with certain rights always reserved for the Allies. When local government was reorganised in the GDR in 1952, East Berlin effectively became the fifteenth district. The seat of government was East Berlin and diplomatic representatives were accommodated there. Yet little things persisted which set East Berlin apart. Its members of the People's Chamber were appointed by the City Council rather than directly elected by the people (until 1981). The SPD organised there (until 1961), a concession that had been made in order to allow the SED to organise in West Berlin. And, of course, there were the occasional patrols by Western soldiers.

Nevertheless, East Berlin's geographical position allowed for a degree of normality that was not afforded West Berlin. The East German Secret Police, the Stasi, was actively involved in the kidnapping of more than 100 people from West Berlin in the 1950s. Periodically, the Soviets and later the GDR police would harass traffic between West Germany and West Berlin: in 1951 this even led briefly to a mini-air transport reminiscent of the days of the Berlin Blockade. In the wake of the Blockade of 1948–9 unemployment rose to 30 per cent in West Berlin in February 1950, so that the federal government declared an economic emergency there in March. The border between the two parts of Berlin was open, trams and the underground criss-crossed the border, and many people lived in one half of the city and worked in the other. It was an almost surreal situation.

West Berlin was also left feeling insecure by the insistence of the Western Allies that it could not become a state of the

Federal Republic. Despite the demands of the West Berlin parliament, in July 1949 the Western Allies banned direct elections to the Bundestag in West Berlin. When, in August 1950, the West Berlin parliament approved a new constitution describing the city as a state of the Federal Republic, this clause was annulled by the Allies. West German laws would only apply to West Berlin if they were approved by the West Berlin parliament. In practice, a procedure was established by which they were adopted almost automatically, subject to an Allied veto.

In 1958 Khrushchev issued a so-called 'Berlin Ultimatum'. In October, SED leader Ulbricht claimed that West Berlin was part of the sovereign territory of the GDR, a claim that was rejected by the West Berlin mayor, Willy Brandt. In November, in Moscow, Khrushchev claimed that the West had not honoured the four-power agreements on Berlin. He demanded that the Allies withdraw from West Berlin and that it be turned into a demilitarised free city within six months, or else the Soviet Union would sign a separate peace treaty with the GDR and hand over control of the transit routes to the GDR authorities. On 31 December, the Western Allies formally rejected this ultimatum and insisted that the agreements on Berlin remained in place. At the same time they expressed a willingness to engage in discussions on European security as long as the ultimatum was withdrawn.

Khrushchev did not hold to his ultimatum. What his motives for issuing it may have been is not known. Partly he seems to have been confident of Soviet superiority after putting the first man in space in October 1957. Partly he undoubtedly wanted to neutralise West Berlin as a centre of subversion against Eastern Europe. He was also attempting to secure Western recognition of the GDR, a state that was still unrecognised by anyone other than Soviet allies and Yugoslavia. And he wanted to help resolve the problem of East Germans fleeing to the West. Yet Khrushchev backed down. Negotiations held in 1959 produced no agreement.

When Khrushchev met the new US President, John F. Kennedy, in Vienna in June 1961, he adopted an aggressive stance, even threatening war if the USA refused to compromise over Berlin. Kennedy made it plain that he was prepared to go to war over the issue of access to West Berlin, even nuclear war (Dennis, 2000, pp. 90–3).

The problem remained of the refugees, who represented a massive 'brain drain' and a significant annual loss to the GDR economy. West Berlin was the escape route for most, since the border between East and West Germany had been sealed years previously. If a diplomatic solution could not be found, then the GDR might be threatened with collapse. The alternative put forward by Ulbricht in early 1961 was to seal the border with West Berlin. Publicly he denied this: in June 1961 Ulbricht stated categorically to a reporter that 'no-one intends to build a wall'. Khrushchev was initially reluctant, since he saw it as a massive admission of failure on the part of socialism. Nevertheless, after the Vienna meeting they felt that they had few options. At a meeting of the First Secretaries of the Communist Parties of the Warsaw Pact on 3–5 August 1961 in Moscow, approval was given. On the morning of 13 August 1961 Berliners woke up to find that the two parts of their city were separated by barbed wire, which was gradually replaced by concrete blocks. Some East Berliners escaped in the next few days, but the problem of mass emigration had been resolved. People on all sides were unhappy about this step, even some communists regarding it as an admission of failure. President Kennedy's words perhaps best sum up reactions: 'It's not a nice solution . . . but a hell of a lot better than war' (Dennis, 2000, pp. 93–4).

Adenauer and CDU Success

When the border was sealed Adenauer was on an electoral campaigning tour in West Germany. He finally went to Berlin nine days later. By contrast, the mayor of West Berlin and SPD candidate for Chancellor, Willy Brandt, stopped campaigning and returned to Berlin immediately. The different reactions were seen by many as an indication of Adenauer's true attitude to Berlin and to German unification.

Konrad Adenauer was the towering figure in West German political life until the early 1960s. Born in 1876 in the Catholic Rhineland, he had been mayor of Cologne from 1917 to 1933 and President of the Prussian State Council from 1924 to 1933, when the Nazis removed him from both posts. Though the Nazis imprisoned him for two short periods, he was never engaged in opposition to them. Rather, he was a conservative politician of the Catholic Centre Party, who essentially retreated into the private sphere after 1933. He re-emerged as the American-appointed mayor of Cologne in 1945, but was sacked by the British the same year as someone they found to be too obstructive. Yet he quickly rose to prominence within the CDU and was the obvious choice for Chancellor after the 1949 election.

If Erhard may be seen as the father of the economic miracle, then Adenauer was without doubt the father of Western integration. The reasons for this are unclear. Time and again in Adenauer's biography he appears first and foremost to be not a German nationalist but a Rhinelander with a pro-Western orientation typical of that region. One of his biographers has titled a chapter on him 'Rheinland, Rheinland über alles' ('Rhineland, Rhineland above all'). This play on the words of the German national anthem ('Deutschland, Deutschland über alles') gives a clear indication of what many saw as his real political orientation (von Uexküll, 1998, p. 29). At the end of the First World War, Adenauer had briefly been involved in a political movement for Rhineland autonomy, until he saw that Germany was, after all, likely to remain united, at which point he turned away from the separatists. Yet the episode showed his pro-Western convictions, which were at odds with the idea of a united, Berlin-led Germany that looked as much to the East as to the West. In some ways the 'Bonn Republic' was a larger version of the 1918 project for Rhineland autonomy. Bonn, a small town on the Rhine, was chosen over Frankfurt as capital of the Federal Republic in a vote by the Parliamentary Council in May 1949.

Adenauer's policy was, however, not simply about the Rhineland. Rather, he identified clearly with what he saw as West European values such as Catholic conservatism and liberal democracy. He himself regarded his decision to opt for a pro-Western policy as the most important decision he made in 1949. In choosing this path he was not without enemies. Some of the most rabid anti-communists in his own ranks were not particularly pro-Western. However, the most vehement opposition in the Federal Republic came from the SPD, led until his death in 1952 by Kurt Schumacher.

Schumacher was a left-wing German nationalist who opposed both the pro-Moscow attitude of the SED (he had opposed the amalgamation of SPD and KPD in 1946) and the pro-Western policies of Adenauer. He was a cutting rhetorician who frequently clashed with Adenauer in the Bundestag. Schumacher, who had been in Nazi concentration camps from 1933 to 1944, when he was released on health grounds, rejected the Ruhr Statute, the Saar Convention, the creation of the ECSC and the policy of re-arming Germany, all of which he saw as harming the potential for unification. He was at the head of the SPD when it lost the first Bundestag election, but died in 1952 from bad health caused by wounds received in the First World War.

Schumacher's SPD, led from 1952 by Erich Ollenhauer, was still to some extent the radical, working-class party with a Marxist agenda that it had been before 1933. It advocated widespread nationalisation of industry, and defence policies that were opposed to atomic and nuclear weapons and also opposed to any significant re-arming of Germany. The party represented a course that was radically different from Adenauer's pro-Western stance, and that left it out of touch with popular opinion.

The 1953 election showed that Adenauer was winning the hearts and minds of most West Germans. The election was held in September, just a few months after events on the streets of East Berlin and in a society that was already beginning to show signs of increasing wealth. Adenauer's CDU, together with its sister party the Bavarian CSU, reaped the benefit. Together they won 45.2 per cent of the vote, an increase of 14 per cent, and fell just one seat short of an outright majority. The SPD vote actually dropped slightly, from 29.2 per cent to 28.8 per cent. The Free Democrats, the League of Expellees, the German Party and the Centre Party (the latter two thanks to local agreements with the CDU) all won seats. Adenauer formed a coalition with these parties (except the Centre) and enjoyed a two-thirds majority in parliament.

In 1957, the CDU/CSU improved further, winning 50.2 per cent of the vote and an outright majority of seats. The SPD recovered only slightly, winning 31.8 per cent, while the FDP and German Party were again represented. Adenauer formed a coalition government with the German Party, whose leading members joined the CDU in 1959. The CDU, led by its by now 81-year-old Chancellor, was thus guaranteed another four years in government.

Adenauer created what many have termed a 'chancellor democracy' in 1950s West Germany. His style was almost presidential, and he combined the roles of Chancellor and Foreign Minister in the early years, thus retaining ultimate control of both national and foreign policy while leaving the economics to Erhard. Adenauer's power derived partly from his strength of character. He appointed weak ministers, whom he saw more as advisers, and he used his position to avoid holding meetings when he thought his power might be challenged. Some have argued that his desire for 'yes-men' was one reason for the large number of ex-Nazis in his cabinet, since they were in no position to challenge him. Partly, however, the Basic Law and electoral law put the Chancellor in a strong position. The list system gave him influence over the choice of nominees. He was responsible for policy guidelines and could only be removed by a constructive vote of no confidence. However, he also had the power to dissolve the Bundestag if such a vote was inconclusive. Ultimately, all these factors combined to make Adenauer a strong chancellor. His successors were generally weak and lasted only a few years. The expression 'chancellor democracy' ultimately relates only to Adenauer's term of office.

Conclusion

Adenauer and the CDU made West Germany in the 1950s their own. They brought economic prosperity, material wealth, political stability and relative security to a population that wished to move on and put the recent past behind it. CDU-led governments were seen to be responsible for this prosperity, and the voters rewarded them with spectacular increases in their vote; 1957 remains to date the only time in the history of the Federal Republic that one party obtained an outright majority of votes. Adenauer also secured for the Federal Republic a respected place in the international community, thanks to a policy of co-operation with neighbours and of reparations towards Israel.

The SPD learned from Adenauer's success. In November 1959 it jettisoned its Marxist, anti-Western policies in favour of the 'Godesberger Programme', which redefined the party as a mass movement, rather than a workers' party. It now advocated a form of democratic socialism, accepted the market economy and supported the need for national defence, implicitly in a Western setting, while rejecting nuclear weapons. The 1960s were to bring it greater success.

In the GDR, the SED strengthened its control over all aspects of daily life, and also led the population to a degree of material wealth that was high by East European standards but lower than in West Germany. That wealth was not enough for some, however, so that in the end, only the building of a wall could guarantee continued SED control and increasing prosperity to the population.

By 1961, the policies of the leaders in both German states had led to the reinforcement of the division of the country in a state of mutual hostility. The SED was 'building socialism' in the GDR, while the CDU had successfully built a capitalist system in the West. What has been called the 'discourse of a divided Germany' was a more or less permanent propaganda war in which it was 'not so much the facts as how these were presented' that mattered (Thomaneck and Niven, 2001, p. 37). West Germany succeeded in putting the blame for division, in the eyes of most Westerners, on the Soviets and the GDR, conveniently downplaying the consequences of its own pro-Western stance. The national division that took such concrete form in Berlin in August 1961 remained, for many Germans, the bitterest legacy of the Second World War. But it was also, in part, a result of German political intransigence on both sides after 1945.

3

SEPARATE PATHS, 1961–9

Introduction

When the 1960s began, Adenauer had an absolute majority in parliament and the CDU was the party of economic prosperity in West Germany. His government was conservative and anti-communist and it pursued a policy of Western integration and complete hostility to the East. Few if any of its members had opposed the Nazis, while some had actively supported that regime. Yet by 1969, Adenauer and many more of his era were dead, while both the President and Chancellor of the West German state were men who had actively opposed Nazism.

By 1961 two completely distinct and mutually hostile German states existed. They each still paid lip service to the concept of unity, but as the 1960s progressed it became clear that they were destined to pursue quite separate paths in political development. Stalinist and neo-Stalinist control-thinking remained dominant in the leadership of the SED, so that the GDR had to wait some ten years after the building of the Wall for a period of liberalisation. By contrast, the Federal Republic changed radically in the 1960s. It is for that reason that this chapter concentrates on developments in West Germany.

The 1961 Election

The SPD under its new candidate for Chancellor, Willy Brandt, who was ruling mayor in Berlin, hoped to make gains that would enable it to form a coalition with the CDU. Certainly, Brandt had received widespread favourable publicity in the wake of his response to the events of 13 August in Berlin. Brandt's attitude contrasted sharply with that of Adenauer, who took more than a week after the building of the Wall to go to Berlin. Bitterness towards Adenauer remained in Berlin long after his death: such behaviour seemed to confirm the widely held belief that for him anything east of the River Elbe was Siberia (Stratenschulte, 1997, p. 101).

Nevertheless, the CDU and FDP profited from the increased tension and resultant fear of the left in general and communism in particular, and also from their association with the benefits of the economic miracle and the stability that this had brought. The electorate's frustration with Adenauer resulted in a shift from the CDU and smaller parties to both the Social Democrats and the FDP, which had campaigned for a coalition with the CDU led by Erhard rather than Adenauer. The CDU/CSU dropped 4.9 per cent to 45.3 per cent, thereby losing its outright majority, while the Free Democrats gained 5.1 per cent, achieving their best result to date in the history of post-1945 Germany, 12.8 per cent. The SPD also increased, up by 4.5 per cent to 36.2 per cent. All of the smaller parties were eliminated from parliament at this election, leaving just a three-party system.

Despite its pledge not to enter a coalition led by Adenauer, the FDP did just that after long negotiations, though on condition that Adenauer agree to hand over to a successor before the next election in 1965. Nevertheless, the FDP's credibility suffered, and its performance in a series of state elections in 1962 and 1963 was significantly lower than its national performance in 1961.

The *Der Spiegel* Affair and the End of Adenauer

The Bavarian conservative and CSU deputy chairman Franz Josef Strauss had been Minister for Defence under Adenauer since 1956, and was thus a central figure in the creation of the new army, the Bundeswehr. As early as 1950 Strauss had pleaded for the re-arming of the Federal Republic in the context of a Western alliance. Strauss had made a particular enemy of many Free Democrats, and he was thoroughly disliked in the SPD and among peace activists, but he had the full backing of Adenauer.

On 10 October 1962 the weekly news magazine *Der Spiegel*, which had been created in 1947 and was closely modelled on the US *Time* magazine, published an article by its deputy editor and defence expert Conrad Ahlers on the Nato military exercise 'Fallex 62'. On the charge that the article contained some classified material, police occupied the editorial offices of the magazine on 26 October and also asked General Franco's police to arrest Ahlers, who was on holiday in Spain at the time. Two days later Ahlers was handed over to the German authorities, while the magazine's publisher, Rudolf Augstein, and other journalists were arrested and had their homes searched. Two army colonels were also arrested a few weeks later. *Der Spiegel*'s offices remained occupied by the police until the end of November, by which time some 20 million documents had been looked at and many had been confiscated.

This spectacular action provoked massive protest. Its legality was dubious from the start. Strauss had not even informed the Minister of Justice, FDP politician Wolfgang Stammberger, beforehand, for fear that he would alert *Spiegel* staff. The Interior Minister, Hermann Höcherl, admitted that the arrest of Ahlers in Spain had been 'somewhat outside the bounds of legality'. Adenauer, meanwhile, claimed in the Bundestag on 7 November that there was treason afoot in the country.

Almost all German newspapers condemned the action as an attack on the freedom of the press. Various publishers and newspapers gave *Der Spiegel* the use of rooms in order to ensure its continued publication. On 28 October 1962, 49 prominent writers, including Günter Grass and Uwe Johnson, made public their opposition to the attack on *Der Spiegel*. On 16 November, the FDP announced that it could not remain in government with Strauss. On 19 November, its ministers resigned and on 27 November, the government resigned to prevent a vote of no confidence in Strauss alone. This gave Adenauer time to form a new coalition. He approached the SPD, but it rejected a coalition led by him. In December, the FDP agreed to enter a new coalition with the CDU/CSU on condition that Adenauer agree to step down in autumn 1963. Strauss was replaced as Minister for Defence by Kai-Uwe von Hassel, while Stammberger also left the government.

The *Der Spiegel* Affair was an important turning point in the history of West Germany because it marked the beginning of the end of Adenauer's tenure in government. As an event it was in many ways symbolic of the arrogance that had crept into government after 13 years of unbroken conservative rule. It also represented an old, authoritarian German attitude to government and citizens' rights, one which was roundly rejected by the population as a whole and, ultimately, by the courts, too. Ahlers and Augstein were acquitted of treason by the Federal Supreme Court in May 1963 (Nicholls, 1997, pp. 177–8). No one arrested was ever convicted, nor was anyone involved in carrying out this semi-legal operation ever charged with law-breaking.

Adenauer was 86 years old at the time of the *Der Spiegel* Affair and he regarded the West German state almost as his own. It was certainly largely his creation, but by now voices were being raised to suggest that new approaches were needed to the main political issues, not least East–West relations. Knowing that his term in office was drawing to a close, Adenauer tried one last manoeuvre in early 1963. He attempted to prevent the CDU from nominating Ludwig Erhard as his successor, suggesting his former Foreign Minister, Heinrich von Brentano, among others, as an alternative. Despite this, in April 1963 the CDU/CSU parliamentary party voted for Erhard to succeed him, and on 16 October

1963 the Bundestag duly elected Erhard as Chancellor. Adenauer remained as CDU chairman until 1966, still with some influence. It is a measure of the prominence and acceptance that he had gained for the Federal Republic that when he died in May 1967 heads of state and government leaders from around the world attended his funeral. Among them were US President Lyndon B. Johnson, British Prime Minister Harold Wilson and French President Charles de Gaulle.

Erhard as Chancellor

In some ways Erhard was a logical successor to Adenauer. As the father of the Economic miracle (though he disliked the term 'miracle') and Economics Minister since the creation of the Federal Republic he represented the prosperity and success of West Germany almost as much as Adenauer did. Under Erhard, West Germans had come to acquire most of the luxury goods that they desired, as well as the ability to travel and visit countries across Europe and beyond. In less than twenty years since the crushing defeat of Nazi Germany, a new, wealthy West German society had emerged.

One aspect of this new society was the gradual disappearance of the smaller parties. Nine political parties and four individuals had been represented in the first Bundestag in 1949. In 1953 only six parties remained, and in 1957 this was further reduced to just four. From 1961 until 1983 only three political parties were ever represented in the Bundestag, all of whom identified with the social market economy and the need for consensus politics. The extent to which the West German population supported the stability and continuity that this brought is best illustrated by the total vote for the three main parties: CDU/CSU, FDP and SPD. In 1949 these parties obtained 72.1 per cent of the vote. By 1961 they had 94.4 per cent of the vote. In the 1965 election, fought under Erhard as Chancellor, this increased again to 96.4 per cent. With only a minor blip in 1969 (for reasons discussed later in this chapter) this trend continued into the mid-1970s (see Appendix 1).

West German society was somewhat self-satisfied in this period, and the election result from 1965, in which the CDU regained some of the ground lost in 1961 but just fell short of an outright majority (47.6 per cent), reflected widespread approval of Erhard and all that he represented. To be sure, the SPD also gained ground, almost reaching 40 per cent, and the FDP dropped to 9.5 per cent from its 1961 peak, but the election was nevertheless a clear victory for the CDU/CSU. Willy Brandt, who had once again been the SPD's candidate for Chancellor, 'returned to Berlin in despair, believing his career had reached a dead end' (Nicholls, 1997, p. 185).

Despite his electoral success, Erhard faced problems. Adenauer continued to needle him from his position as CDU chairman. The party was also split between so-called Atlanticists such as Erhard and his Foreign Minister, Gerhard Schröder, who favoured more liberal foreign policies and closer co-operation with the USA and Great Britain, and the so-called Gaullists, such as Adenauer and Strauss, who favoured a hard line towards the East and closer co-operation with France, even to the extent of supporting de Gaulle's veto on British entry to the European Economic Community. However, the main problem facing Erhard was a minor economic recession that set in in the mid-1960s, coupled with increased hostility between the CDU and the FDP and a growing willingness in sections of the CDU to enter a coalition with the SPD. On a personal level, Erhard's own lack of ruthlessness perhaps also contributed to his downfall (Nicholls, 1997, pp. 187–8).

When he became Chancellor in 1963 Erhard represented continuity rather than innovation. He resigned as Chancellor in late November 1966 after just three years in office. A new era in West German politics was heralded by the creation of a grand coalition between the CDU/CSU and the SPD. The economic and political background to the creation of this 'Grand Coalition' will be discussed below. Before that, let us turn to German foreign policy.

Foreign Policy

West German foreign policy in the early 1960s was still centred on the idea that the Federal Republic was the sole representative of all Germans. Adenauer's pro-Western policies were never seriously questioned as the basis of foreign policy, even if some right-wingers in the CDU and CSU wished to pursue a more independent, German nationalist policy.

It is a measure of the agreement among the various shades of opinion in the party that one of the key issues, the debate between Atlanticists and Gaullists, was regarded almost as a non-issue. On the one hand, West Germany was keen to participate in Nato structures; on the other hand, the French under de Gaulle distrusted American leadership, and Adenauer wanted a close relationship with France. Tension increased when John F. Kennedy 'came to power with a team of intellectuals who took an unemotional view of the German situation and were anxious to reach a *modus vivendi* with the Soviet Union on the European sector of the cold war' (Grosser, 1974, p. 475).

The Franco-German Treaty of 22 January 1963 was in many ways the crowning glory of Adenauer's years of rapprochement with France. Though he had rejected political union when de Gaulle proposed this in 1960, Adenauer favoured close co-operation with France, and he was prepared to engage in this even as de Gaulle was signalling his rejection of 'Anglo-Saxon' (i.e. British and American) influence by resisting British membership of the EEC. On 29 January 1963, de Gaulle finally vetoed Britain's application.

In Bonn many politicians were so annoyed with Adenauer's stance that before ratifying the treaty, the Bundestag added a preamble stressing West Germany's commitment to

Nato and European Union. Though de Gaulle saw this as a negation of the treaty, Adenauer reassured him that it was not. After Adenauer, it became clear that Erhard was on far more friendly terms with US President Johnson than with de Gaulle. He also disliked the kinds of economic controls that he felt the French imposed on the economy, favouring instead his free market model.

Israel and the Arab Countries

The biggest foreign policy challenges facing West Germany in the 1960s related to the maintenance of the Hallstein Doctrine and to its policy of improving relations with Israel. The two issues were closely linked.

Despite his determination to help Israel as a sign of atonement for the Holocaust, Adenauer never established formal diplomatic relations with Israel. On several occasions he made it clear that this was largely due to the delicate situation that existed in Germany and between Israel and the Arab countries. In concrete terms, Adenauer was afraid that if West Germany recognised Israel, then the Arab countries would recognise the GDR. In this particular context the Hallstein Doctrine had become a millstone around West Germany's neck.

Nevertheless, both Adenauer's and Erhard's government continued the policy of reparations payments to Israel. In 1964, Israel and the Federal Republic signed a protocol on the implementation of the 1952 agreement, which envisaged payments totalling DM250 million to Israel. Finally, in 1965, Erhard's government grasped the nettle. When it became known in January of that year that the SED leader Walter Ulbricht was to visit Egypt, West Germany threatened to break off diplomatic relations. Instead, Erhard established diplomatic relations with Israel in May 1965, whereupon nine Arab countries, including Egypt, Saudi Arabia and Algeria, broke off relations with West Germany, though without establishing diplomatic relations with the GDR. Egypt only did so in July 1969, by which time the Hallstein Doctrine was already resting on very shaky foundations.

The trials of war criminals in West Germany continued throughout the 1960s, with notorious trials of defendants who were accused of participating in mass murder in Auschwitz, Treblinka and other Nazi death camps or of having been actively involved in implementing euthanasia programmes in the Nazi period. Concentration camp survivors and others ensured that attempts by some conservatives to simply forget the past were not successful, so that the West German state was forced to continue its efforts to come to terms with and atone for the Nazi past.

In the context of dealing with the Nazi past, two events stand out. One was the various debates over the statute of limitations for murder, which was fifteen years. As such, Nazi war criminals would have been free from prosecution after 1960. Survivors' groups were joined by the Soviet Union, Israel and others in protesting in strong terms that this would amount to an amnesty for war criminals. In debates held in 1960, 1965, 1969 and 1979 the Bundestag decided to extend the statute of limitations for Nazi crimes. Later the statute of limitations for genocide and murder were removed completely.

The other event was the trial in Israel of Adolf Eichmann, a Nazi bureaucrat who had played a senior administrative role in the organisation of the Holocaust. Eichmann had been kidnapped by the Israeli secret service in Argentina in 1960 and taken to Israel. His trial, which was widely reported throughout the world at the time, most notably in a series of articles for the *New Yorker* magazine by Hannah Arendt, exposed what Arendt controversially called 'The Banality of Evil' (Arendt, 1994). Eichmann was apparently quite dispassionate about the role he had played in the attempted genocide of the Jews. He was found guilty and executed in May 1963, and there was little echo to this in Germany.

One other event indicated the extent to which there had been a massive shift in opinion since 1945 among (West) Germans on the subject of Jews. When, in June 1967, Israel fought the Six-Day War against its Arab neighbours, West German public opinion was largely behind the Israelis, with only small sections of the left wing opposing Israel's actions. The shift in just over twenty years from support for Nazism to support for the Jewish State at war was a massive one in any terms. One problematic aspect of that support was that some conservative newspapers' backing of Israel appeared to be motivated more by admiration for Israel's stunningly successful military campaign than by support for the Jewish State as such.

German–German Relations

The building of the Berlin Wall forced West Germany to rethink its attitude to the East. Some people, especially those on the right wing of the CDU and CSU, retained their belief in a hard-line approach and in maintaining the Federal Republic's claim to speak for all Germans. Similarly, the Hallstein Doctrine remained in place, and when Fidel Castro's Cuba established diplomatic relations with the GDR in 1963 it became the second country with which West Germany broke off diplomatic relations.

Yet the reality was that on some issues West Germany now had no choice but to deal with the GDR. Of course, right through the 1950s there had been trade agreements, but now it became necessary to negotiate access to East Berlin and East Germany for West German citizens. The Wall and the East–West German border divided mothers and fathers from their sons and daughters, children from their grandparents, and siblings from each other. Adenauer's hard-line approach was often answered in kind by the GDR, with the result that families could not meet.

Egon Bahr, a spokesman for the highly popular ruling mayor of Berlin and SPD candidate for Chancellor, Willy Brandt, enunciated a new, more flexible approach to the GDR which would make life easier for families divided by the Wall and also, hopefully, promote reform in the GDR itself. Brandt was a massively popular figure in West Berlin: in January 1963 the SPD, led by him, had won 61.9 per cent of the vote in the state election there. In July 1963, Bahr promoted the idea of 'change through moving close together' (*Wandel durch Annäherung*). In suggesting this, Bahr was taking up US President Kennedy's proposition that the two German states should recognise each other's legitimate interests and co-operate in such areas. In June, Kennedy had visited Berlin and, asserting that West Berlin stood for the free world, proclaimed: 'Ich bin ein Berliner' to a crowd of around 300,000 people. Kennedy's hope was for German unity within the North Atlantic alliance, which he rightly saw as likely to be achieved neither quickly nor easily. Nevertheless, he made a massive impression in the city, and the square on which he had made his speech was renamed in his honour just 24 hours after his assassination in November 1963 (Baumann, 2001, p. 325).

The most tangible result of Brandt's new approach was the agreement in December 1963 between West Berlin and the GDR which allowed West Berliners to visit relatives in the East, the so-called 'Permit Agreement'. After the building of the Wall only West Germans, but not West Berliners, had been allowed to visit the east of the city. Between 19 December 1963 and 5 January 1964 over 700,000 West Berliners visited East Berlin, some of them several times, to meet with relatives they had not seen for more than two years. Criticism from Erhard that this separate agreement was lending credence to the East German theory that Germany was now three political entities (East Germany always emphasised that West Berlin was not a full part of the Federal Republic) caused negotiations for a similar agreement at Easter 1964 to break down. However, after a meeting with Erhard, Brandt was given more room to negotiate, and further agreements followed at Christmas 1964, Christmas 1965, and at Easter and Whitsun 1966, leading to more than one million visits each time. Subsequent disputes about the political status of the agreements led to a breakdown in July 1966, and no new accords were reached until 1972. West Berliners could only visit relatives in cases of emergency in this period.

Despite Brandt's approach, steps were taken by both sides which drove the two states further apart. In late 1961, members of the FDJ engaged in an aggressive campaign to prevent East Germans from watching Western television. This 'Ochsenkopf' campaign, named after a Bavarian mountain near the border, on which a large transmitter was situated, was ended only after several citizens threatened to take FDJ members to court. In June 1964, a suggestion from Ulbricht that newspapers from each state be sold in the other was rejected by Erhard on the grounds that this would contravene the ban on the Communist Party, a decision for which he was criticised by the SPD, FDP and even sections of his own party. In December 1964, the GDR introduced a compulsory minimum exchange of currency for Western visitors: the amount was DM5 at a rate of 1:1. In 1965, the GDR called for a united socialist Germany, a prospect so unrealistic that this was effectively a declaration that it was no longer really interested in unification. The GDR was also admitted to the International Olympic Committee that year, and in Mexico in 1968 two separate German teams competed in the Olympic Games for the first time. In 1967, the GDR created its own citizenship, thereby abandoning the notion of a single German citizenship. In 1968 a new constitution described the GDR as a 'Socialist State of the German Nation', thus reinforcing the separate citizenship and moving away from the 1949 constitution's declaration of Germany as an indivisible republic. In 1967, the SED also began pressuring the churches to split from the all-German organisations and set up separate GDR umbrella bodies. In 1968, the Eastern Region of the United Evangelical Lutheran Church of Germany became the first church to split from the all-German parent church. Finally, in 1969, the main Protestant Church of Germany (EKD) split, with the Eastern branches forming a 'League of Protestant Churches in the GDR'. The Catholic Church, very much a minority church in the GDR, reorganised its diocesan boundaries in the early 1970s.

Meanwhile, in the mid- and late 1960s the Hallstein Doctrine began to lose its force. In 1967, West Germany established diplomatic relations with Romania, despite that country's diplomatic ties to the GDR, a move which indicated only that the Hallstein Doctrine no longer applied to communist countries. It was still regarded as applying to neutral countries, so that in July 1969, despite opposition from Brandt, who was by now Vice-Chancellor in the Grand Coalition (see below), West Germany broke off diplomatic relationships with South Yemen after it had established relations with the GDR. After the 1969 federal election the Doctrine became defunct, though it was not formally abandoned until 1972.

The 1960s may be seen as a somewhat contradictory period in German–German relations. The GDR continued to strive for recognition as a separate state, but with limited success. In the West, progressive forces, centred around Brandt but including members of all parties, battled with conservatives to establish a new, more open policy towards the East. The real breakthrough in East–West German relations, indeed in West Germany's relations with the entire Soviet Bloc, came in the early 1970s, and will be discussed in the next chapter.

The GDR in the 1960s

If relations with West Germany were contradictory in the 1960s, then the political atmosphere within the GDR also went from conservative to liberal and back again. Ulbricht remained in control throughout this period; there was no question of the GDR being anything other than a loyal member of the Soviet Bloc, and the SED retained the reins of power. Still, younger politicians were coming through, and many writers and others saw, somewhat paradoxically, a new opportunity for openness in the wake of the building of the Wall. Rather than engaging in direct confrontation with the West and thus blaming the West for its own ills, the GDR would now have to try to resolve its contradictions internally. As the writer and singer Wolf Biermann has put it: now that the lid was on, the kettle might boil more quickly. Any steam that existed in society would now be kept in rather than let out to West Germany.

One of the first measures was the introduction of the New Economic System of Planning and Leadership (NÖSPL) in 1963. Based on the ideas of the Soviet economist Evsei S. Liberman, the new system involved a degree of decentralisation and also of rewarding increased production on a regional and individual basis. The aim was clear: in the face of an ever-increasing gap in the living standards of East Europeans compared with West Europeans, the system needed to be reformed to increase productivity and, by extension, the prosperity of ordinary East Germans. More enterprise autonomy and more material incentives were the key to these reforms. The task of carrying out the reforms was entrusted to Erich Apel, a former rocket scientist under the Nazis and, from 1946 to 1952, in the Soviet Union, who had little time for ideology. The Soviet Union appears to have tolerated rather than supported these reforms (Liberman's ideas were not implemented in the Soviet Union), and a number of SED conservatives such as Erich Honecker, Willi Stoph and Hermann Axen feared that they might mean moving closer to the West (Dennis, 2000, pp. 105–7).

Walter Ulbricht was a conservative who, somewhat surprisingly, supported the NÖSPL. But it met with increased opposition after Khrushchev's removal from power in the

Soviet Union in 1964. His successor Leonid Brezhnev singularly failed to give his backing to the experiment, and also
insisted on a new five-year trade agreement in 1965 that was,
once again, highly unfavourable to the GDR. Honecker and
others felt strengthened by Brezhnev's attitude to the
NÖSPL and began criticising Apel. It was claimed that the
system of incentives and bonuses could lead to 'socialist
millionaires'. Some in the party felt that their political position was being undermined by ideologically uncommitted
bureaucrats. Faced with mounting criticism, Apel committed
suicide in December 1965. Ironically, in 1966 the fruits of his
planning combined with a minor economic recession in the
West caused the GDR's economy to grow at a greater rate
than West Germany's for the first time since 1955. The
annual growth rate of 3.8 per cent was maintained for
three years before decreasing again from 1969. The system
was renamed the 'Economic System of Socialism' (ÖSS) in
1967, and ultimately it may be seen as only a half-reform,
since there was never any question of the SED giving up state
control of the economy. Some in the SED felt that the system
of bonuses undermined one of the party's key aims, which
was the achievement of social equality. The biggest problem
remained the setting of exaggerated goals. For all its successes, the new economic system was never likely to cause
standards of living in the GDR to overtake those in West
Germany.

Nevertheless, living standards did increase, and there is
strong evidence from West German opinion researchers that
young East Germans increasingly came to identify with the
GDR, favouring diplomatic recognition of their state, while
also maintaining a sense of German nationality. This duality
is similar to the official government stance adopted by the
GDR somewhat later (in 1974): 'Nationality: German. Citizenship: GDR.' In the 1960s the SED began emphasising the
'GDR' aspect of this dual identity and encouraged identification with the state. As part of this the FDJ tried to promote
a livelier image, organising evenings in which previously

forbidden Western music was played and danced to, or evenings of song at which popular singers such as Wolf Biermann performed. A high point was reached at the *Deutschlandtreffen* ('Germany Meeting') in East Berlin at Whitsun 1964 when 'thousands of young East and West Germans gathered in a relaxed atmosphere' and danced to jazz and rock music on Unter den Linden, East Berlin's main thoroughfare (Dennis, 2000, pp. 112–13). Sport assumed a top priority, and the success of GDR athletes within the last all-German Olympic team in 1964 (they won 23 medals) was built on for 1968, when the GDR came third behind the Soviet Union and the USA in the medals table. The GDR enjoyed massive success in sport throughout the 1970s and 1980s, which boosted its prestige, even if we know now that this success was in no small measure due to the practices of illegal drug taking, much of it administered to children without their parents' consent.

In the midst of this it was clear that under no circumstances would the SED relinquish control. The first tentative steps towards liberalism, which saw the publication of novels such as Christa Wolf's *Divided Heaven* in 1963, provoked a backlash at the 11th Plenary Meeting of the SED Central Committee in 1965. At that meeting Erich Honecker launched a massive attack on writers and artists, including some of the GDR's most prominent writers such as Stefan Heym, Heiner Müller and Wolf Biermann. The entire year's production of films from the DEFA studio in Babelsberg was banned, with one exception, Erik Neutsch's *Spur der Steine*, but when it came to be shown in 1966, protesting mobs organised by the SED caused its removal from cinemas. In August 1968, when Soviet tanks crushed the brave reform movement in Czechoslovakia that had attempted to implement a more liberal, democratic system, known as the 'Prague Spring', Ulbricht's GDR was an enthusiastic supporter of the tanks (Frank, 2001, p. 393). Its radio station, which broadcast in Czech and Slovak, was so hard-line that the Czechoslovak communists asked the SED to stop broadcasting. Many teachers, lecturers and others who refused to sign a document supporting the invasion lost their jobs. Despite rumours to the contrary in 1968 and after, however, archival evidence now shows that the GDR did not participate militarily in the invasion (Baumann, 2001, pp. 425–6).

The 1960s in the GDR can thus be summed up as a period of economic experimentation and growth coupled with very limited attempts at liberalisation under strict SED control. Though some have argued that Ulbricht was more of a liberal than has generally been assumed (Grieder, 1999, pp. 160–83), when it came to the crunch he almost always retreated into a hard-line position. Economic growth brought success and an increased sense of identification with the state. In 1966 the GDR opened its first nuclear power plant, a clear sign, at the time, of economic advancement. By 1969, 70 per cent of households had a television, while 50 per cent had a refrigerator and a similar number owned a washing machine. All of this occurred in the context of increased emphasis by the SED on the separateness of the GDR from West Germany. It was an attitude that the West Germans were only slowly beginning to accept, on a political level at least.

Economic Recession in the West

The years of economic growth in West Germany in the 1950s had in part been fuelled by the steady supply of labour from the GDR. Despite this, there were not enough people to fill all the jobs available. By 1960, for example, the average number of unemployed people was 241,000, or 1.3 per cent, while there were 570,000 job vacancies in the country. After 1961, when the building of the Wall caused the supply of labour from the East to dry up, the recruitment of foreigners, mostly southern Europeans, to work in West Germany intensified. In 1960 the average number of 'guest workers' in the Federal Republic was 270,000. In 1964 the millionth guest worker arrived. By 1973 they accounted for 10 per cent of the workforce.

In 1966, a minor economic recession began in West Germany. By the standards of the 1920s and 1930s or even the 1970s and 1980s it was insignificant. The unemployment rate never rose above 3.2 per cent, and by September 1968, when the unemployment rate was down to 0.8 per cent, effectively signalling full employment, it was over. The 'recession', such as it was, involved shortened working hours in such successful companies as Volkswagen (December 1966) and the steel industry (January 1967). For three years, economic growth in the GDR exceeded that of West Germany, a fact that was something of a shock to all concerned.

The effect of this economic slowdown was to shatter the myth of invincibility. After some fifteen years of continuous growth and the achievement of full employment, hundreds of thousands of Germans found themselves unemployed. The reactions to this were varied. Some blamed foreign workers for taking 'German' jobs, and began to vote for the NPD. Others took to the streets and protested. Some went on strike, such as 300,000 coal miners in March 1966, demanding protection against cheap imports of coal, and 30,000 farmers in March 1967, demanding greater subsidies for agriculture.

At a political level there were joint measures between the government and employers to subsidise those industries most threatened. The Federal Economics Minster, Karl Schiller, tried to organise a degree of concerted action between government and industry, while a major steel industrialist, Krupp, received large loans from the government in April 1967. In May 1967, parliament passed a law to promote the stability of economic growth, which provided a specific framework for greater government intervention in the economy. In November 1967, the government passed another law aimed at retraining coal miners for employment in other areas: almost 60,000 miners had lost their jobs that year. The success of these measures has already been mentioned. In many ways they were made possible precisely because the two largest parties in parliament, the CDU/CSU and the SPD, had joined forces in 1966 to form a grand coalition.

The Grand Coalition

Internal politics began to change in the 1960s in West Germany. Throughout the period the FDP had been growing increasingly restless with its role as a junior partner in CDU-led governments. In October 1966, proposed CDU measures that included higher taxation to deal with the economic downturn were rejected by the FDP, whose ministers resigned. This was different from the aftermath of the *Spiegel* Affair in 1962, when a new cabinet was formed through a reshuffle in the wake of FDP resignations. The SPD had been putting forward the idea for some time that it was ready to assume responsibility for government. When the upper house of parliament, the Bundesrat, rejected the budget unanimously, Erhard suffered a serious loss of prestige. On 2 November 1966 he announced that he was prepared to resign.

One week later the CDU leadership nominated the state president of Baden-Württemberg, Kurt Georg Kiesinger, as Erhard's successor. Negotiations on a new coalition between the CDU and FDP failed, whereupon the FDP, in its self-appointed role as 'kingmaker' in West German politics, attempted to form a coalition with the SPD. However, since the SPD leader Brandt could not be sure of support from all sections of the FDP, his party opted for a grand coalition with the CDU/CSU. On 1 December 1966, Kiesinger was elected Chancellor. Kiesinger's past (he had been a member of the Nazi Party from 1933 to 1945, though he was not implicated in any war crimes, working instead as a propagandist) led to some criticism of the appointment abroad. In stark contrast to this, his new Deputy Chancellor and

Foreign Minister, Willy Brandt of the SPD, had been an opponent of the Nazis who actively campaigned against them in exile in Scandinavia. In his first declaration on 13 December 1966, Kiesinger announced his priorities: passing emergency laws, improving relations with eastern Europe and consolidating state finances and the economy. In respect of the GDR he said: 'We want to ease and not harden the situation, to overcome rifts and not deepen them.'

Relations with the East entered an ambiguous phase in December 1966 that was only finally resolved after 1969. The Grand Coalition was also faced with other problems. Emergency laws became just one of the major issues of the coalition's period of office. The biggest problem was the lack of parliamentary opposition: the government had 447 seats in parliament, while the FDP as sole opposition had only 49 seats. And if there was no opposition in parliament, there were those who felt that opposition would then have to be organised outside the Bundestag (Glees, 1996, p. 151). This came from both right and left, on the streets and in the state parliaments.

Neo-Nazism in West Germany

Nazism had never completely disappeared from the West German political scene after 1945. We have already seen that the Socialist Reich Party was banned in 1952 and that other neo-Nazi parties enjoyed periodic electoral success in the 1950s. The most successful nationalist conservative party was the German Party (DP), a party that contained both conservatives, many of whom left to join the CDU in 1959, and some neo-Nazis, who re-formed the party in 1962 after the 1959 split. In 1963 the DP again won seats in Bremen state elections.

In 1964 there was a call by the German Reich Party (DRP) to the plethora of neo-Nazi groups to 'unite the national camp'. In November of that year in Hanover some seventy groups united to form the National Democratic Party of Germany (NPD), a party which aimed to unite all Germans in the 'national interest' and against what it regarded as foreign influence. In the federal election of 1965 it obtained a disappointing 2 per cent of the vote and no seats.

Despite this, the situation was in some ways ripe for a resurgence of neo-Nazism. The minor economic recession evoked fears of a repeat of the economic slumps of the 1920s and early 1930s, so that as in the 1930s, some saw extremism as the solution. Also, xenophobia was on the rise now that there were more than a million foreign workers in the country, workers who were easy scapegoats at a time of recession. In any case, there was residual sympathy in some sections of the population for Nazism. Thousands of civil servants, judges and others who had served under the Nazis were among the voting population, and many of them were still in office, or had been until recently. As late as 1961, 143 judges who had been judges in the Nazi system were able to retire on a full pension without their activities being investigated. There were also many Germans, both old and young, who felt that twenty years after the war they should no longer be required to carry the burden of Germany's Nazi past. Finally, a degree of tiredness with the perpetual bickering between the CDU and FDP crept in. When this was resolved by the creation of a grand coalition in December 1966, in which conservatives shared power with socialists, some voters felt that the NPD was now the only true party of the right.

The NPD's first breakthrough came in the state election in Hesse on 6 November 1966, just ten days after the FDP had left the federal government. It won 7.9 per cent of the vote, securing 8 seats (out of 100) in the state parliament. Further success came two weeks later in Bavaria, when it won 7.4 per cent. In 1967 the party was successful in four state elections in Rhineland-Palatinate, Schleswig-Holstein, Lower Saxony and Bremen. In April 1968 the NPD achieved its greatest success to date, 9.8 per cent in Baden-Württemberg.

It was now represented in seven out of ten West German states.

After these successes the party's greatest aim was to achieve a national breakthrough in the federal election scheduled for 1969. Yet when the election came, in September, the NPD fell short of the 5 per cent required to be awarded any seats. It won just 4.3 per cent of the vote, a failure that led to internal party fighting and, in 1970–2, to the loss of all the seats that had been won in 1966–8.

The reasons for the NPD's poor performance in 1969 are many. To some extent the wind was taken out of the party's sails by the long period since its last success: after winning seats in seven elections in an eighteen-month period between November 1966 and April 1968 the party had to wait another eighteen months for the federal election. But there were other reasons, too. Most Germans were not willing to vote for a party that echoed the evil of Nazism, an evil that had ultimately brought so much destruction on Germany. Many were also conscious of the damage done to West Germany's reputation every time the NPD had been successful in elections. Others were simply put off by the sight of NPD orderlies at demonstrations, who frequently attacked reporters and who reminded them of nothing so much as jackbooted SA men from the 1930s. Most of all, the economic recession of the mid-1960s began to recede within a couple of years. All in all, it may be said that the NPD came close to a breakthrough but just failed. It was to be another twenty years before neo-Nazis again had a measure of electoral success.

Student Protests, Emergency Laws and Opposition outside Parliament

The late 1960s in West Germany saw widespread protests which, though initially led by students, went far beyond the student movement. They came to encompass protest against a range of issues, from the situation at the universities to the Vietnam War, and from the issue of emergency laws to the lack of parliamentary opposition. Nevertheless, the origins of the protest lie firmly in the student movement and the situation at the universities.

In February 1964, university representatives highlighted major shortcomings in the West German system, including massive numbers of students for whom there was little room in lecture theatres, which led to poor results and thus a shortage of suitably qualified personnel for academia and for industry. One analyst, Georg Picht, highlighted in a series of newspaper articles in spring 1964 the decreasing numbers of candidates for the school-leaving examination, and the shortage of teachers, a situation that he called an 'educational state of emergency'. His prognosis was that as a result, the economic growth of recent years would not be sustainable, because of the lack of a skilled and qualified workforce. He showed that in school-leaving statistics West Germany was comparable to some of the poorest European countries, including Ireland, Portugal and Yugoslavia. One initial response from the federal government was the founding of five new universities, announced in March 1964.

West Berlin became a centre of opposition to the federal government. In part this was because compulsory military service did not apply there and the city thus attracted more radical students than elsewhere. In May 1965, students at the Free University (FU) in West Berlin went on strike. The initial cause was the imposition of a ban on the journalist Erich Kuby, who was to have spoken about the role of the USA in the Vietnam War. However, there were two main issues. One was the serious staff shortages and over-filled lecture theatres. In June 1965, the Union of German Student Unions (VDS) called for an increase in the budget for universities to help overcome this. The other was that students saw universities as hierarchical, authoritarian places in which a small minority of those involved, the professors, had all of the power. The Free University in West Berlin was the only West German university in which there was a representative body through which students had a say in the running of the institution. Student protesters wanted more financial support for education and more student say in university affairs.

In February 1966, 2500 students participated in a demonstration against US involvement in the Vietnam War. Eggs were thrown at the America House there, which led to a confrontation with riot police. The Socialist German Student Union (SDS), one of whose leaders was the sociology student Rudi Dutschke, was the most active student group at this time. In June 1966, students at the FU organised a US-style 'sit-in', demanding an end to the ban on freedom of assembly there and also a greater say in university affairs. In that same year, the Federal Minister of Science, Gerhard Stoltenberg, announced increased expenditure on education and research, though it was not enough to cover the increase in student numbers, which at 260,000 in 1966 was double the 1955 figure.

At the same time that students were protesting about education and the Vietnam War, the trade unions were becoming active on other issues. After the bad experience of a divided trade union movement in Weimar, the German Federation of Trade Unions (DGB) had been set up in April 1947 in the British Zone as an umbrella organisation for 16 trade unions, aimed at co-ordinating their activities and industrial power. Later, in October 1949, the movement was extended to cover West Germany as a whole. It thus became the German equivalent of the British TUC or the American AFL–CIO.

The DGB became the main centre of opposition to the emergency laws which CDU-led governments had been attempting to introduce since 1958. At that time the Federal Interior Minister, Gerhard Schröder, claimed that existing laws would be insufficient to counter a communist threat in an emergency situation in which the government was under threat. By contrast, many citizens felt that such laws were

potentially authoritarian and might be too similar to the so-
called 'enabling laws' that had been used by Hitler in the
1930s to remove all other political parties and create a one-
party state. Various attempts to introduce such laws, which
needed a two-thirds majority in parliament, were successfully
opposed by the SPD in 1960, 1962 and 1965, in the latter
case after a massive trade union demonstration in Cologne.
Nevertheless, the CDU and CSU remained committed to the
concept of emergency legislation. The SPD, meanwhile, had
opposed only the actual draft laws, not the principle. Opposition outside parliament remained, and in October 1966,
20,000 people demonstrated against such laws, among
them the writer Hans Magnus Enzensberger and the philosopher Ernst Bloch.

Bloch was one of a number of university professors whose
political sympathies were largely with the protesting students
and trade unionists, whether on the issue of university
reform, emergency laws or the Vietnam War. Others included
Theodor Adorno, a philosophy professor in Frankfurt who
had been an exile from the Nazis in the USA, and his pupil
Jürgen Habermas. Among the prominent writers were Heinrich Böll, Günter Grass and Erich Fried, an Austrian refugee
from the Nazis who lived in London. Perhaps the greatest
influence on the students was Herbert Marcuse, a German
exile from the Nazis who had taught at Harvard and Brandeis
universities and was now in San Diego. Marcuse argued that
whereas early industrial societies had been open to radical
political change, modern affluent society was not, because
people settled for material pleasures and thus abandoned
attempts to reform and create a more just world (K. Bullivant
and C. J. Rice, in Burns, 1995, pp. 242–3). The students and
many trade unionists were motivated by a desire to reform
society.

Some were also motivated by a desire to overthrow the
Western system of government. The SDS was partly engaged
in establishing communal living forms such as 'Kommune
1', set up in West Berlin in January 1967. Police methods

against them often amounted to a massive over-reaction, such as in April 1967, when police raided the commune on the eve of a visit to West Berlin by US Vice-President Hubert Humphrey. The 'bombs' that police found were full of blancmange.

On 2 June 1967 the situation changed radically. During a demonstration in West Berlin against a visit by the Shah of Iran, who was accused of human rights abuses, a student, Benno Ohnesorg, was shot dead by a policeman, Karl Heinz Kurras. Kurras claimed to have acted in self-defence and was acquitted of manslaughter (second-degree murder) by a court in November 1967. The death led to massive protests against what some saw as state-sanctioned murder, whereas the tabloid press blamed the students. More than 100,000 people protested at various West German universities, and much of the anger was directed at the tabloid press, especially the *Bild* newspaper and its owner, the Axel Springer publishing house. In September Berlin's ruling mayor, Interior Minister and Chief of Police, who had all supported Kurras, were forced to resign.

The opposition outside parliament (Apo) protested against tendencies in West German society and abroad that it regarded as unjust and problematic. One was the failure of West Germany properly to deal with Germany's Nazi past. Apart from paying reparations to Israel there had been no serious public discussion of the subject. Students in the mid- and late 1960s were the sons and daughters of those who had fought for Germany in the Second World War, and many began to ask the simple question: 'What did you do in the War, Dad?' The older generation frequently did not want to answer, indeed, did not even want to remember. Too often it seemed as if West Germany tried to pretend that before 1945 there was nothing. The concept of 1945 as 'zero hour' was widespread in West German politics. (In East Germany a different lie was propagated, one that saw East Germans as people 'liberated' from Nazism, like the Poles and Czechs, rather than as defeated Germans.) Another cause for protest was West German support for the US in Vietnam. In West Germany (and throughout the world), the left wing saw American participation in the Vietnam War was immoral, an example of colonial aggression against a people fighting a war of liberation. They felt that the US had no right to be there.

In February and March 1968, protests intensified against the education policies, the Vietnam War and the planned emergency laws; 3000 people took part in an International Vietnam Conference in West Berlin in February, at which an SDS spokesman, Rudi Dutschke, called on US soldiers to desert rather than fight in Vietnam. A day later 12,000 people protested against the US in West Berlin. Against this, 80,000 West Berliners demanded three days later that 'West Berlin should not become Saigon', a clear rejection of student violence. Nevertheless, the student protests in West Germany should be seen as part of a world-wide movement. In France there were massive protests that threatened to topple the government there, and there was also a large anti-Vietnam War movement in the USA at this time.

On 11 April 1968 a right-wing terrorist, Josef Erwin Bachmann, shot and seriously wounded Rudi Dutschke (the injuries finally took his life in 1979). Thousands protested immediately against the Springer media empire as the 'spiritual instigator' of the attack and called for the expropriation of the company. (In May 1968 a government report expressed concern at Springer's domination of the press, whereupon the company sold off five of its newspapers, representing one-quarter of its total circulation.) Hundreds of thousands took to the streets in protest at the attack on Dutschke. Riots ensued, which were roundly condemned by Chancellor Kiesinger on 13 April as the actions of a small, militant minority of students led by 'radical ringleaders'. To many it seemed as if the government would not listen to their protests.

In the Bundestag, Kiesinger claimed that the protesters were opposed to the 'free, democratic basic order' of the

Federal Republic. This was undoubtedly true of a minority. The SDS became ever more radical (it was classified as anti-constitutional in November 1968), and some protesters, such as Andreas Baader and Gudrun Ensslin, even turned to terrorist methods (this is discussed in Chapter 4). However, many others less radical were extremely concerned at the planned emergency laws. The DGB, which had supported the demonstration against student violence in Berlin in February 1968, was at the forefront of organising demonstrations against the emergency laws. Despite the fact that the SPD was in government and thus helping to bring these laws into being, many SPD politicians joined with the DGB, the FDP and others in protesting against the proposals. Critics feared the potential in the law for limiting individual freedoms: the law specifically stated that in the event of serious political tension then all mail could be intercepted and telephones tapped, apartments and houses searched and restrictions placed on people's movements and jobs. The biggest problem was that there was no clear definition of 'serious political tension'. Despite widespread opposition, the law was passed in the Bundestag on 30 May 1968 by 384 votes to 100, with 1 CDU and 53 SPD members joining the FDP opposition to oppose the measure. Two weeks later the Bundesrat approved the law and it came into force on 28 June 1968.

In January 1968, the West German Conference of University Presidents agreed a reform programme which went some way to meeting the student's demands for democratisation and modernisation of the universities. In April 1968, the state Ministers for Culture approved a reform of the university system to give students the right to a share in decision-making while also restricting the rights of professors, a measure that led to a protest resolution against the change by 1500 professors in June 1968. Nevertheless, the demands for reform continued into 1969 and beyond, with the SDS gaining control of the national student organisation, the VDS, and reorganising it along communist lines in

March 1969, while the Social Democratic University Union (SHB), the SPD's university group, moved politically closer to the SDS. In March 1969 the VDS lost its government funding, while the SHB lost its SPD funding. Further reforms to the education system in 1969 did not prevent more demonstrations, with the one at Göttingen in June 1969 leading to violence.

The political turbulence that existed in West Germany had peaked by 1969. In the midst of what many saw as largely repressive measures, such as support for the US war effort in Vietnam and the passing of the emergency laws, there were some attempts at reform of education, while one or two small measures of liberalisation were tolerated. The Communist Party of Germany (KPD), banned in 1956, was allowed to re-form as the German Communist Party (DKP), while the warrant for the arrest of the KPD chairman, Max Reimann, was lifted, and he returned from the GDR. West Germany was, despite the turbulence, moving towards a new era. That new era began with the election of September 1969.

Brandt's Success

In March of 1969 the first sign of the potential for change had been given when the FDP supported the SPD's candidate for Federal President. Gustav Heinemann, the Protestant minister who had opposed the Nazis and resigned as CDU Minister of the Interior in 1950 over rearmament and who had joined the SPD in the late 1950s, became the first Social Democratic President of the Federal Republic.

In 1968–9, towards the end of the Grand Coalition, the differences between the Social Democrats and Christian Democrats had become more apparent. For a while the parties had worked very well together: the SPD Minister for Economics, Karl Schiller, for example, had been able to co-operate surprisingly well with the CSU Finance Minister,

Franz Josef Strauss, he of the *Der Spiegel* Affair. Despite this, there were strong differences of opinion, not least on the subject of policy towards the East, or 'Ostpolitik'. Many in the SPD wanted to attempt government without the CDU, going into coalition with the FDP instead. The SPD's transformation from a Marxist party, begun in 1959, had continued throughout the 1960s, and its three years in government with the CDU/CSU had shown many West Germans that the party was now capable of government.

Crucially, there had also been a shift in power within the FDP. The Free Democrats had always been a coalition of various strands of liberal thinking, from left-leaning social liberals who were close to the SPD to secular conservatives who agreed with the CDU on most issues except the 'Christian' label. Erich Mende, the party leader since 1960, was a cautious figure, and in January 1968 he was replaced by Walter Scheel, who made no secret of his preference for the SPD.

The election was held on 28 September 1969, and the SPD's candidate for Chancellor was the same Willy Brandt who had lost to Adenauer in 1961 and to Erhard in 1965 before becoming Vice-Chancellor in the Grand Coalition. The result was close. The CDU/CSU lost 1.5 per cent and 3 seats, leaving them with 242 seats in parliament. The SPD gained 3.4 per cent, scoring over 40 per cent (42.7 per cent) for the first time in West Germany's history and taking 224 seats. After the significant losses in 1965, the FDP lost another 3.7 per cent to achieve just 5.8 per cent of the vote and 30 seats. The NPD failed to cross the 5 per cent barrier. Both the large parties attempted to form a coalition with the FDP, but Scheel had already made his preference clear. On 21 October 1969 Willy Brandt became the first Social Democratic Chancellor of West Germany. His Deputy and Foreign Minister was Walter Scheel of the FDP. Their government only had a very thin majority of 12 seats over the CDU/CSU, something that was to make life precarious during the next three years.

Thus, in October 1969, West Germany's President and Chancellor were both anti-Nazis. It was an historic break with 1945 and with CDU domination of postwar German politics. Many saw it as the beginning of a new era. It was Brandt who said when he became Chancellor, exaggerating only slightly, that 'Today Hitler finally lost the War' (Glees, 1996, pp. 156–7).

4

NEW BEGINNINGS, 1969–77

Introduction

Despite its small majority in the Bundestag and uncertainty about the loyalties of some FDP representatives, the new SPD–FDP coalition set about its radical programme of reform with alacrity. Brandt and Scheel not only wished to fundamentally transform relations with Eastern Europe and with East Germany, they also had far-reaching internal reform plans for the Federal Republic itself.

Brandt's desire to engage in less confrontational politics with Eastern Europe is the aspect of his time in office that has gained most recognition, both at home and abroad. The word 'Ostpolitik', meaning politics towards the east, passed into the English language at this time. There were limits to what Brandt's Ostpolitik could achieve: with the best will in the world he could never accept the GDR's demand that it be treated by West Germany as just another foreign country. Brandt insisted that though there were two states in Germany, they could never be regarded as foreign (*Ausland*) to each other. Still, he was prepared to engage in unprecedented levels of co-operation with the GDR and with Poland, Czechoslovakia and the Soviet Union.

For this to work, Brandt needed partners in the East. Brezhnev, Soviet leader since 1964, appeared willing to try to improve relations with the West, and Poland and Czechoslovakia were also similarly inclined. Of course, they too had preconditions, especially in relation to territories lost by Germany in 1945, which Germany still claimed were legally

German, but they were prepared to negotiate. By contrast, Ulbricht seemed incapable of grasping the nettle, and he was replaced in 1971 by Erich Honecker, who pursued a twofold policy of negotiating with the West to improve relations while insisting on the GDR's separateness from West Germany. This opened the door to compromise.

By the same token, Brandt had ambitious plans for internal reforms in the areas of education, gender equality, women's rights and personal freedom. In the early 1970s he found himself having to combat terrorist activity, and he also introduced an ill-judged law to exclude 'extremists' from civil service jobs. In the GDR, Honecker introduced an era of liberalisation that was welcomed in many quarters but which always had its limits: it was liberalisation by SED standards only.

Ostpolitik 1: Moscow

Three fundamental aims lay behind Brandt's new Ostpolitik: (i) to improve the situation of Germans in the East; (ii) to contribute to the easing of tensions in Europe; and (iii) to work towards the elimination of fear and thus towards the possible reunification of Germany. The latter aim was definitely a very long-term one, but the first two were aims that could be achieved rather more quickly by concerted effort on the part of a West German leader coupled with goodwill from partners in the East. Brandt decided, very early on, the best way to avoid any suspicion that his real policy was to subvert Soviet influence in Eastern Europe. He dealt first with Moscow.

On 30 January 1970 Egon Bahr, a state secretary in the Chancellor's Office, began negotiations in Moscow on a treaty in which each side would renounce the use of force. By May, Bahr had reached agreement with the Soviet Foreign Minister, Andrei Gromyko, on a 10-point paper. When the document was leaked in June and July it caused massive controversy, with the CDU/CSU and even sections of the government opposed to the ideas it contained. However, Brandt and Scheel went ahead with the plan and signed the Moscow Treaty in Moscow on 12 August 1970. Essentially, each side agreed to refrain from the use or threat of violence, to resolve all disagreements peacefully, and to acknowledge the existing borders in Europe, specifically the Oder–Neisse Line and the East–West German border, as inviolable. Given that the Basic Law (constitution) of the Federal Republic still claimed that West Germany existed *de jure* in its 1937 borders (i.e. including the GDR and much of postwar Poland), this was a brave step by Brandt. In a 'Letter on German Unity', submitted after the signing by Brandt and accepted by the Soviets, Brandt said that none of this precluded German reunification or a final settlement of borders when a peace treaty between Germany and the Allies was finally signed. (There had as yet been no peace treaty because the Allies could not agree on which German state was competent to sign such a treaty.) Brandt proposed to submit the treaty to the Bundestag for ratification only when the Berlin question had been satisfactorily resolved.

Ostpolitik 2: Warsaw

On 4 February 1970 negotiations also began between State Secretary Georg Duckwitz and the Polish Deputy Foreign Minister, Józef Winiewicz, in Warsaw on normalising relations between the two countries. After long negotiations and the conclusion of the Moscow Treaty, the Warsaw Treaty was signed in Warsaw on 7 December 1970 by Brandt, Scheel, the Chairman of the Polish Council of Ministers and the Polish Foreign Minister. As in Moscow, each side agreed to refrain from the use of violence, and West Germany also recognised the Oder–Neisse Line as Poland's western border, subject to a final peace treaty. Again, Brandt made ratification conditional upon satisfactory regulation of the Berlin question.

The historical significance of the treaty, and Brandt's determination to engage Germany in reconciliation with its neighbours, was underscored by one small act of massive significance. Laying a wreath, on 7 December, at the memorial to the Jewish victims of the Warsaw Ghetto uprising, Willy Brandt suddenly went down on both knees and bowed his head in a mark of respect. He was praised throughout the world for this, though it was extremely controversial at home, with public opinion divided roughly evenly on whether it was an appropriate gesture.

Berlin

On 26 March 1970, the ambassadors of the USA, Great Britain and France in West Germany and the Soviet ambassador in the GDR began negotiations on a four-power agreement for Berlin. A resolution of the Berlin problem was necessary from a Western point of view because of ongoing GDR measures that hindered access to West Berlin, measures made possible because in 1945 the occupying powers had simply overlooked the question of access to West Berlin from the West. Negotiations proceeded for almost eighteen months, and an agreement was finally signed on 3 September 1971 in Berlin. The agreement was a compromise. Civilian access to the city was guaranteed, and West Germany obtained certain rights to external representation for West Berlin, which nevertheless remained a special political entity rather than an integral part of the Federal Republic, a point emphasised by the provision for opening a Soviet consulate there.

One point on which the four powers had not been able to agree was whether the provisions of the agreement applied to all of Berlin (the Western view) or just West Berlin (the Soviet view). In the end an expression was found that would render almost any legal contract null and void: the treaty refers simply to 'the territory concerned'. Nevertheless, for West Germany this treaty was the real success, and the federal government issued a statement broadly welcoming it. Though the West German desire for incorporation of West Berlin into the Federal Republic was not achieved, the 'essentials' outlined by President Kennedy some years earlier were: links to West Germany, access, and a guaranteed Western military presence in the city. When he met Brezhnev in the Crimea shortly after the signing, Brandt spoke of a 'decisive turn' in East–West relations. 'The way now seemed clear for a treaty on the relations between the two Germanies' (Fulbrook, 1991, pp. 208–9).

The End of Ulbricht

Ulbricht's strict policy of modernisation of industry in the late 1960s had not produced the desired results. The hard winter of 1969–70 led to production shortfalls, so that the population as a whole was suffering from shortages in a range of areas. Inefficiency was one of the biggest factors in the economic downturn that threatened after the growth years 1966–8. As a result, in September 1970 the Politburo called a halt to a number of investment projects in favour of more building of apartments.

At the same meeting of the Politburo, which Ulbricht did not attend, Willi Stoph, the GDR's Prime Minister since 1964, voiced criticism of Ulbricht's economic policies, especially the concentration on building up 'prestigious areas' in town centres (not least East Berlin) at the expense of the countryside and of consumer goods. Another member of the Politburo, Erich Honecker, began to gain support. Despite this, in December 1970 and in January 1971 Ulbricht was able to rally the party leadership behind him once again. These were his last victories. Thirteen Politburo members wrote to Brezhnev in March 1971 asking him to intervene with Ulbricht to persuade him to step down, which Brezhnev did in April. In May, Erich Honecker was elected as the new First Secretary of the SED. Ulbricht became 'Chairman of the SED', a previously unknown post that was not re-filled after his death in 1973, and he remained as 'Chairman of the State Council', but these were mere honorary functions (Frank, 2001, pp. 427–8). Two years after the major change in West Germany, the GDR also had a new, younger leader.

Honecker's First Years: Liberalisation and Demarcation

Erich Honecker was not by any means known as a liberal in the SED hierarchy. Born in the Saarland in 1912 he had joined the Communist Youth Movement in 1926 and followed his father into the Communist Party in 1929. After 1933 he engaged in anti-Nazi activity in Germany and was arrested in 1935. He served ten years in Nazi prisons before being freed by the Soviet Army. He became a KPD and then SED activist immediately and was a central figure in the creation of the Free German Youth (FDJ). A full member of the Politburo from 1958, he was also responsible for the massive attacks on writers and artists at the SED Central Committee's 11th Plenary Meeting in 1965.

It was therefore something of a shock when, in December 1971, Honecker stated to the SED Central Committee that 'if one proceeds from the solid premise of socialism, there can in my view be no taboos in the realm of art and literature'. For the first time in GDR history an SED leader seemed prepared to forgo the use of 'aesthetic' excuses for banning literature. Some writers and publishers took him at his word, so that novels such as Stefan Heym's Stalinism critique in biblical clothing, *The King David Report*, and Ulrich Plenzdorf's story of youthful disillusionment, *The Sorrows of Young W*, modelled to some extent on J. D. Salinger's *Catcher in the Rye*, were published. Jeans, which had been regarded as Western and decadent in the 1960s, were now sold; beat music was allowed; and long hair and short skirts were tolerated. A film, *The Legend of Paul and Paula*, in which Paul takes off his FDJ shirt before making love to Paula on a flower bed, was given the go ahead by Honecker himself (Dennis, 2000, p. 145). In 1975 there was even a political debate in the pages of the newspapers after a meeting of world communist parties in East Berlin, with relatively open discussion of a new concept, Eurocommunism, which no longer bowed automatically to Soviet leadership.

In social policy the country became somewhat more liberal, too, with a greater focus on the family rather than the overbearing state. The 1966 Family Code had determined the ideal family to be a married couple finding fulfilment in the birth and raising of children. In 1972 practical measures were introduced to support this idea. Maternity leave was improved, and significant allowances for the birth of children were introduced, with the allowances becoming greater with each child. In 1976 even more generous measures were introduced, including the so-called 'baby year', a year off work on 65–90 per cent of pay for the second and every subsequent child, in addition to maternity leave of 26 weeks. Working mothers were given shorter working hours and longer holidays. The provision of pre-school care expanded: by 1980 there were free kindergarten places for 92 per cent of children and crèche facilities for 61 per cent, an increase over 1970 of 30 per cent in each case. The weakness in this policy was that most of the work at home tended to fall to women, even though by 1970, 82 per cent of women also had a full-time job. The male-dominated SED hierarchy had no real concept of gender politics. Despite this, one point that should be made is that in contrast to these family-oriented measures, which were partly in response to the decline in the population of working age, the GDR in 1972 also introduced abortion on demand during the first twelve weeks of pregnancy. This was the only time until October 1989 that a vote in the GDR parliament, the Volkskammer, was not unanimous: fourteen CDU deputies opposed the motion, while another eight abstained.

In September 1971, Honecker also announced a change in economic direction, replacing Ulbricht's modernisation with what he called the 'unity of economic and social policies'. A range of measures promoting the building of apartments for large families, improvements in social insurance, increases in wages and pensions and a reduction in the cost of children's clothing all contributed to Honecker's initial popularity. His economic measures were initially successful: in the period 1973–5 the rate of economic growth in the GDR at 4 per cent per annum was, for the second time in under a decade, higher than in West Germany, albeit a West Germany in recession. In addition, the provision of household goods and cars increased significantly over the next 10–12 years, so that by 1983, 42 per cent of families had a car (1970: 16 per cent), 87 per cent a washing machine (1970: 54 per cent), 91 per cent a television (1970: 70 per cent), and 93 per cent a refrigerator (1970: 91 per cent). These statistics are broadly comparable to equivalent West German ones for the 1980s, although, interestingly, West Germans had more cars (65 per cent) but fewer refrigerators (also 65 per cent) than East Germans. Of course, it is generally agreed that the quality of West German goods was far superior.

If Honecker was aiming for more liberalisation in the GDR, his attitude to West Germany was somewhat harder. On the one hand he was, unlike Ulbricht, willing to engage in attempts at negotiating a better *modus vivendi* with the Federal Republic than had existed throughout the 1950s and 1960s. On the other hand, the basis for such understanding he saw as a clear acceptance of the existence of two mutually foreign political entities. As such, even while it negotiated a treaty with the Federal Republic (see below), Honecker's GDR also continued to introduce measures designed to remove, as far as possible, any remnants of an all-German identity. From 1 July 1970, GDR goods had borne the label 'Made in GDR' instead of 'Made in Germany'. In February 1972, 'German Television' was renamed 'TV of the GDR'. From June 1972, West Germans required a visa to visit the GDR, just like other 'foreigners', while areas close to the West German border were effectively closed to all but the few who lived there. The new 1974 constitution removed the reference to a 'socialist state of the German nation' and replaced it with a 'socialist state of workers and peasants'. In that year East German cars also discarded the national symbol D (for Deutschland) and replaced it with DDR. In the midst of the desire to remove all references to 'Germany' it is ironic that the journalistic bastion of GDR communism, the party newspaper *Neues Deutschland* (New Germany), kept its title unchanged.

Ostpolitik 3: Brandt and the GDR

When Willy Brandt came to power in 1969 East and West German concepts of the nation were mutually irreconcilable. The GDR constitution of 1968 still talked about the 'German nation', but the SED had created a new citizenship and it officially saw the Federal Republic as a foreign country. By contrast, when Brandt made his first governmental declaration in January 1970 he was absolutely clear that West Germany could never accept Ulbricht's notion that the two German states were foreign to each other. Brandt's basic premise was that in Germany there were two states, one nation. This was in marked contrast to the old CDU attitude, which argued that in Germany there was one state and one nation, the eastern part of which was temporarily a 'zone of occupation'.

Having initiated the Moscow and Warsaw negotiations in the first two months of 1970, Brandt went to Erfurt in March 1970 to meet the GDR's Prime Minister, Willi Stoph. Each leader merely reiterated his position. Nevertheless, in May 1970 Stoph returned the compliment by visiting Brandt in

Kassel. At this meeting they agreed to a 'time out', so that the negotiations with Moscow could be concluded and digested. In November 1970 formal negotiations on a basic treaty began between Egon Bahr, who had led the negotiations with Moscow, and Michael Kohl, a state secretary in the GDR government. Ulbricht was intensely sceptical of Brandt's intentions (Frank, 2001, pp. 401–2) but he had little choice when the Soviets accepted Brandt's overtures.

In January 1971, after the conclusion of the Moscow and Warsaw Treaties, Brandt made it clear in his 'State of the Nation Report' to the Bundestag that a treaty with the GDR would also be necessary. He asserted that such a treaty would not be allowed to affect the legal status of West Berlin. The CDU was critical, claiming that Brandt was in the process of selling out German unity. Herbert Czaja, the president of the League of Expellee Associations, played on the German word *Verzicht*, which can mean renunciation or relinquishment, and accused Brandt of pursuing a policy of relinquishing German territory rather than merely renouncing the use of force. Nevertheless, Brandt was not to be deterred, and his policy also led to some relaxation in tension with the GDR. When Chile established diplomatic relations with the GDR in March 1972, the Hallstein Doctrine was not applied at all. Restrictions on the sale of GDR publications in West Germany were lifted in the same month. In June, the official 1961 map-drawing guidelines, which insisted that Germany's 1937 borders be shown and that the GDR be called the 'Soviet Zone of Occupation', were discarded. Brandt was determined to move forward.

The main sticking point was the GDR's insistence that the Federal Republic accord it full diplomatic recognition as a foreign country. This was, quite simply, a non-starter. Brandt would never have found a majority for such a proposition even in his own SPD, let alone in the FDP or the CDU/CSU. Brandt was prepared to recognise the *fact* of the GDR's existence, but he could never recognise the *legality* of the political division of Germany. Eventually, 'after pressure from Moscow, East Berlin dropped its demand for *de jure* recognition and no longer insisted on the exchange of ambassadors' (Kettenacker, 1997, p. 73).

In December 1972, Bahr and Kohl signed the Basic Treaty between the Federal Republic and the GDR in East Berlin. Under the provisions of the treaty the two states agreed to maintain normal neighbourly relations with each other, to resolve all disagreements peacefully, not to claim to represent the other internationally, and to limit the application of their laws to their respective territory. A number of humanitarian issues were also addressed, especially the reuniting of families divided by the border. The two states also agreed to establish diplomatic relations, with offices in each other's capital, Bonn and East Berlin. However, in deference to the West German insistence that these could not be embassies, a title reserved for the diplomatic offices of *foreign* governments, these offices would be known as 'Permanent Representations'. Finally, in a 'Letter on German Unity', Brandt's government made plain that the treaty did not cover citizenship, which it still saw in singular terms for the citizens of both states. The Basic Treaty was subject to ratification in the Bundestag and in the East German parliament (see below). It was in the Bundestag that Brandt had been in trouble since 1970.

Opposition, Defections and an Early Election

From the beginning of his term of office Brandt met with stiff opposition from within the ranks of the CDU and CSU, as well as from sections of the FDP. Twenty years of government had left many in the CDU and CSU considering themselves the natural parties of government. Some ultra-conservatives in these parties even saw Brandt's exile from Nazi Germany as treason to the fatherland rather than principled opposition. In the Bundestag vote to elect him, the quality of some of the opposition was shown by one voting paper, which carried the words 'Frahm Nein'. This was a reference to Willy Brandt's birth name, Herbert Frahm, which he had changed in exile to avoid discovery by the Nazis. He then kept the new name on his return to Germany in 1945.

Despite the personal attacks, much of the opposition was to Brandt's policies. One of the first consequences came in October 1970, when Erich Mende, a former leader of the FDP, and two other FDP members of the Bundestag defected to the CDU. Mende was on the national liberal wing of the FDP, which had been defeated by Scheel in 1968. This wing of the party was never entirely happy with either the social–liberal coalition or Brandt's Ostpolitik. In addition to the new Ostpolitik, the three also criticised the government's economic policies.

Their action cut the government's majority from twelve seats to six. In March 1972, two SPD members of the Bundestag also defected to the CDU. One, Herbert Hupka, was the chairman of the Association of Expellees from Silesia, a formerly German territory now recognised by Brandt as being in Poland. The government majority was now just two seats. In April, two further FDP members declared that they would not support Brandt in a vote of no confidence in the Bundestag. The CDU/CSU seemed assured of a majority in such a vote, so on 24 April they used the 'constructive vote of no confidence' (see Chapter 1) to propose that their parliamentary chairman, Rainer Barzel, replace Brandt as Chancellor. In the end, because of two defections from the ranks of the CDU, Barzel obtained only 247 votes instead of the necessary 249. Brandt survived in office. The defections were the subject of a later, inconclusive inquiry into allegations of bribery.

Brandt's precarious position in the Bundestag made co-operation with the CDU imperative. Some of the realists in the CDU, such as Barzel, the leader of the Christian Democratic Trade Union, Norbert Blüm, and the later President of the Federal Republic, Richard von Weizsäcker, saw that a majority of the population supported Brandt's policies. They therefore engaged in constructive opposition, aiming to modify rather than completely reject his proposals. In February 1972, during the first reading in the Bundestag of the Moscow and Warsaw Treaties, Barzel suggested three conditions that would be necessary for their acceptance: Soviet recognition of the European Economic Community (EEC), confirmation of the right to self-determination of the German people, and the declared intention to establish freedom of movement in Germany. In March 1972, Brezhnev responded positively to the first two demands. In May, after the failed vote of no confidence, Brandt and Barzel agreed on a 'Joint Declaration' in the Bundestag which reasserted the German right to self-determination, treaties notwithstanding. The Soviets declared their readiness to accept this declaration.

Even with most of his demands met, Barzel was still unable to persuade the CDU/CSU to support the treaties. Instead, most CDU/CSU members of the Bundestag abstained. On 17 May 1972, the Moscow Treaty was passed in the Bundestag by 248 votes to 10, with 238 abstentions. On the same day the Warsaw Treaty was approved by 248 votes to 17, with 231 abstentions. The Joint Declaration was approved by 491–0, with 5 abstentions. The treaties became law a few days later, after the Bundesrat had also signalled its approval. Within two weeks the Soviet and Polish parliaments had also ratified the respective treaties, though the Poles rejected the Joint Declaration.

The Basic Treaty with the GDR was the next major obstacle, and it seemed under even greater threat. Brandt had no majority in parliament, and he used the rejection of the budget on a vote of 247–247 to call for a vote of confidence, in which he and his ministers abstained. The resulting early election, called in November 1972, was essentially a referendum on Brandt's Ostpolitik. Social issues played little or no role in the campaign. The SPD and FDP were united as never before. The CDU/CSU were opposed, but their campaign suffered from a lack of credibility because of their abstention rather than outright opposition in the crucial votes earlier in the year.

The result was a massive endorsement of the new Ostpolitik. In the highest turnout ever recorded in a federal election, 91.1 per cent, the SPD became the largest party for the first time, winning 45.8 per cent, up by 3.1 per cent. This remains its best ever result in the history of the Federal Republic. The FDP vote also jumped 2.6 per cent to 8.4 per cent. The CDU/CSU lost 1.2 per cent and finished on 44.9 per cent, its worst result since the election of 1949. The SPD–FDP coalition now had a solid majority in the Bundestag of 46 seats. Brandt and Scheel had been entirely vindicated. When the Basic Treaty was submitted to the Bundestag for approval in May 1973 it was passed on a vote of 268–217. Attempts by Strauss and the CSU to have it declared unconstitutional failed. In the GDR it was unanimously approved in the People's Chamber in June 1973.

Consequences of the Basic Treaty

The Basic Treaty allowed the two German states to take their place in the community of nations alongside each other. It introduced a degree of normality in relations between the two states – in so far as any neighbourly (or brotherly) relationship based on fenced and walled borders can ever be normal. The GDR got its wish to be recognised as a separate political entity with its own representation and profile abroad: the Basic Treaty meant the formal end to the Hallstein Doctrine. West Germany, on the other hand, while recognising East Germany's existence, retained its aspiration to German unification. One slightly piquant consequence of this new normality occurred during the 1974 soccer World Cup finals, which were staged in West Germany. On the way to winning the Cup, West Germany had to face the GDR in the first round of matches, and the East Germans won 1–0.

In November 1972, just a month before the signing of the treaty, both states had been admitted to the Conference on Security and Co-operation in Europe (CSCE) in Helsinki. In September 1973, after the treaty had been ratified by the parliaments of both states, they were admitted to membership of the United Nations. In March 1974 the protocol for the establishment of diplomatic representatives was agreed, and in May these offices were opened in Bonn and East Berlin. The slightly contorted nature of the negotiations reflected each side's different attitude to the other state: the West German representative in East Berlin, Günter Gaus, was called a 'state secretary' but was accredited to the GDR's Foreign Office (State Department). The GDR representative in Bonn, Michael Kohl, was called an 'ambassador' but was accredited to the Chancellor's Office, not the Foreign Office. Internationally, the GDR established diplomatic relations with Great Britain and France in February 1973 and with the USA in September 1974. The GDR now had diplomatic relations with all the postwar Occupying Powers, a position West Germany had been in since 1955.

A range of other agreements regulating transit to West Berlin, travel between the two states, and trade were also concluded in this period. The number of visits from West Germany and West Berlin to the GDR increased significantly in 1973. However, the situation remained an abnormal one. There were several incidents in which West Germans, and in one case, an Italian, were shot by GDR border guards. The border was mined, and electronically activated machine-guns were also installed. The GDR sometimes reacted to decisions about West Berlin that it disliked (such as establishing West German institutions there) by harassing transit traffic, so that in December 1973 Brandt appealed to Brezhnev to force the GDR to 'act in the new spirit of Ostpolitik' (Marshall, 1990, p. 96). In one instance in May 1975, a West Berlin child was left to drown after falling into the river, because GDR border guards would not allow anyone to dive in to save it (Baumann, 2001, p. 559). The incident caused such outrage that the GDR reached an agreement with the West Berlin authorities some months later to allow rescue from the West in such cases. Yet the political normality achieved by the treaty created a daily normality that was, in many ways, anything but normal.

Ostpolitik 4: Prague

There was one final piece to the Ostpolitik jigsaw. More than 3 million Sudeten Germans had been expelled from Czechoslovakia after 1945, because the Czechoslovak government never again wanted a situation to arise like that which led to the Munich Agreement of 1938. Basically, Hitler had used the German-speaking majority in the border areas of Czechoslovakia to argue for the dismemberment of the country, with these areas being given to Germany. Britain and France had agreed to this, though they were condemned in some quarters for their 'appeasement' of Hitler.

There were many such Germans, from the Sudetenland, Silesia, East Prussia etc., in the GDR, but the post-1945 territorial changes and expulsions were accepted by the SED and discussion of a return to their former homelands was absolutely forbidden. Not so in West Germany, where the Sudeten Germans were a vocal minority. Yet their situation was different from that of the refugees from other eastern territories because the Sudetenland had never been part of Germany apart from the brief period under Hitler. Until 1918 the Sudeten Germans had been citizens of Austria-Hungary and thereafter of Czechoslovakia. This was not a question of lost territory. For the Sudeten Germans the issue was, however, that they had lost their homes. For the Czechoslovaks the issue was that the Munich Agreement was technically still valid.

In the end the Prague Treaty did not discuss the issue of the Sudeten Germans and the loss of their homes. The Czechoslovak government simply refused to do so. Instead, the treaty declared the Munich Agreement of 1938 and its legal consequences to be null and void, while both sides renounced violence against each other and recognised existing borders. Other questions, such as reuniting families divided by the border, were also discussed. Brandt, in a broadcast from Prague on West German television, claimed that the treaty had 'conceded nothing that had not in fact been lost a long time ago'.

The treaty was opposed by the CDU/CSU, largely because of its failure to mention the Sudeten Germans and their 'right to self-determination'. The CDU/CSU majority in the Bundesrat rejected the treaty in March 1974, but the SPD–FDP majority in the Bundestag over-ruled them and ratified the treaty in June and July of that year. West Germany had now found a way of co-existing peacefully with all of its closest neighbours to the east.

International Relations

The international situation in the early 1970s was marked by increasing détente, and Brandt's contribution to that process should not be under-estimated. The USA was slightly unsettled by Brandt's attitude to the East, and in April 1973 he travelled to the United States to reassure the Americans about the Federal Republic's pro-Western sympathies. In May 1973, Brezhnev became the first Soviet leader to visit West Germany.

The spirit of détente was exemplified by the CSCE, whose origins lay in a suggestion made in January 1965 by the Warsaw Pact states that a conference of all European states be called to discuss guaranteeing collective security in Europe (Baumann, 2001, p. 371). Events in Czechoslovakia in 1968 on the one hand reinforced Soviet domination in Eastern Europe. On the other hand, voices in East and West which called for an acceptance of the political status quo became louder. Neither the Eastern nor the Western military bloc in Europe was likely to be able to dominate, or win any significant victory over, the other. Thus, when in March 1969 the Warsaw Pact again signalled a readiness to call such a conference, the West was not opposed to the idea. Finally, in November 1972 a preparatory conference was held in Helsinki, the capital of neutral Finland.

The conference itself started in July 1973, with 33 European states plus the USA and Canada taking part. Negotiations took place in various sessions over the next two years in Helsinki and Geneva. The end result was a mixed bag of agreements on the recognition of existing borders in Europe and the sovereignty of existing states, the renunciation of force as a means of resolving disputes, non-interference in states' internal affairs and respect for human rights and freedom of conscience and religion. The final agreement was signed by all 35 states in the summer of 1975.

The end result has been interpreted by its Western critics as essentially a victory for the Soviet Union, which got recognition of its 'empire' in Eastern Europe while giving little in return (Pearson, 1998, pp. 86–7). They argue that the United States had been weakened by the Watergate scandal in 1972 and also by criticism of its war in Vietnam, which was drawing towards a final defeat for the US and its South Vietnamese allies in 1975. Others, however, have seen Helsinki, in conjunction with the treaties relating to Germany, as simply a 'post-war peace settlement based on acceptance of the continent's division' (Young, 1996, p. 31). Critics of Helsinki forget that no one in the West rushed to help East Europeans in 1953, 1956 or 1968. That people there lived under Soviet domination was hard reality.

Certainly, though human rights were meant to be one of the main issues in Helsinki, there was little change in the Soviet or East European attitude to dissent after 1975. The GDR Foreign Ministry regarded the relevant sections as having been 'safeguarded' (i.e. weakened) to such an extent that 'direct negative effects on our social relations can be ruled out' (Baumann, 2001, p. 572). Critics such as Andrei

Sakharov in the Soviet Union were still harassed, while members of the Czechoslovak group Charter 77, established to monitor human rights, were arrested in 1979 (Young, 1996, p. 32). Nevertheless, one positive aspect in the years after 1975 was the increased contact between East and West at a cultural level. This in turn led to the promotion of ideas in the East that might be seen as somewhat subversive. West German peace and anti-nuclear movements, for example, had a significant effect on similar movements in the GDR. Some argue that Helsinki opened the way for quiet subversion of the East from within, despite the ostensible victory for a Soviet definition of peaceful co-existence.

Israelis, Arabs and Oil

Brandt's attitude to Israel was substantially the same as Adenauer's. In February 1970, Abba Eban became the first member of an Israeli government to visit West Germany, where he had talks with Brandt and Scheel. In June 1973, Brandt became the first West German Chancellor to visit Israel. (Adenauer had gone there in 1966, after his period in office.) West Germany's close relationship with Israel precluded it from being a mediator in the increasingly tense situation in the Middle East that year. Indeed, after the Yom Kippur War between Israel and the Arab States in October 1973 it became known that West Germany had secretly been supplying weapons to Israel. West German sympathy for Israel was still strong, though left-wing voices in West Germany as elsewhere in Western Europe were increasingly calling on Israel to vacate the territories it had occupied after the Six Day War in 1967, including the West Bank, Gaza and East Jerusalem.

The Middle Eastern conflict came to Germany during the Munich Olympic Games in September 1972. A Palestinian terrorist group known as 'Black September' attacked the Israeli team in its apartments, killing two people and taking nine hostages. An attempt by German police to free the hostages failed miserably: all nine were killed, together with five terrorists and one policeman. Three terrorists were captured, but were released later in response to a demand by Palestinians who had hijacked a Lufthansa aeroplane flying between Frankfurt and Damascus.

The 1973 Yom Kippur War was the first Middle Eastern conflict to have a significant effect on the economies of Western nations. US airlifts on behalf of Israel provoked the oil-rich Arab States into using oil as an economic weapon. On 17 October 1973, twelve days into the war, 'the Organisation of Arab Petroleum Exporting Countries (OAPEC) announced a reduction in oil production until Israel withdrew from her 1967 conquests' (Fraser, 1995, p. 102). Shortly afterwards they announced a total embargo on exports to the USA and the Netherlands, the latter because it supplied much of Western Europe through the port of Rotterdam. Since the US had become a net importer of oil, it was unable to replace the Arab supplies with oil of its own.

The impact on Western economies was severe. Whereas only 5 per cent of energy consumption in the USA was dependent on Arab oil, in West Germany and Britain the figure was 40 per cent, in France 51 per cent, in Japan 59 per cent and in Italy 61 per cent (Baumann, 2001, pp. 521–2). The price of a barrel of oil rose between October 1973 and January 1974 from $2.70 to $11.60. Arab oil accounted for approximately 75 per cent of total West German oil imports and the effect of such price increases was almost immediate.

Economic Recession and Guest Workers

The early period of Brandt's time in office saw significant economic growth in West Germany. In 1969 the economy grew by 12 per cent, forcing the new government to revalue the Deutschmark by 8.5 per cent against the dollar in October of that year. Continued growth into the 1970s, coupled with the effects of a weakening US dollar, caused the Bundesbank to float the DM in May 1971. In December 1971 a devaluation of the dollar meant an effective revaluation of the DM by 13.6 per cent. In January 1973 the dollar was devalued by a further 10 per cent, again increasing the value of the DM. That year saw a wave of strikes in West Germany, as unions sought to win some of the benefits of economic expansion for their members in the form of significant wage increases. None of this appeared to affect West Germany's economic growth. A change came in October 1973.

Since the oil boycott affected only Western countries, it initially made little difference to the GDR, which enjoyed three boom years from 1973 before the increased cost of oil from the Soviet Union began to have an effect. By contrast, this use of oil as a political weapon was the prime cause of the first serious economic crisis in the history of the Federal Republic, easily overshadowing the minor recession of the mid- to late 1960s. The country's GNP increased by 5.3 per cent in 1973 as part of the ongoing boom, but stagnated in 1974 (+0.4 per cent) and actually decreased in 1975 (−3.4 per cent). The unemployment rate increased from 1.2 per cent in 1973 to an average of 4.7 per cent in 1975, even briefly crossing the 5 per cent threshold in early 1975.

One consequence of the economic uncertainty was an almost immediate end to the recruitment of guest workers from the countries of southern Europe. The one-millionth guest worker had arrived in West Germany in 1964, but at that early stage many came, stayed for a few years, and went home again. Others stayed for long years, visiting their families only during holidays and on long weekends. It was not untypical for guest workers from Yugoslavia to be based in south Germany and to board buses on a Friday to visit a wife and children in Zagreb or Sarajevo, returning in the small hours of Monday morning. With time, however, many of them obtained permission for their families to move to Germany. In addition, one million guest workers were recruited during the boom years of 1969–71, so that by 1973 the total number of guest workers in West Germany was 2.5 million (Nicholls, 1997, p. 248).

The first guest workers (*Gastarbeiter*, a term coined in preference to the Nazi word *Fremdarbeiter*, which means 'foreign workers') had been recruited under an agreement with the Italian government in 1955. At a time when the West German economy was expanding rapidly, guest workers were brought in to do essentially menial and unskilled work on lower pay and with worse working conditions than most Germans were prepared to accept. In 1964 one-third of all guest workers were employed in the coal and steel industries and one-quarter in the construction industry. Though it is a simplification, there is a core of truth in the statement that the economic miracle was a product of German brains, American money, and guest workers' sweat.

Though the first agreement was for 100,000 Italians, workers followed from all the countries of southern Europe. Agreements with Spain and Greece were concluded in 1960, while the millionth guest worker, in 1964, was Portuguese. Turks and Yugoslavs also followed in large numbers, especially after the building of the Berlin Wall had ended the labour flow from the East. During the minor recession there had been calls for an end to immigration and to the recruitment of guest workers, not least from the ranks of the NPD. Now, in November 1973, the Federal Minister for Employment ordered a stop to the recruitment of foreign workers. In 1975, Baden-Württemberg became the first state to offer guest workers one-off payments to return to their native country. The Bundestag also found it necessary to increase penalties for employers who employed illegal foreign labour.

Nevertheless, attempts to reduce the number of foreigners in Germany were futile. In 1970, when there were 3 million foreigners in total in West Germany (4.8 per cent of the population), Italians were the largest single group (19 per cent), followed closely by Yugoslavs (17 per cent) and Turks (16 per cent). By 1999, Turks made up 28 per cent of the total number of foreigners, easily the largest contingent, while the total number of foreigners had increased to 8 million, or 10 per cent of the population of united Germany. Though many guest workers did return to their home country, others had children who had been born in Germany but who, because German nationality law is based on blood rather than place of birth, were not accorded citizenship. Thus thousands of those who are regarded as 'foreigners' were actually born in Germany and have lived there all their lives. The law was not relaxed until the 1990s (see Chapter 7).

By 1976, the economy had begun to improve again and the recession was regarded as over. West Germany achieved a 5.5 per cent increase in GNP that year. The guest workers, who had borne much of the consequences of economic recession, remained a political issue, while employment rates never again reached the dizzy heights (over 99 per cent) of the pre-1973 period.

Terrorism and the 'German Autumn'

After the election of Willy Brandt in 1969 the Apo dissolved fairly rapidly, almost in response to his new Ostpolitik and internal reforms. However, in the midst of this success a radical fringe of Apo had become utterly disillusioned with politics and switched to terrorist methods. The Baader–Meinhof Gang, also known as the Red Army Faction (RAF), was a strange mixture of on the one hand revolutionary idealists and on the other hand criminals armed with a smattering of anti-capitalist rhetoric. Ulrike Meinhof, Andreas Baader and Gudrun Ensslin were the three main figures in this movement.

All three were of the generation born in the 1940s that had difficulty grasping their parents' behaviour when Nazi crimes were being committed. All were from a middle-class background. Meinhof was a gifted journalist who sought a just world and opposed, amongst other things, the US war in Vietnam. Ensslin was the daughter of a Protestant pastor who hated the church and identified it with social injustice. By contrast, there is some evidence that Baader, though he was the son of a university professor, enjoyed the thrills of the movement but was an ideological lightweight. Whereas other radicals believed in taking over the state from within (by way of a 'long march through the institutions'), the RAF was united in support of violence by a belief that intellectual argument would be unable to combat the power of the established parties and the influence of the Springer press.

Baader had been jailed in 1968 for setting fire to a department store, had escaped in 1969, was re-arrested but freed again in May 1970 by Meinhof and Ensslin. They and their gang then engaged in a series of criminal operations. In 1971 two terrorists and one policeman were shot dead in different incidents. In 1972 a policeman and a terrorist were shot dead, while bomb attacks were carried out against US Army bases in Frankfurt and Heidelberg, against Springer's headquarters in Hamburg and against a judge investigating the RAF. The largest search operation in West German history, begun on 31 May 1972, led to the arrest of Baader, Ensslin, Meinhof and others within a few short weeks.

The killing of Israeli athletes in 1972 had been carried out by Palestinians, but their actions found an echo in the West German terrorist scene. Ulrike Meinhof wrote a polemic in support of the Black September group's action and suggested that the RAF should forget about debate and stick to machine-gunning (Glees, 1996, p. 164). Meinhof's followers took her at her word. In the next few years a number of industrialists such as the president of the Employers' Confederation, Hanns-Martin Schleyer, as well as legal figures such as the West Berlin Chief Justice, Günter von Drenkmann, and the Attorney-General, Siegfried Buback, were murdered. There was a bomb attack on the Chair of the West Berlin Jewish community, Heinz Galinski, whom the RAF accused of 'being an agent of the Zionist regime'.

In February 1975 the CDU chairman in West Berlin was kidnapped to secure the release of RAF terrorists, who were flown out to South Yemen, whereupon Lorenz was released unharmed. In April 1975, German terrorists occupied the German embassy in Stockholm demanding the release of the entire RAF leadership. Two hostages were shot dead before police stormed the building to free the others, killing two terrorists and arresting the other five in the process. In June 1976, a Palestinian group hijacked an Air France jet and demanded the release of 53 people worldwide, among them six RAF members. An Israeli raid on the plane in Entebbe, Uganda, killed 31 people but freed the remaining hostages.

The government reacted with new laws limiting some individual freedoms, while sections of the press reacted almost hysterically to the wave of terrorist attacks. In June 1972, new laws regulated the possession of firearms and the use of the Border Police in emergency circumstances. In 1974, laws were introduced which limited access to lawyers for terrorist suspects and also restricted a lawyer's ability to bring several suspects together by acting for all of them. In 1976, a new law against the 'formation of terrorist groups' was passed. Political life at the time became notorious for the presence of armed guards, including armoured vehicles, around government offices and the Bundestag in Bonn. The heated political atmosphere and the poisonous reporting by some newspapers, especially the Springer press, against anyone who criticised such measures became known as the 'German autumn'. Helmut Schmidt described it as the most serious political crisis for a state based on the rule of law.

The reaction on the part of the press and some politicians even in the early days caused the writer Heinrich Böll, who received the Nobel Prize for Literature in 1972, to warn in January 1972 against an over-reaction to terrorism. Böll was demonised by the Springer press for his comments, but got his reward when a novel about the press and the denial of civil liberties, *The Lost Honour of Katharina Blum*, topped the

West German bestseller lists for several months after its release in 1974. It was a rare success for criticism in a paranoid era. Nevertheless, the political atmosphere continued to be such that anyone criticising the government's response was branded in conservative circles as a 'sympathiser' with terrorism: Franz Josef Strauss even went so far as to claim that there were terrorist sympathisers in the SPD and FDP parliamentary parties (Thränhardt, 1996, p. 234). The CDU chairman in Hesse, Alfred Dregger, branded a number of left-wing intellectuals, even those who had publicly distanced themselves from the terror, such as Herbert Marcuse and some from the Frankfurt School of philosophers, as 'intellectual instigators' of the violence.

Those RAF members who had been caught were subjected to the due process of law. In 1974 Meinhof, Baader, Ensslin and others were all sentenced to long jail terms. They were joined by Horst Mahler, a lawyer who had used his position to give illegal help to the RAF. In May 1976, Meinhof was found hanged in her cell. The authorities said it was suicide, but this was doubted by supporters, who rioted in a number of cities, while supporters elsewhere bombed German buildings abroad in reaction to the news. In October 1977, a plane hijacked by Palestinians demanding the release of eleven German terrorists was stormed by an elite West German military unit, the GSG9, in Mogadishu, Somalia, and all passengers were freed. The next morning Baader was found shot and Ensslin hanged in their cells in Stuttgart prison. Once again the official verdict of suicide was doubted, and there were protests at home and abroad.

More laws were passed in the years that followed, more arrests were made, and occasional attacks followed, but terrorism in West Germany in many ways reached its peak in 1976–7. The RAF had never been a mass movement and had never enjoyed widespread support. Its members had contacts with a number of international terrorist groups at the time, including the Italian Red Brigades and some Palestinian groups, though it seems to have had little contact with

the IRA. Perhaps the most significant aspect of the groups
was the middle-class background of most of its activists.
Their revolutionary ideals were a potent mixture and their
actions were deadly. Though some members remained on
the run for years afterwards, and more attacks were carried
out, the group faded after 1978.

Mogadishu was a turning point in West German terrorism.
As we shall see, the RAF did not disappear completely after
1977. Nevertheless, the paranoid reaction provoked by its
campaign in the 1970s was not repeated in response to
individual acts of terror that continued on a sporadic basis
into the 1990s. We shall see in Chapter 5 that in the late
1970s many West German radicals turned instead to politics.

Liberalisation and 'Radicals' in West Germany

Terrorism was one problem facing Brandt in the wake of his
1969 success. Another was the promise by some of the radical left who were not engaged in terrorism that they would
instead undertake a 'long march through the institutions' to
take control of West German politics. Quite how they proposed to do this in a multi-party electoral system was never
entirely clear. However, in January 1972 the Interior Minister, Hans-Dietrich Genscher, and the Minister Presidents of
the states passed the so-called *Berufsverbot*, or employment
ban, allowing for the political vetting of everyone applying
for a state job (which included train drivers and postmen as
well as civil servants). As a result, between 1972 and 1976 half
a million applicants for state jobs were tested for political
loyalty, and 430 were rejected.

Supporters of this law see it as an attempt to make consistent, across all the states, practices that already existed.
Opponents rejected it as an example of the old-style authori-
tarianism that had been practised under Adenauer (Glees,
1996, p. 165). The law also seemed to be used much more
against those from a radical communist background than

against neo-Nazis. Large sections of the SPD doubted the wisdom of the law, partly because it was felt that the grounds for rejecting candidates often would not stand up in a court case. An attempt by the Bundestag to reform the law in October 1975 was blocked by the Bundesrat in February 1976, so that the original law remained, controversially, in place.

In contrast to this illiberal move, the SPD–FDP coalition governments of 1969–77 introduced a range of reforms that liberalised social law. Under the Grand Coalition in 1969, homosexuality had been decriminalised, while children born outside marriage were given the same rights as those born in marriage. Widows' pensions were increased. In 1971 a form of financial support for students was introduced that would enable the children of working-class families to go to university: at that time such children were only 7 per cent of the student population. Compulsory military service was reduced from 18 to 15 months in 1972, while non-military service undertaken by conscientious objectors was made equal in value to military service in July 1973. A further reform in 1976, to make it easier to opt for non-military service, was rejected by the Federal Constitutional Court. In 1974, 18-year-olds were given the right to be elected – 1969 had been the first federal election in which they had been able to vote, and they had voted massively for Brandt. In June 1976, husbands and wives were given equal rights before the law, while divorce without blame was made possible.

In 1971 a debate also began in West Germany on reforming the abortion law. A new law was passed in April 1974 allowing abortion within the first three months as long as a woman first spoke to her doctor. The CDU/CSU opposed the law, and the Federal Constitutional Court declared it unconstitutional ten months later. It was replaced in 1976 by a so-called 'indication law', which allowed abortion in the first twelve weeks, based on various medical, psychological and, controversially, social 'indicators'. The law remained unchanged until the 1990s.

Brandt's attempts at liberalising West German society were overshadowed somewhat by his achievements in foreign policy. He also had difficulties with the conservative establishment, especially the Federal Constitutional Court, which even when it did not reject his laws, often put conditions on them. At times it seemed that Brandt and many on the left of his party over-estimated the extent to which any established society can be radically changed from within. That did not prevent their attempts at reform.

The End of Brandt

The end of Brandt's time as Chancellor came unexpectedly. Tensions within the government had been apparent for some time, but the cause of Brandt's downfall was the discovery that one of the advisers in his Office, Günter Guillaume, was a GDR spy. Brandt himself was not responsible for this: when the head of the security service discovered Guillaume's identity he reported it not to Brandt but to Herbert Wehner, to whom he owed his appointment. Wehner shared the information with Schmidt and Genscher before he told Brandt. When the news came out on 24 April 1974, Brandt 'received very little support from his party lieutenants, Wehner and Schmidt, both of whom advised him to leave office' (Nicholls, 1997, p. 250). On 6 May, Brandt accepted full responsibility for the affair and resigned.

His resignation brought a stunning era of political change in the Federal Republic to an end. There was a certain irony in the fact that the man who had done most to create a new atmosphere between West and East Germany was brought down by an East German spy. There was a massively sympathetic response in the public at large, both at home and abroad. Even the conservative *Times* of London praised this Social Democratic Chancellor, while also commenting that his job was done. Going down on one knee in Warsaw was the most memorable single gesture of his career, and it was for his Ostpolitik that he was awarded the Nobel Prize for Peace in 1971. He had represented a new, different Germany from the one that had been infamous in the 1930s and 1940s. He also represented a more humane approach to resolving differences than did the Cold Warriors of the 1950s and 1960s. The argument about whether his Ostpolitik reinforced the division of Germany or helped create the circumstances in which that division could be overcome must remain unresolved.

Brandt did not retire from politics. He remained as Chairman of the SPD until 1987 and was President of the Socialist International 1976–92. His successor as Chancellor, Helmut Schmidt, had none of his vision. Schmidt was a pragmatist who had acquired a reputation for straightforward action as Hamburg's Interior Minister (1962–6), Federal Defence Minister (1969–72) and Finance Minister (1972–4). Ostensibly he continued Brandt's policies, but there were no new major developments with the East. Rather, Schmidt reinforced West Germany's position in the Western Alliance, an attitude that made some sections of his party uneasy.

The End of Liberalisation

The period of liberalisation in the GDR always had its limits. Some writers were still not allowed to publish. Novels such as Stefan Heym's *Five Days in June*, which is about the June 1953 uprising, still could not appear. Then, in 1976, what liberalisation there was came to an abrupt end, when the singer and poet Wolf Biermann, who was giving a concert tour of West Germany sponsored by the Trade Union Federation (DGB), used a concert in Cologne on 13 November 1976 to criticise the GDR leadership. His criticisms, though couched in terms that made it plain that he still regarded the GDR as the better German state, were too much for the SED leadership, and three days later they announced that they had stripped him of his citizenship. Biermann was the son of a communist Jewish father who had moved to East Berlin from Hamburg as a 17-year-old in 1953. He was no opponent of communism; rather, he saw himself as a critical communist. The GDR leadership claimed that his Cologne performance had been hostile to the socialist state.

The SED was completely unprepared for the scale of the reaction to this decision. The action provoked thirteen leading writers and artists, among them Stefan Heym, Stephan Hermlin, Volker Braun, Heiner Müller, Christa Wolf and Jurek Becker, into writing an open letter in Biermann's defence. In it, they argued that the socialist state should be able to tolerate uncomfortable criticism and asked the party leadership to reconsider its decision. They asked the party newspaper, *Neues Deutschland,* to publish their letter but also sent a copy to a Western press agency lest they be ignored in the East. The letter was only published in the West, but within five days a further 93 artists and writers had signed. More signatures were added later.

The state's reaction was hard-line. Four of the first thirteen signatories were expelled from the SED and three others were disciplined. Other signatories were arrested, while a series of prominent artists and writers left the GDR for the West in the years following. The GDR lost some of its best people in the cultural and intellectual sphere because it insisted essentially on loyalty without significant criticism. The Biermann Affair permanently ruptured the relationship between the SED and the intellectuals. Liberalisation was at an end.

Brandt's period of liberalisation in the West came to an end for altogether different reasons. Resistance from conservative institutions was partly responsible, but the main factor was Schmidt's lack of reforming idealism. He was essentially a managerial liberal who, in common with the FDP, saw himself as a 'guardian[s] of a prosperous, well-managed economy' (Kettenacker, 1997, p. 146). The economic recession came to be well managed by him after 1975, though at the expense of more, potentially expensive social reform. In 1976 the coalition held onto power by the skin of its teeth. The CDU/CSU captured 48.6 per cent of the vote and 243 seats in the Bundestag. For the first time since 1953 the SPD's share of the vote dropped, by 3.3 per cent to 42.5 per cent. The FDP's share also dropped slightly, to 7.9 per cent. Together, the coalition parties had 253 seats, a majority of just ten. Though this was similar to the 1969 position, there were now no FDP members who wished to defect to the CDU. Schmidt was confirmed in power.

Conclusion

The period 1969–74 is characterised by a pioneering spirit in international relations in which West Germany put its relationship with the East on an entirely new footing. The GDR responded with a period of relative liberalisation that lasted until 1976. The motives behind Brandt's actions seem clear: he was in many ways an idealist who wished to force his fellow West Germans to face up to the hard reality of division. While there is no doubt that Brandt never gave up the hope that one day Germany would be reunited, he was, nevertheless, 'a German patriot [for whom] Germany seemed increasingly a cultural, and not a political concept' (Glees, 1996, p. 195). Honecker was someone prepared to accept the reaffirmation of West Berlin's ties with West Germany in return for a strengthening of the GDR's international position as a separate state. This was, essentially, the compromise that was reached.

By the mid- to late 1970s liberalisation came to an end in both states, and détente, the era of co-operation between capitalist and communist states, was also in decline, despite the achievement of the Helsinki Agreement in 1975. Honecker and the SED were again fighting writers and intellectuals and stifling dissent, in much the same way that they had done in the 1950s and 1960s. Schmidt's SPD-led government was fighting terrorism and economic problems that had already begun to take the shine off West Germany's postwar economic achievements. Internationally, two German states had taken their respective places in the world's community of nations. They had also found a less hostile way of co-existing in a Europe that was still divided along a line that ran down the middle of Germany. By the late 1970s the division of Germany seemed more or less permanent.

5

TWO NATIONS? 1977–89

Introduction

By 1977, German politics were no longer about new beginnings. Rather, the two states settled down to a neighbourly if not quite friendly relationship. In West Germany terrorism reached a peak, the economy settled down, and Helmut Schmidt led a period of unexciting economic management. When the SPD–FDP coalition ended in 1982 and was replaced by a CDU–FDP coalition, it merely marked a transition to continuity. There was no radical change in government politics, not even on the 'German Question'. Throughout this period in the GDR, Honecker reaffirmed SED control of the state and its institutions, which remained in place until 1989.

Each state seemed to be governed by consensus, even if a repressive apparatus lay behind the outward show of loyalty offered by most citizens in the GDR. In the absence of any big political crusade led by the dominant parties in either state, people began to reflect on their lives, their welfare, their environment and their identities. The anti-nuclear and environmental movements were an obvious manifestation of this in West Germany, and an environmental movement even sprang up in the GDR. West Germany became more self-absorbed and moved into an era when the concept of German unification was something that few thought would ever be realised. In its own eyes it became 'Germany', with the GDR being something quite distinct. In the GDR people developed an ability to lead a dual life in which outward loyalty to the state was complemented by a retreat into a private, niche existence outside of work and political meetings. Young people maintained a sense of Germanness that was fundamentally different from West Germany's sense of Germanness.

'The long 1980s' seems an appropriate name for this period. The two states settled into quite different political agendas, and the division of Germany seemed to no one to be a contemporary political issue. Yet changes were taking place in both states, slowly, almost imperceptibly in some cases. In West Germany the real political challenge came from a rise of environmentalism in the political shape of 'the Greens', who started winning seats in elections from 1979 on. In the GDR, slow change culminated in a 'big bang', the fall of the Berlin Wall, which is discussed in Chapter 6.

Global Politics

The 1970s may be seen as the decisive decade in détente, even if the process broke down a little in 1978–80 over issues such as the neutron bomb and the 1979 Soviet invasion of Afghanistan. (The latter led to a boycott of the 1980 Moscow Olympic Games by the USA and West Germany, among others.) Peaceful co-existence is the key description of this phase in the Cold War, even if proxy wars were still fought between US and Soviet surrogates in places such as Angola. The first Strategic Arms Limitation Treaty (SALT I), signed in 1972, limited the number of nuclear warheads held by the US and the Soviets. Even in the middle of a relatively cold period in US–Soviet relations a second treaty, SALT II, was signed in 1979. In response to the invasion of Afghanistan the US never ratified the treaty, though it did basically adhere to its provisions (Thränhardt, 1996, pp. 244–7). In a similar vein there was a reduction in the number of Soviet troops stationed in the GDR in 1979.

Ronald Reagan's accession to the US Presidency in January 1981 led to an intensification of anti-American sentiment in Europe. In part this was because of his very obvious ultra-conservative foreign policy agenda: Reagan supported oppressive military dictators such as Pinochet in Chile and Galtieri in Argentina while being obsessed with overthrowing the left-wing Sandinistas in Nicaragua. The poisonous atmosphere was illustrated on the one hand by the Soviet Union's continuation of the war in Afghanistan and on the other by Reagan's massive financial support for the right-wing Contras, who were fighting a war with the Sandinistas. Kohl threw in his tuppence-worth in 1986 when, after a meeting in Reykjavik between Reagan and the new Soviet leader, Gorbachev, he claimed that Gorbachev's propaganda methods were comparable to those of Josef Goebbels, Hitler's propaganda chief.

Whatever happened concerning words and surrogate wars, it was in the realm of nuclear armaments that the East–West conflict was most prominent in the 1980s, and it was this issue that provoked massive demonstrations in West Germany, and even stirred some opposition in the GDR.

Nuclear Weapons

A section of West German political opinion had always been against atomic and then nuclear arms – there had been protests as far back as the early 1950s against the stationing of atomic weapons in Germany, and the development of the neutron bomb in the late 1970s saw a major revival of anti-nuclear protests. SPD politician Egon Bahr described the new bomb, which killed people without causing either significant damage to buildings or long-term radioactive contamination, as a 'symbol of the perversion of human thinking' (Baumann, 2001, p. 631). In 1978, the CDU/CSU opposition in the Bundestag called on Schmidt's government to support the production of the new weapon and its deployment by Nato. Schmidt rejected such an open demonstration of support, saying the matter was for the US to decide. Despite this, after discussions between Genscher and US Secretary of State Cyrus Vance, Bonn agreed to arming Nato with the weapons, though US President Jimmy Carter decided in April 1978 to delay production, a move criticised by Strauss as weakness in the face of the Soviet Union.

In June 1979, Carter and Soviet leader Leonid Brezhnev signed the SALT II Treaty in Vienna, a treaty that did not cover the short- and medium-range missiles stationed in Europe. In the mid-1970s the Soviets had surprised most observers in Western Europe by replacing outdated missiles stationed in Eastern Europe with new ones of the type SS-20, which could hit targets in Europe but not in the USA. This was seen by many as an attempt to drive a wedge between the USA and Western Europe by suggesting that the US was no longer a target. In December 1979, Nato responded with the so-called 'Twin Track' strategy. Nato offered the Soviets talks on further disarmament, while also making clear that if the talks failed to reach agreement Nato would begin, in 1983, stationing new short-range Pershing II missiles in West Germany and medium-range Cruise missiles in the Netherlands, Belgium, West Germany and Italy. The weapons would be under US control. Negotiations on arms limitation were designed to make the stationing of the new weapons superfluous. Helmut Schmidt was one of the prime movers behind this decision.

The Twin Track decision was extremely controversial in the Federal Republic, and it gave a massive boost to the peace movement there. Various appeals were made by prominent individuals from public life, and mass demonstrations were organised, including one in Bonn in October 1981 attended by 300,000 people, and another there in June 1982 on the occasion of a Nato summit, which attracted 400,000 people. The main Protestant Church in Germany criticised the Twin Track decision in 1981. The SPD supported the decision, despite vehement opposition from sections of the party, but agreed to a special conference on whether the missiles should be stationed on German soil.

Many West Germans saw this as an issue not just of peace, but of the survival of Germans. It seemed to some that the two superpowers were prepared to station short- and medium-range weapons that could wipe out the whole of Germany and most of central Europe, while leaving the US and much of the Soviet Union untouched. Schmidt, supported by his coalition partners the FDP and by the CDU/CSU opposition but opposed by much of his own party, saw a need for military strength to face up to the perceived Soviet threat. Supporters of the Twin Track strategy argued that they were sincere about negotiating for disarmament. Critics could not see any sincerity in putting a missile to Soviet heads while negotiating with them.

The issue was one that helped bring about the downfall of the SPD–FDP coalition in late 1982 (see below). Schmidt's government was replaced by a CDU/CSU–FDP coalition led by Helmut Kohl, which was much more sympathetic to the tationing of nuclear weapons; 1983 saw further massive demonstrations throughout the Federal Republic against the stationing of Pershing and Cruise missiles. 700,000 people took part in Easter marches for peace in April, 20,000 demonstrated against a visit to Krefeld by US Vice-President George C. Bush in June, and for three days in September several thousand people blockaded the entrance to the US military depot at Mutlangen, where the Pershing missiles were to be stationed. On 5 October, five million people observed a Trade Union call for 'five minutes silence for peace', while 1.3 million people participated in a week of demonstrations in late October, including 300,000 in Bonn and 200,000 who formed a 108-kilometer (68-mile) human chain between Stuttgart and Ulm. In November 1983, a special SPD conference voted against the stationing of the missiles by 383 votes to 14. Nevertheless, a few days later, on 22 November, the Bundestag approved the measure by 286 votes to 225, and the next day the first missiles were flown in.

This did not signal the end of anti-nuclear demonstrations. When, in 1985, US President Ronald Reagan announced his intention to launch the 'Strategic Defence Initiative' (SDI, also known as 'Star Wars'), Chancellor Kohl supported him, but many in West Germany did not. France was also vehemently opposed. One spectacular act of opposition was undertaken in January 1987 by 20 judges, who were arrested for blockading the US depot at Mutlangen. Negotiations between the superpowers on arms limitation continued, and in December 1987 Reagan and the Soviet leader, Gorbachev, signed an agreement in Washington on a so-called 'zero option', by which all nuclear weapons with a range between 300 and 3000 miles would be removed. Ironically, some conservatives, such as Kohl, feared that this left the Soviets in a stronger position because of their superior conventional forces on the ground (Young, 1996, pp. 36–7).

Both German states had a secondary role in these negotiations. The main players were the USA and the Soviet Union. Nevertheless, these political developments stirred opposition in both states. We shall see that in the GDR this opposition was part of a wider, largely church-based opposition movement that developed in the 1980s. In West Germany the issue of nuclear arms, though it was separate from the environmental issue and was certainly never the concern of just one political party, nevertheless became closely linked to environmental issues. The result was the creation of a strong new political movement that changed the face of West German politics.

Nuclear Energy, the Environment and the Greens

Protection of the environment was traditionally a conservative issue that saw rural communities opposed to industrial expansion, the building of motorways, etc. By the 1970s in West Germany and many other developed countries it became more of a left-wing issue, with ecologists and environmentalists opposed to the expansionist plans of global industrial concerns and the polluting effects of their activities. Even atomic/nuclear energy, which many protesters against atomic weapons in the 1950s had seen as essentially clean, became an issue when the heavy cost to the environment of cleaning up old plants became apparent. Some conservatives supported the environmentalist movement in the 1970s and 1980s, but many shared Franz Josef Strauss's extreme view that environmentalist campaigners were 'ecological nut cases' (Thränhardt, 1996, p. 216) or the view of the Minister President of Baden-Württemberg, Hans Filbinger, who in 1975 called protesters against a nuclear power plant at Wyhl 'anarchists and communists'.

The environmental lobby campaigned on a plethora of issues, all of them geared towards protecting an environment that had been severely damaged by the industrial success of the Federal Republic. Imposing a speed limit on West German motorways was one issue, but the powerful pro-automobile lobby resisted this proposal, with the result that even today there is no speed limit on some German 'autobahns'. The promotion of lead-free petrol was another, and this has largely been achieved, despite similar opposition. Reducing toxic emissions from factories has been another issue, not least because the emissions have contributed significantly to the killing of trees and the reduction of forested areas: the German word for 'the dying of the forests', *waldsterben*, has passed into several European languages since the 1970s.

In 1975, demonstrators occupied the site of a proposed nuclear power plant at Wyhl on the Upper Rhine. The authorities had sanctioned the building of the plant despite the fact that the licence was due to be challenged in court. In November 1976, 30,000 people protested against the planned construction of another plant at Brokdorf in

Schleswig-Holstein. In March 1977, 15,000 people demonstrated against the planned construction of a nuclear reprocessing plant at Gorleben in Lower Saxony. Meanwhile, the legal authorities in some areas began demonstrating a willingness to insist that the companies running these plants show that they were taking their environmental responsibilities seriously. In March 1977 a regional court in Freiburg annulled the building licence for Wyhl because the possible bursting of a pressure container, though unlikely, could not be called a 'minimal risk' (Baumann, 2001, p. 611).

The demonstrations that took place often erupted into fighting between demonstrators and police. Demonstrators sometimes felt justified in resisting what they saw as heavy-handed and semi-legal tactics on the part of the authorities, while the police on occasion used somewhat more than minimal force in response to resistance from demonstrators. It is probably also true that some hard-line left-wing elements that became involved were determined to maximise the potential for confrontation. What is clear is that most of those involved in environmental protests did not see their views represented in any of the mainstream political parties. As a result they began to organise their own political groups. In many ways this was another legacy of the Apo, but taken one step further in organisational terms.

The first environmental groups had been citizens' groups formed in 1972, and the protests throughout that decade were largely co-ordinated by *ad hoc* committees. In July 1978 this began to change, when West Germany's first national environmental party, Green Action for the Future (GAZ) was formed in Bonn. In that same year environmental groupings took between 2 per cent and 4.5 per cent of the votes in various regional elections. In January 1979, the state government of North Rhine-Westphalia was forced to issue the first ever widespread smog alarm in the Federal Republic when the level of sulphur dioxide in the atmosphere in the Ruhr industrial area passed the critical limit of 0.8 mg/m^3. Environmentalist candidates then enjoyed some success in local elections in North Rhine-Westphalia that year. The nuclear accident at Harrisburg, Pennsylvania, in March/April 1979 provoked a strong reaction in West Germany, and growing doubts were expressed about the plant at Gorleben, forcing Lower Saxony's Minister President to admit that politically the plant could not be constructed. In October 1979, 100,000 people took part in the largest antinuclear power demonstration to date. In that same month a Green List made a first breakthrough, taking 5.1 per cent of the vote and 4 seats in the Bremen state parliament.

In January 1980, 'the Greens' were formed as a national political party with an essentially left-wing and environmentalist platform, though some conservative politicians also joined. The common denominator was a desire to protect the environment. New aspects to this issue came up regularly. In Frankfurt, a proposal to build a new airport runway, 'Startbahn West', was met with fierce opposition in a campaign that lasted years. In Gorleben, plans to build a storage depot in place of the reprocessing plant were met with resistance and the creation there of a self-declared 'Free Republic of Wendland' by environmentalists. In March 1980, the Greens won 5.3 per cent of the vote and 6 seats in Baden-Württemberg state elections. However, in the national election in October 1980 they took just 1.5 per cent and no seats.

Nevertheless, environmental issues remained alive and the SPD in particular began to pay more attention, for fear that its support could be reduced by the attractiveness of Green politics to young voters. A demonstration by 100,000 people at Brokdorf in February 1981 led to internal SPD disputes in nearby Hamburg, which caused the resignation of the mayor, Hans-Ulrich Klose. An Alternative List allied to the Greens won 7.2 per cent and 9 seats in the West Berlin parliament in May 1981. Conservative environmentalists left the Greens that year, to form a separate party, which has never enjoyed electoral success. In 1982 the Greens won seats in the state parliaments in Lower Saxony, Hamburg and Hesse. Finally, in 1983, the Greens won 5.6 per cent in the national election, thus becoming the first new party to win seats in the Bundestag since the 1950s.

1983 was not the end of their successes. In 1984 the Greens tolerated an SPD minority government in Hesse, but in 1985 they went into coalition, with Joschka Fischer as Minister for the Environment. The decision to go into government brought to a head a crucial debate that had been going on within the Greens between the so-called 'Fundis', or fundamentalists, who believed firmly that the party should be in opposition attempting to change society, and the 'Realos', or realists, who felt that they should be prepared to change society from within. It was not until 1990 that the debate was finally resolved with a resounding defeat for the Fundis. By then the Realos' strategy had appeared confirmed by further successes at state level and a jump from 5.6 per cent to 8.3 per cent in the 1987 federal election. The 1987 success was at least partly attributable to fears generated by the atomic reactor explosion at Chernobyl in the Ukraine in April 1986, which sent radioactive clouds to the furthest fringes of western Europe and beyond.

The Greens had what was in many ways a simple message: protection of the environment was more important than economic growth; and this appealed to many younger voters who might otherwise have opted for the SPD or the FDP. They also insisted on more grassroots democracy and greater human rights (especially women's rights), and they were opposed to nuclear armaments (indeed, many were pacifists). Their support was strongest among younger, educated voters: the proportion of their voters with a university education was twice the West German average. One response from the larger parties was to set up environmental ministries at both federal and state level. Their successes provoked governments into tackling the political issues that they raised, though their early successes were in part due to Schmidt's indifference to environmental issues (Kettenacker, 1997, pp. 150–2).

'The German Autumn'

The terrorist activity of the RAF had left the state with little tolerance of violent dissent and it continued to hunt down terrorists, who themselves carried out some high-profile assassinations. Various governments continued to pass laws that limited the rights of defendants in terrorist trials and broadened police powers in the search for suspects. There was also increased co-ordination of anti-terrorist activity with neighbouring states, including Austria, Switzerland and Italy. Attacks on US targets in West Germany were stepped up: a bomb attack on the European Headquarters of the US Air Force at Ramstein in August 1981 injured 20, while more attacks on various bases were launched in the years following. Attacks on *British* Army bases in this period were a different issue, being generally the work of the IRA rather than the RAF.

In 1982 the police arrested some of the leading RAF terrorists, including Brigitte Mohnhaupt, and discovered 13 weapons dumps. Yet the RAF continued its attacks. In 1985 a Munich industrialist was murdered, and two people were killed in an attack on a US air base in Frankfurt. In 1986 a member of the board at the global concern Siemens and his driver were murdered near Munich, as was a leading West German diplomat in Bonn. In 1989 a spokesman for the Deutsche Bank was killed. Though many terrorists were captured and jailed, many were never caught. After 1990 it transpired that some had been given new identities and allowed to live in the GDR.

Criticism of the state's measures against terrorism was widespread, even among many who had no sympathy for the terrorists themselves. Critics also pointed to the misuse of some laws by the security apparatus, to invade people's privacy in the name of protecting the state. There was also ongoing criticism of Brandt's 'employment ban', which was seen as an attempt to exert state control in areas in which it was not necessary. Certainly, there is much evidence that the

'Federal News Service' (BND), as the West German secret service was officially called, used its powers to keep people out of jobs in which they posed no threat to the state. Secret police are by no means the preserve of communist states, and the West German BND operated in a manner which, though legal in defence of the state, was frequently at the expense of individuals' rights. The law was revised, so that individuals applying for state positions were no longer auto- matically checked by the BND from 1979, while in 1985 Saarland became the first state to abolish the law. It has, however, never been superseded. Terrorism itself also re- fused to disappear completely (though the RAF announced its own dissolution in April 1998), but the extreme situation of the 1970s has never returned.

West German Economics and Social Policy

Following the period of economic recession in the early to mid-1970s, when many Western economies were hit by what the American economist Fritz Stern called 'stagflation' (in- flation without economic growth), West Germany made a major recovery in the period 1976–8. By 1979 unemployment in West Germany stood at just 3.8 per cent. Throughout the 1970s the Deutschmark had continually strengthened against the US dollar: while the price of gold and oil soared, the dollar weakened, sinking to just DM1.71 in December 1979, which was less than half of the DM3.65 it had been worth in 1970.

Helmut Schmidt had a good reputation in business circles as a manager who was not too troubled by ideology. He wished to see an economically strong Federal Republic. He introduced economic measures that pleased his coalition partners in the FDP, such as tax cuts for industry and the wealthier in society, while increasing VAT, thereby penalis- ing the less well off, but these measures alienated many in his own party. Willy Brandt, who was still Party Chairman, shielded Schmidt from some of his strongest critics, but he himself 'felt that the SPD was moving too far to the right and was in danger of losing its constituency' (Nicholls, 1997, p. 271). In particular, Brandt was afraid that younger voters, many of whom were beginning to question the whole notion of economic growth, might be attracted by radical measures to support the environment, such as taxing environmentally-unfriendly businesses. Schmidt refused to countenance such radicalism, and he was supported by some on the right of his party.

In the early 1980s economic and financial problems began to mount for Schmidt. Unemployment had never returned to the low levels of the 1950s, but now it began to rise again, reaching 1.8 million (7.6 per cent) in 1982 and hitting 2.5 million (10.4 per cent) in February 1983, the highest level in the history of the Federal Republic, by which time Schmidt had lost his job. Inflation was at 5 per cent. In 1981 it became apparent that the budget for 1982 would require an emergency savings package if it were not to be in deficit from the start. An agreement between the coalition partners SPD and FDP was vetoed by the CDU/CSU majority in the Bundesrat. Cuts in child welfare, social welfare and housing allowances, amongst other things, were necessary before the revised package was approved. These revised measures were deeply unpopular in the SPD. The same economic difficulties recurred in 1982 and this time they could not be resolved. The FDP's proposals for deep cuts in the provision of social welfare were unacceptable even to Schmidt, who issued an ultimatum that forced the FDP out of government. In the end it was the SPD who lost office as the FDP combined with the opposition to elect Helmut Kohl as Chancellor in October 1982 (see below).

Large sections of the SPD were dismayed that Schmidt preferred to cut social spending and taxes on business while increasing VAT. The new government from October 1982 had no such qualms. It imposed a range of cuts in unemployment benefit, it made sick benefit and Christmas and holiday bonuses liable for pension contributions and it cut maternity benefit from January 1984. It insisted on more flexible working hours for trainees and young people, and also allowed retirement from age 58. Unemployment stabilised at around 9.3 per cent for the next four years, but only began to decline in 1988. Even then it only dropped to 7.2 per cent in 1990. In 1987, the Federal Government introduced a major tax reform which favoured those on medium and high incomes, with a progressive rate of income tax going from 19 per cent up to a top rate of 53 per cent.

West Germany remained a wealthy society, but by the 1980s it had changed somewhat from the society that had existed in the wake of the economic miracle. Full employment was no longer guaranteed. In 1972 the CDU politician Norbert Blüm estimated that 1.7 per cent of the population owned 70 per cent of the means of production. If anything, this concentration of wealth in the hands of a tiny minority continued. In addition to the many who were unemployed, many more worked shorter hours. So-called 'guest workers' were a permanent feature of the West German economy, many of them with children who had been born in West Germany and who knew no other society, but who were not accorded citizenship. In the 1980s there were some 4 million foreigners in a West German population of 61 million. 'The 1980s were a period when class distinctions were replaced by a new social division into those in and out of employment' (Kettenacker, 1997, p. 148). Some referred to West Germany as the 'two-thirds society', in which two-thirds of the population were comfortable and had a political voice while one-third was poor and ignored. Housing became a major issue in some towns, especially Frankfurt and Hamburg, as speculators pulled down old, working-class areas to make room for business developments and upmarket apartments. In Frankfurt, this became the subject of a play by Rainer Werner Fassbinder called *Garbage, the City and Death,* which faced protests and accusations of anti-Semitism because the chief property speculator was Jewish.

The extent to which the mainstream of West German politics began to shrink is illustrated by some electoral statistics. The 1970s were the high point of West German political involvement with the three main parties, the CDU/CSU, the FDP and the SPD. In all federal elections from 1961 through to 1980 only these three parties succeeded in winning seats in the Bundestag. Such was the concentration of votes that in 1972 they took 99.1 per cent of the vote on a 91.1 per cent turnout. In other words, 90.3 per cent of all those of voting age in West Germany supported the three main parties. A similar figure shows for 1976: 99.1 per cent on a 90.7 per cent turnout, giving 89.9 per cent of all voters. Just over ten years later this had dropped significantly: in the January 1987 election the three main parties obtained 90.4 per cent of the vote on a turnout of 84.3 per cent. Together, they now took the votes of just 76.2 per cent of voters. This was the lowest percentage for the three main parties since the 1950s (see Appendix 1). The proportion of voters now voting for other parties or abstaining had risen to one-quarter of the electorate, up from just 10 per cent in 1972 and 1976. Clearly, there was increasing disillusionment with the mainstream parties and what they represented. It is their performance and the things that they, as parties, represented that we will now investigate.

West German Political Parties and Elections

A Marxist criticism of West German politics in the 1970s and, indeed, of most capitalist systems is that 'there is, in effect, little real choice between conservative and professedly socialist parties, since both must operate in a manner which allows capitalism to flourish' (Fulbrook, 1991, p. 257). Certainly, there are many respects in which, despite the hard-line rhetoric of some right-wingers like Strauss, the choice in West Germany in the 1970s was between three variations on a single theme, that theme being a social market economy in a federal political system. The difference between the parties was one of emphasis rather than policy, with the exception of Ostpolitik, though by 1983 even that difference had disappeared. To be sure, differences opened up in the 1980s on the question of nuclear weapons, but even here there was agreement that West Germany should still belong to the Atlantic alliance. West German politics in the 1970s and early 1980s were built on consensus and a large degree of uniformity.

Nevertheless, there were politicians on the right wing of the CDU and CSU who sought confrontation at every opportunity. Franz Josef Strauss was the epitome of such confrontational politics, a man who regarded any politicians to the left of the CDU (and even some in the CDU) as at best crypto-communists, at worst, open subversives. With CDU politicians such as Hans Filbinger in Baden-Württemberg and Alfred Dregger in Hesse he openly campaigned with slogans such as 'Freedom or Socialism' and 'Freedom instead of Socialism', the clear implication being that an SPD-led government was little better than one led by the SED. The CDU chairman, Helmut Kohl, who despite being kept in opposition by the SPD–FDP coalition had led the CDU/CSU to its second best result ever in 1976, was no real friend of Strauss. Still, the support Strauss gained from conservatives in the CDU enabled his election as joint CDU/CSU 'Candidate for Chancellor' for the 1980 federal election, defeating Kohl's nominee, Ernst Albrecht, in the process.

Schmidt for the SPD and Genscher for the FDP agreed early in 1980 on a renewal of the SPD–FDP coalition if they won the election. They also succeeded in turning the election into something akin to a referendum on Strauss's confrontational style of politics. The result was that, despite an indirect appeal by the Catholic bishops in September 1980 for support for the CDU/CSU, Strauss led the Union to its worst electoral performance since 1949. It won 44.3 per cent of the vote. The SPD held its ground, but the main beneficiaries were the FDP, who scored 10.6 per cent. Clearly there were many liberal conservatives who could not stomach Strauss. The SPD–FDP coalition increased its majority from 10 seats to 45.

The success of the coalition parties in 1980 could not hide the divisions that existed, which were getting stronger by the day. The SPD had barely increased its vote (+0.3 per cent), and its position had been saved only by Strauss's extremism. It was not the unified and quite single-minded mass party of the 1972 election, when it had enjoyed its biggest success. Rather, it was riven by internal divisions, with a leadership elite around Schmidt close to the FDP, but more and more of the ordinary party members opposed to the FDP, the Nato Twin Track decision, cuts in social spending and a range of other policies. The FDP quickly showed that it was also beginning to look in other directions. After state elections in Berlin in 1981 it tolerated a minority CDU government rather than investigate joining a coalition with the SPD and the Alternative List. A series of defeats in state elections in 1981 and 1982, in most of which it failed to win any seats, showed the unpopularity of the party, unpopularity which some of its leaders attributed to its continued participation in government with the SPD.

The financial crisis that beset Schmidt in his last two years as Chancellor was brought to a head by 'machinations within the Free Democratic Party' (Nicholls, 1997, p. 275). Its leader, Hans-Dietrich Genscher, was a more conservative figure than his predecessor, Walter Scheel, and he enjoyed a personal friendship with Kohl. Economically, his sympathies lay with the CDU, a party that was acceptable to him now that Strauss had been sidelined, but he was also determined to preserve the benefits of Brandt's Ostpolitik. Kohl was agreeable to this. In the summer of 1982 it became obvious that the FDP was preparing to change sides. The FDP Economics Minister, Count Otto Lambsdorff, told a tabloid newspaper that if the voters in the regional election in Hesse decided that the FDP should change coalition partners there, this would be signal for Bonn. In the event, the

FDP lost all of its seats in Hesse and was replaced in parliament there by the Greens. Schmidt went on the offensive and ordered Lambsdorff to present his ideas for the development of the economy. Lambsdorff's prescription was so geared towards free market economics that neither his own FDP nor the CDU fully supported it. Strauss, in typically aggressive fashion, asked whether Lambsdorff, who had been a member of the social–liberal coalition for thirteen years, had actually been in Siberia or the Indian jungle for all that time. Schmidt decided to blame his coalition partners for a breakdown in government and try to provoke new elections. Genscher and the other FDP ministers then resigned on 17 September 1982 and started negotiations with the CDU/CSU. Despite opposition in the ranks of the FDP, and despite calls for fresh elections in order to provide a mandate for any new government, on 1 October Helmut Kohl became Chancellor by using the constructive vote of no confidence in the Bundestag, with Genscher once again Foreign Minister. Six months later, in March 1983, Kohl and Genscher contrived to hold early elections, which duly confirmed them in power. This was the election that also saw the Greens enter the Bundestag for the first time, winning votes largely at the expense of the SPD.

In power, Kohl promised the politics of continuity. A youthful 52 and a Catholic Rhinelander, he accepted the Ostpolitik of the SPD–FDP coalition, and he continued and intensified the social and economic policies of the Schmidt government, which were now vehemently opposed by the SPD in opposition. He also supported the stationing of nuclear weapons and later Reagan's Star Wars initiative (SDI). Government policy in the remainder of the 1980s was characterised by continuity, in part guaranteed by the continued participation in government of the FDP, albeit under a different senior partner. The SPD, by contrast, became radically opposed to most of the policies that it had, however grudgingly, supported under Schmidt, and it lost votes in 1983 and again in 1987, whereas the Greens in parliament seemed to go from strength to strength, despite their internal divisions.

The manner in which Kohl came to power left a bad taste in many mouths. Though the constitution specifically provides for just such a changeover, many FDP members felt their party had betrayed its electoral mandate of 1980, which was for coalition with the SPD. The youth wing of the party dissociated itself from the FDP, while many of the leading politicians also left, some of them later joining the SPD. Yet the disenchantment caused by the events of September/October 1982 was mild compared to the disillusionment caused by the series of political scandals that beset West German political life in the 1980s.

The Flick scandal showed the extent to which the West German political parties were corruptible. All except the Greens were implicated in receiving donations from Friedrich Karl Flick, one of the richest men in the Federal Republic and the son of the founder of the Flick Industrial Corporation, a company with interests in steel, munitions and explosives, engineering, paper and chemicals. In 1983 the company had a turnover of DM6 billion and spent DM14 million 'buying influence for itself' (Glees, 1996, pp. 208–9). In 1975 Flick had sold a 29 per cent stake in Mercedes Benz, and he sought to avoid paying tax on the profits of this sale. Flick was never found guilty of bribery, but during the investigations it became clear that many leading politicians had received very expensive gifts from him. Strauss, Schmidt, Kohl, Brandt and others were all implicated. In addition, he had made political donations to all of the parties (except the Greens), many handed over in brown paper envelopes and not put through normal party book-keeping: Helmut Kohl was one of those who had to answer questions to the inquiry on this subject. Not one of the parties emerged with its reputation intact. The impression was created of a Federal Republic which could be bought if the price was right (Thränhardt, 1996, p. 277). In February 1987, two former FDP economics ministers, Hans Friderichs and Count Otto

Lambsdorff, and a former general manager of Flick, Eberhard von Brauchitsch, were convicted of tax evasion and fined. Charges of bribery were dropped for lack of evidence (Glees, 1996, p. 207). Ultimately the impression was created that the Flick investigation, despite the best efforts of one of its members, Otto Schily of the Greens, was aimed at burying rather than illuminating the affair. Investigations dragged out, prosecutions were few, and the whole thing left a sour aftertaste in the mouths of many citizens. It undoubtedly contributed to the feeling which became stronger in the 1990s that politics was not worthwhile.

An economic scandal that indirectly touched on politics was the 'Neue Heimat' affair, which erupted in 1982. Leading managers in this, the largest construction company in western Europe, which had built 470,000 municipal apartments (council flats) between 1950 and 1980, were accused of corruption and of having profited from illegal contracts. When it became known in early 1983 that the company owed billions of Marks, the board was forced to resign. Leading figures in the Trade Union movement and some politicians were accused of having been aware of the situation, but no senior politicians were implicated.

In September 1987 another scandal broke, this time in the northern state of Schleswig-Holstein. The CDU Minister President of the state, Uwe Barschel, was accused by *Der Spiegel* of using dirty tricks in the state election campaign against his opponent Björn Engholm of the SPD, including bugging his office and checking his tax returns. The news broke one day before the vote. Barschel initially denied the charges, but within two weeks he had been forced to accept 'political responsibility', and two weeks after that, on 11 October, he was found dead in a hotel bathroom in Geneva. The verdict was suicide. The election itself resulted in an impasse, with the CDU losing its majority and unable to form a coalition with the FDP (together they had 37 out of 74 seats), which also refused to go into government with the SPD. Another election, in May 1988, gave the SPD an absolute majority, with the CDU in opposition there for the first time since 1950.

Politics in West Germany had, in many ways, become normal. Politicians were corruptible, some voters were disillusioned and there was really no single big issue other than, perhaps, the environment. But even this had been brought into mainstream politics by the emergence of the Greens and the adoption of sections of their agenda by the other parties. A majority of voters were concerned with ordinary, everyday political issues such as unemployment, inflation, wage rises, the standard of living, gender issues, the environment, the economy, education, etc. West Germany was a leading power in the moves towards European integration and had developed a very significant friendship with France. It was a strong supporter of the Atlantic alliance, it had a strong economy and a strong currency, and it was, despite the unsatisfactory level of unemployment in the mid-1980s, envied by most other nations in the Western world.

Nevertheless, West Germany was anything but a normal state, because it was still living with the legacy of the 1930s and 1940s. Neo-Nazism and West Germans' attempts to come to terms with the Nazi era were one issue that set West Germany apart from most other Western democracies. Its official yearning for unification with its German-speaking neighbour to the East was the other. These issues remained ever-present though rarely central in political discourse.

The Nazi Past and Contemporary Neo-Nazism

The West German State had made solid attempts to make reparation for Germany's Nazi past through payments to and support for Israel, and also to many of the victims of National Socialism. The left had always supported this agenda, though the right had been divided, as was shown when Adenauer first proposed payments to Israel. After the Six-Day War between Israel and its neighbours in 1967, however, sections of the left in Western Europe as a whole became critical of Israel. They no longer saw Israel as a David facing the Arab Goliath but regarded it rather as an aggressor state which should return to the Arabs the lands it had captured in 1967, something it refused to do until 1979, and then only some land was returned. Even a moderate such as Schmidt criticised the Israeli occupation of the West Bank and supported Palestinian self-determination (in April 1981), for which he was roundly condemned in Israel. This was the most serious criticism of Israel to have come from a leading West German politician, but it was entirely in keeping with most West European thinking at the time.

By contrast, sections of the right-wing German press had been delighted by Israel's military successes in 1967. Support for Israel became stronger in conservative circles after 1967, but this could not disguise the fact that in some sections of West German political life there was still a reluctance to fully accept Germany's responsibility for the murderous policies of the Third Reich. Some had skeletons in the cupboard: Hans Filbinger was forced to resign as Minister President of Baden-Württemberg in 1978 when it became known that he had sentenced German sailors to death in the very last days of World War II. Filbinger displayed no realisation of the seriousness of his actions. Investigations and trials against Germans who were suspected of participation in Nazi war crimes were ongoing: in 1980 it was disclosed that 86,498 people had been investigated since 1945 by the German authorities, of whom just 6446 had been sentenced, while investigations were continuing against another 2450. More than 77,000 had not been prosecuted.

Contemporary West German attitudes to the Nazi past remained contradictory and problematic. Reparations payments to Israel continued. Young Germans were taught in school about the Nazi period and the evils that their grandparents had perpetrated. In contrast to this, associations of expellees from various regions continued to proclaim that the territory lost in 1945 was rightfully theirs, as if there should be no consequences of the Nazi period for them. In 1985 the annual meeting of Silesian expellees was forced to change its slogan (from 'Forty Years of Displacement – Silesia Remains Ours' to 'Forty Years of Displacement – Silesia Remains Our Future – In a Europe of Free Peoples') before Kohl would agree to address them.

On a visit to Israel Kohl said that as someone who was fifteen when World War II ended he had the 'blessing of having been born late', i.e. too late to be directly responsible for Nazism. Young Germans, he argued, were prepared to accept Germany's responsibility for the crimes of Nazism but were not prepared to see themselves as collectively guilty of those crimes. He welcomed this development, though his comments were criticised by some as a veiled attempt to put the Nazi past behind Germany, something Kohl denied he was trying to do.

For all Kohl's frequent sensitivity on such issues, his actions were occasionally clumsy. In 1986 he likened Gorbachev's attempts at publicity to Goebbels's propaganda, a comparison which provoked outrage. In 1985, when Ronald Reagan visited West Germany on the occasion of the 40th anniversary of the end of World War II (the Germans had, unsurprisingly, not been invited to the main event in Normandy), Kohl and Reagan refused to cancel a visit to a military cemetery that also held Waffen-SS graves. Instead, somewhat insensitively, they hastily organised a visit to Belsen concentration camp as well, where Kohl, surprising his critics, spoke eloquently of Germany's crimes.

Other politicians on occasion also displayed a lack of understanding of Germany's past. In November 1988, on the occasion of the 50th anniversary of the *Kristallnacht*, which was a Nazi-organised pogrom against Jews in Germany, the President of the Bundestag, Philipp Jenninger, appeared to justify Nazi crimes, though he claimed that he was misunderstood. Nevertheless, he was forced to resign. By contrast, Richard von Weizsäcker's speech in 1985 as Federal President was a model of mature reflection on Germany's role in

World War II. In it he firmly blamed Germany's suffering not on events after 8 May 1945 (i.e. the end of the war) but on events after 30 January 1933 (i.e. Hitler's accession to power). Germany had to accept its past because 'those who shut their eyes to the past will be blind to the future' (quoted in Nicholls, 1997, p. 292).

The Historians' Debate of 1986–7 illustrated the problematic nature of attempts to characterise Germany's past. Jürgen Habermas, a philosopher of the Frankfurt School, launched the debate by attacking the ideas of historian Ernst Nolte. Nolte had attempted to explain the horrors of Nazism as in part a reaction to the threat of Bolshevism and claimed that much of what Hitler did had already been done by Stalin. Without ever justifying Hitler's atrocities, he called into question the uniqueness of the Holocaust by referring to the Turkish massacre of Armenians in the 1910s and Pol Pot's crimes in Cambodia in the 1970s, and also argued, somewhat ahistorically, that Jewish support for Britain against Hitler may help explain Hitler's measures against the Jews. Another argument was that those who sympathise with the victims of the Holocaust should extend that sympathy to cover those Germans expelled from their homelands after 1945. Habermas saw in Nolte not a crank, but a representative of a conservative school that was engaged in 'a semi-official conspiracy to whitewash German history' (Kettenacker, 1997, p. 169). Many historians became involved and often engaged more in personal attacks than in historical argument. Yet there remained a feeling that Nolte and those who supported him were trying to revise history in a way that would relativise and therefore somehow reduce Germany's guilt. For many conservatives it was 'time to move on'. For others the past would be a permanent reminder of Germany's capabilities.

For some of the more extreme elements in West German society the solution lay in neo-Nazism. Some younger people became involved in neo-Nazi 'sports groups', such as the paramilitary Hoffmann group, which was banned in 1980. Some resorted to terrorist attacks: in 1980 neo-Nazis killed seventeen people in three separate attacks, including two Vietnamese in an attack on a hostel in Hamburg, two Swiss border guards shot on duty, and thirteen people killed in a bomb attack which also injured 200 people, at the Munich Oktoberfest beer festival. Electoral success eluded the neo-Nazis until 1987.

In 1983 a new extreme right-wing party, the 'Republikaner', was founded in Munich by two disenchanted members of the CSU. However, it was another group, the German People's Union (DVU), which made the first electoral breakthrough, winning 3.4 per cent in Bremen but taking a seat because it passed the 5 per cent threshold in Bremerhaven. Then, in January 1989, the Republikaner won 7.5 per cent of the votes and 11 seats in the West Berlin parliament. In May of that year they took 7.1 per cent and 6 seats in the West German election to the European Parliament in Strasbourg. These groups dwelt on social issues but with a racist, national slant. They saw foreigners, refugees and asylum seekers as essentially to blame for West Germany's economic ills. Though they did not make a major breakthrough to equal the widespread success of the NPD in 1966–8, these achievements may be seen as the beginning of a period in which neo-Nazi groups were able to enjoy sporadic successes at regional level through the 1990s. Their major failing is a lack of co-ordination, since three different parties are in competition with each other: the Republikaner, the DVU and the NPD. Their themes are similar, and in the 1990s they found occasionally fertile ground in both eastern and western Germany. Their voters are a mixture of dedicated Nazis who reject the post-1945 consensus, protest voters, and people who see a radical solution to contemporary social problems.

Control of GDR Society

The GDR has often been called a totalitarian state. Certainly, one party, the SED, controlled political and economic life there. 'The Party is always right' was one of the guiding principles in the 1950s, and there were those who felt that this still applied in the 1980s. The SED was determined to create a society that, by its own definition, would be 'socialist in the colours of the GDR' (Allinson, 2002, p. 156). The leadership of the SED and thus of the state consisted, even in the 1980s, of an aged elite that had largely formed its political opinions during and immediately after Hitler's time. The expansion of the SED Central Committee in 1986 to bring in 'new blood' actually increased the average age of the membership from 57 to 60, while the newcomers to the Politburo raised its average age from 60 to 63 (Staritz, 1996, pp. 295–6). It was an old party with an old ideology.

Domination of the party, whose membership reached some 2 million in the 1980s (in a country with a total population of just 17 million), and of parliament was, however, not enough to control society. The GDR relied on a secret service apparatus that was one of the most extensive in the world. The Ministry for State Security, commonly known as the Stasi, had just 2700 employees in 1950. By 1989 this had grown to 91,000. In addition, hundreds of thousands of 'informal collaborators' (IM) worked for it at various stages. This has led to the idea that the GDR was a police state, though a clear definition of a 'police state' is rarely offered.

What the Stasi did effectively was not just compile information about individuals, but also keep a watchful eye and ear to the ground for signs of organised political dissent. It infiltrated movements that wished to challenge SED dominance, and it collaborated very efficiently with other organs of the state, such as the police, the border guards and the army, as well as, of course, the Soviets. Their military presence, as had been demonstrated in 1953, was a last line of defence if all else failed.

The SED also used a range of organisations other than itself to bring people into the system. The aim was to give all citizens a sense of belonging, in one way or another, to the new, socialist society that was being created. Political parties

162

and organisations such as the CDU (for Christians), the NDPD (for ex-Nazis and nationalists), the DBD (for small farmers) and the FDJ (for young people) encouraged a sense of civic responsibility and commitment to 'socialist' ideals. In addition, other organisations promoted active involvement in society and thus, by implication, in the achievement of some or all of the SED's goals. Among them were the Society for German–Soviet Friendship (6 million members in 1989), the German Gymnastics and Sport Association (3.6 million in 1986), the Consumers Co-operative Society (4.5 million in 1985) and the paramilitary Society for Sport and Technology (600,000 members in 1982) (Dennis, 2000, p. 202).

Yet none of this could have functioned without the collaboration, or at least acquiescence, of large sections of the population. Sometimes people went along with the system for reasons of personal gain. Anyone wishing to study medicine, for example, was required to do three years' military service instead of the regulation 18 months, and many young men chose to do this. Some people in any society are simply predisposed to snoop on their neighbours and friends, not to mention their enemies. Some collaborators were blackmailed into working for the Stasi, some were drawn to clandestine activity, some expected personal rewards, others gained a feeling of empowerment, while still others were genuinely committed to the communist ideals of the state. Some have claimed since unification that they infiltrated opposition groups out of a genuine wish to 'prevent the worst', though it seems likely that the Stasi manipulated them rather than the other way round (Dennis, 2000, pp. 219–20).

What is clear is that many people in the GDR were prepared to go along with the state, some in a more active fashion than others. Most took part in annual May Day demonstrations, though it should be said that participation was more or less compulsory. Apart from a brief period in 1953 there was no stage, until late 1989, at which the GDR could be described as a society in which opposed elements were at war with each other, and even in 1989 it was not a war but a peaceful revolution that occurred. Much as some would like it to be, the GDR 'cannot be simply written off as a repressive regime pitted against a heroically oppositional people' (Fulbrook, 1995, p. 61). Neither, however, can the GDR claim to have had the active support of all of its people. Its citizens responded to the repressive regime in a number of ways. One way was to create a private persona and circle that were quite distinct from one's public persona and function.

The Niche Society

Despite attempts by the SED to portray the state as a social unit with its various political and semi-political sub-units, there is ample evidence that the family remained the nuclear unit in the GDR. Many people simply retreated to this private sphere from their work and other public functions and found some release by speaking more openly and freely there than elsewhere. Individuals spent a higher proportion of free time with their families, which was partly a reflection of the lack of social facilities compared with the West. There is evidence that teenagers in the GDR trusted their parents as advisers more than in the West (Dennis, 2000, p. 151). Some of the time together was spent watching West German TV, itself a form of family escape, with the result that the SED complained that its citizens were living only part of their lives in the GDR. Of course, the GDR was in a unique position in this respect: it was the only communist country which shared its language with a capitalist one, and it was this that made it easy for *all* of its citizens to watch Western TV.

Günter Gaus, who was West Germany's Permanent Representative in the GDR from 1974 until 1981, described the GDR as a 'niche society' in his widely acclaimed book on the other German state (Gaus, 1983). He suggested that outward conformity was less than enthusiastic and was coupled with 'private authenticity', a private sphere in which individuals were more open and free with each other. One area in which GDR citizens were successful in defining the limits of their recreational activities despite initial SED opposition was on the beaches. Nude bathing was widespread, so much so that since unification the rather more prudish West Germans have even tried to reclaim some East German beaches for those who prefer bathing costumes. In the private sphere East Germans often resorted to humour, telling jokes about the leadership or about the police, who in standard GDR jokes were a singularly unintelligent breed. An example of often ironic GDR humour was heard when a number of Volkswagen Golfs and Volvos were imported and given the Berlin registration numbers IBN (Golf) and IBM (Volvo). The cars were expensive, and it was joked that the registration numbers stood for the German words for 'I am nouveau riche' and 'I am a millionaire'.

Contact with foreigners was for the most part discouraged. One aspect of the GDR economy was the so-called 'contract workers' from socialist states such as Cuba, Vietnam and Angola, who lived and worked there for a limited number of years before returning to their home country. Almost all of them lived in strictly segregated accommodation, and there was little or no interaction with Germans outside work. The authorities did not desire such contacts, which were difficult to control once initiated.

The private sphere was not entirely free of state interference. Ample evidence has come to light since 1990 of individuals breaking the privacy and confidentiality of the family unit by spying on members of their own family. In addition, as social attitudes changed in the 1970s and 1980s, the traditional family unit became less common: divorce rates soared, there were more single mothers and more people entered into 'trial marriages', which lasted on average just 2.5 years (Dennis, 2000, p. 152). Though some qualifications have been put on the description of the GDR as a niche society (see Fulbrook, 1995, pp. 129–50), it has remained an accepted description of social relations there. In essence, most people seemed resigned to the fact that they could not fundamentally change the political system, so they conformed, outwardly at least. The private sphere was their 'real' life.

Opposition in the GDR

That said, not everyone retreated into the private sphere. At various stages individuals and groups tried to change the political direction of the state from below. June 1953 was one such episode. The internal party struggles of the later 1950s were another. Yet such efforts were always doomed to fail. Change, if it were to come, could really only be effected from above, as when Ulbricht was removed at the request of other Politburo members, or when, in 1971, Honecker announced that there would be 'no taboos' in culture. Nevertheless, opposition formed in the GDR, and in the 1980s it was a constant presence, though it was small and very much on the edge of society. It took many forms, including internal party opposition, intellectual opposition and, most threateningly of all, the many church and peace groups which formed in the 1970s and 1980s.

Wolfgang Harich and others had been tried in the 1950s for their oppositional views as members of the SED. In the 1960s Robert Havemann, a professor at the Humboldt University in East Berlin, had expressed principled Marxist opposition to what he saw as the East German perversion of Marxism. In the 1970s the most prominent internal party critic was Rudolf Bahro. In his 1977 book *The Alternative*, published only in West Germany, he described the type of Soviet-influenced system that existed in the GDR as an 'asiatic development dictatorship' that was a hindrance to the further development of mankind. In the wake of the Biermann Affair, publishing in the West was dangerous. To publish such outspoken views was essentially to invite trouble.

Bahro was arrested in 1977 and sentenced to eight years' imprisonment in 1978 for 'spying' for a foreign power. Various international organisations attempted to intervene on his behalf and in 1979 he was released and went to West Germany, where he became active in the Greens. A reformist SED manifesto, published anonymously in *Der Spiegel* in 1978, had little effect. Its author, Hermann von Berg, was a professor of Marxism–Leninism in East Berlin. He was briefly held in custody before being allowed to resume his career. It was only in 1985, when he published a critical book in West Germany, that he lost his job and was allowed to leave for West Germany.

It is undoubtedly true that most GDR dissident intellectuals were Marxists of one sort or another. Their dissidence lay in the fact that they attempted to offer alternative Marxist views in a monolithic state. This was also true of some writers. The criticisms that came in the wake of the expulsion of Biermann had been aimed at reforming the state, not destroying it, but the SED reaction was hard-line. When in 1979 Stefan Heym allowed publication in the West of a new novel, *Collin*, he was denied permission to make a trip to the West and fined 9000 Marks for 'breaking currency regulations'. Other authors simply left the GDR for the West, some surrendering their citizenship, like Reiner Kunze, others with long-term visas, such as Jurek Becker, who moved from East to West Berlin, Günter Kunert, who went to West Germany, and Wolfgang Harich, who went to Austria. Some were expelled from the Writers' Union and/or the SED, while others were jailed. In that year the law was significantly tightened in respect of contacts with the West: passing even non-secret information to Western news agencies became an offence. Essentially, this was a catch-all law that could be used by the authorities as required, to persecute individuals on political grounds.

Censorship remained a problem for writers in the GDR. The various publishing houses all employed individuals who read books in search of 'unacceptable' passages. Sometimes such passages were simply edited out, as in the case of Christa Wolf's comments about nuclear war in her novel *Kassandra*, published in 1983. Jurek Becker's 1978 novel *Schlaflose Tage* (*Sleepless Days*) was simply not allowed to appear in the GDR. Indeed, the number of novels, plays and collections of short stories and poetry by GDR authors which were published only in the West increased dramatically after 1976. What could not be measured was the degree of self-censorship that authors exercised. Many admitted to censoring themselves, though some claimed that they did so in order that less critical passages or an overall message might see the light of day in the GDR. Thus writers like Volker Braun published novels and short stories that clearly satirised the SED without calling into question the basic social and political order. Still, censorship was a sore point, and in 1987 at the annual meeting of the Writers' Union the playwright, novelist and essayist Christoph Hein rounded on censorship as 'anti-human, anti-national, illegal and punishable' and called for its immediate removal. He ironically thanked the newspapers for being so boring and monotonous, claiming that this increased readership of fiction, which portrayed life more realistically than did the media. Sadly, censorship remained in place until 1989.

Most threatening of all to the established order in the GDR were the many protest groups which sprang up in the 1970s and 1980s, usually under the umbrella of the Protestant churches. The Church occupied a somewhat controversial position in the GDR. It had split from the united German church in the late 1960s under pressure from the SED leadership. Nevertheless, the SED, as a Marxist party, was still avowedly atheist and saw religion as an anachronism. Church membership declined continuously throughout the history of the GDR, so that by 1989 it was probably less than 50 per cent, down from 93 per cent in 1950. Largely this was because active membership of a church brought disadvantages, among them difficulty in gaining admittance to university courses other than theology. In August 1976 a

Protestant minister, Oskar Brüsewitz, protested against the 'oppression of the churches in schools' by burning himself to death in the main square in the small town of Zeitz. The SED's reaction was to publish critical articles about the minister in the days that followed, despite the international criticism of the GDR that followed Brüsewitz's death.

The main Protestant Church reached an accord with the SED in 1978, describing itself as a 'Church in socialism'. This was an uneasy peace, and various small, autonomous groups began to form under the church's informal protection. These groups represented an alternative political culture in which unofficial ideas on peace, nuclear weapons, ecological issues, human rights, gay rights and Third World issues were addressed. Of course, these groups had no access to official GDR media. As a result, they often used Church gatherings as a forum for discussion and expression of their ideas, because the Protestant Church was 'the only major public institution with a significant measure of control over its own affairs' (Dennis, 2000, p. 241). Most of these groups wished to reform the existing system, not overthrow it. The groups were certainly influenced by West German environmentalist and anti-nuclear groups, but there was little talk of German unity, a subject considered taboo by the SED. Among the most prominent groups were the 'Church from Below', an ecological group called 'Ark', and environmental libraries in Berlin, Leipzig and other places.

The Stasi infiltrated all of these groups, and some even disbanded themselves because they felt that they had been infiltrated. Stasi activity was thorough, but it could not always control the activities of the groups. One famous campaign which necessitated *public* action by the authorities was the 'swords to ploughshares' movement begun in 1980. This quote from the Bible was cleverly set beside a statue that the Soviet Union had presented to the United Nations in 1959. The initiators of the movement collected signatures for peace and were supported by sections of the main Protestant Church. They simply did not accept the standard

GDR line that socialist nuclear weapons were peaceful while capitalist ones were aggressive. The badge that they created was worn as an armband by increasing numbers of GDR citizens until, ultimately, it was banned. The SED could not tolerate such an open display of dissent. When the badge was banned for the Dresden Peace Forum in February 1982, even the Church stated publicly that it could no longer protect those who wore it.

These groups continued to organise throughout the 1980s and the state's reaction was sometimes heavy-handed. In November 1987 the Stasi broke into the Environmental Library in the Zion Church in East Berlin, confiscated a printing press and large amounts of material, and arrested 20 people. This provoked protests in a number of other towns and cities. Groups were adept at using Marxist symbols and quotations to support their cause. The Soviet statue was one such. Another was the use of Rosa Luxemburg's words 'Freedom is always the Freedom to think differently.' Luxemburg had been a founder member of the KPD, whose murder at the hands of right-wingers in 1919 was commemorated in Berlin every January. In 1988, 120 protesters were arrested for disrupting this commemoration.

The Church had some reservations about these groups. It was suspected that many activists were non-Christians who were simply using the Church for protection. Certainly, the emptiness of places like the Berlin Zion Church after 1990, when Germany was unified, contrasts sharply with the packed house that that church frequently enjoyed in GDR times, which retrospectively lends credence to the Church's suspicion. Though the Church shared many of the activists' aims, the methods used by some groups had the potential to damage the delicate relationship between it and the state.

The various groups created in the 1980s were in many ways peripheral to society. They rarely impinged on the lives of ordinary, apolitical GDR citizens, even if most people were aware of their existence. Nor did most of the groups play a significant role in the political events of 1989–1990, though some leading individuals did rise to prominence in 1989. The essential legacy of these groups is that they contributed to an atmosphere in the GDR in which challenging orthodoxy did not automatically bring down repressive measures on the heads of the challengers. In many ways this helped create the atmosphere in which the events of 1989 could happen. The SED was still in control of the GDR in the 1980s, but society was, gradually, becoming a little less monolithic and, unofficially at least, a little more pluralist.

Economic and Political Weaknesses

The GDR economy was, by Western standards, a curious one. For many, its greatest social achievement was that there was no unemployment, and the state took pride in this statistic. Others regarded this as economically disastrous, claiming that many of the jobs in GDR industry were artificially maintained even when they were no longer economically justified. These differing analyses are essentially a dispute between those who argue that organising the economy carries with it a degree of social responsibility and those who see economics primarily in business terms.

The economy faced a range of pressures. One was to maintain a level of production that could provide its citizens with material wealth, including consumer goods, that was comparable to that of West Germany. In this it failed, though it certainly maintained a standard of production and a degree of wealth that was the envy of most other communist states. It also continually tried to introduce new consumer goods, such as colour televisions, better refrigerators, etc. Cars were imported from the West on occasion (such as 22,000 VW Golfs and 1000 Volvos in 1977), partly because the waiting times for a new GDR car (up to 18 years) meant that second-hand cars, which could be purchased immediately, were more expensive than new ones. Other goods, such as wine, coffee and other items with Western brand names, were sold in new, more expensive shops that were created in 1978. In addition, some GDR citizens had access to Western goods via relatives, though fears were expressed that this could create a 'two-class' system – those with Western relatives against those without.

Officially there was no inflation in the GDR, either. One way around the policy of having no inflation was to allow goods to sell out and disappear for a while, then reintroduce them in different packaging and with a higher price, officially as a new product. The state also subsidised basic foodstuffs, travel and accommodation at levels that gradually became unsustainable. It was forced to pay more and more for raw materials, of which it had little of its own, but the cost was not being passed on to its citizens. In particular, the knock-on effect of the 1973 oil crisis, which hit the Comecon countries in 1975, and the sudden doubling of oil prices in 1979–80, which forced the Soviet Union, faced with massive debts of its own, to cut oil supplies to Comecon countries, had a serious effect on the GDR's balance of payments. It ran into debt with most of its trading partners. In addition, it was investing less of its total income in industry, which could help reduce debt, and more in social projects such as housing. (The three-millionth apartment built in the GDR since 1950 was constructed in 1988.) One possibly apocryphal story has it that Japanese visitors to a GDR computer factory, Robotron, thought it was actually a museum. Attempts to bring this deficit to the attention of the SED leadership and to change current practices in the late 1970s were fruitless (Dennis, 2000, pp. 161–4). In 1981, GDP actually decreased by 1.1 per cent, the worst performance in the GDR's history.

The GDR leadership had a secret reserve of hard, i.e. Western, currency built up since the mid-1960s by a special organisation within the Ministry for Foreign Trade called 'Commercial Co-ordination' or 'KoKo', led by Alexander Schalck-Golodkowski. Payments made by West Germany and by Western visitors, who had to convert DM into East German Marks at the artificial rate of 1:1 on each visit, also increased reserves. The amount to be converted on each visit varied, but by the 1980s it was DM25 per day. Nevertheless, by mid-1982 it was likely that the GDR would be unable to acquire new credits from Western banks. In one of the more surprising twists in post-1945 German politics it was none other than the arch-conservative and anti-communist Bavarian premier, Franz Josef Strauss, who arranged credits, guaranteed by the federal government, of DM1 billion and DM950 million in 1983 and 1984. (The move was extremely controversial in the CSU and was one of the causes of the breakaway that led to the creation of the Republikaner.)

The GDR did not use these credits to purchase. Rather they were left with banks as deposits, and repaid at the end of each year. By late 1984 the GDR was once again considered to be credit-worthy. On the other hand, production was still well below Western levels, and the economy was becoming continually weaker by comparison. In 1988 the GDR's GDP was just 9 per cent of West Germany's, compared with 18 per cent in 1950. More and more GDR Marks needed to be spent to earn just one DM: from 2.20 in 1980 to 4.40 by 1989. The leadership was either unwilling or unable to grasp the nettle and come to terms with the need for a radical restructuring of its pricing policies and the level of subsidy it maintained. The reason for this lay in ideology: the GDR leadership wished to create a society that was based on a degree of equality, and that meant making basic needs easily affordable. They saw the inequalities that existed in capitalism as inexcusable in systems that professed to be democratic. Unfortunately, the global economic conditions in which the SED attempted to achieve equality were dictated more and more by the inequalities of a capitalist world economy.

Conclusion: German States East and West

In the 1950s and 1960s both German states officially supported the concept of a single German nation. Their

173

populations also believed in this concept. Brandt's Ostpolitik had accepted the political realities of the division of Germany (and Europe) without ever surrendering the concept of a single German nation. Throughout the 1970s and 1980s, when official East Germany had redefined the GDR as a socialist nation separate from the West German nation, official West Germany continued to argue that, despite political division, a single German nation continued to exist.

The problem was that the behaviour and attitudes of the mass of the population in each state was at variance with the attitudes of the leaders. West German leaders paid lip service to unification, it was enshrined in the constitution and few politicians dared to challenge the concept. Yet the population had moved on. West Germany became, for most people, simply 'Germany'. People readily used the phrase *Deutschland und die DDR* (Germany and the GDR), clearly implying that the GDR was not Germany. In sporting competitions West German athletes could set a new 'German' record even when they came second to athletes from Leipzig, Dresden or Brandenburg in the East. In the 1974 Soccer World Cup 'Germany' became world champions, even though the GDR had played (and beaten) the 'German' team in an earlier round. Many West Germans took pride in the achievements of the Federal Republic, though some left-wingers derided them for this as 'DM nationalists' (Fulbrook, 1999, p. 186). Some saw the GDR as at times even more foreign than Austria, another German-speaking country.

Regionalism played a part in this. Germany had only been united for the first time in 1871, and many Germans' individual identity is based more on a pride in the dialect and customs of Bavaria, Westphalia, Swabia or Friesland than on a sense of Germanness. Post-Holocaust it was also difficult to take pride in Germanness, so a sense of regional identity or pride in post-1945 achievements was substituted for the type of patriotism that was more common in other countries. West Germans also threw themselves into the European project and became enthusiastic supporters of

European Union. In 1984 Chancellor Kohl spoke to the Bundestag of leading the way towards European Union with the objective of a 'United States of Europe' (Nicholls, 1997, p. 298). By contrast, in 1987 he said that while an awareness of the unity of the German nation was still alive, it was not on the current agenda of world politics. Unification became a kind of holy grail, something lost, to be sought for but with no realistic prospect of it ever being found. In contrast to the 35 per cent of West Germans who considered unification the most important political problem in the mid-1960s, never more than 1 per cent took this view from the mid-1970s on (Garton Ash, 1994, pp. 133–4). Others, such as the writer Günter Grass, spoke of Germany as a 'cultural nation' rather than a political one (Grass, 1990).

The GDR, by contrast, had officially created its own citizenship in the 1960s and no longer supported the concept of a single German nation. Rather unconvincing attempts were made to define the 'GDR nation' in economic terms, and a distinction was drawn between 'nationality', which was still considered to be German on linguistic and historical grounds, and 'nation', which was social, political and economic and was very definitely 'GDR'. Honecker had noted as early as 1974 that many GDR citizens were having difficulty with the distinction between nationality and citizenship and argued that it was simple: 'Nationality: German. Citizenship: GDR' (Staritz, 1996, p. 290). In an attempt to delegitimise West Germany's claim to the word 'Germany', the GDR used the abbreviation 'BRD' (Bundesrepublik Deutschland – Federal Republic of Germany) for West Germany, an abbreviation that was explicitly rejected in 1981 by the culture ministers of the West German states. (The ministers also insisted that atlases used in schools should continue to show a united Germany in its 1937 borders, i.e. including both the GDR and the eastern territories lost in 1945.)

West Germany's claim that there was a single German nation was explicitly rejected by the SED. In 1980 Honecker submitted a list of demands, including recognition of GDR citizenship by West Germany and the transformation of the diplomatic representations in Bonn and East Berlin into full embassies. Honecker's so-called 'Gera Demands' were simply ignored in the West. Yet there remained a degree of ambiguity in the GDR approach. The distinction between citizenship and nationality was never fully accepted by its citizens. In 1981 Honecker also blurred the lines by saying that the question of German unification would be open again in the rather unlikely event that West Germany became socialist.

East Germans were certainly ambiguous about their identity. Regionalism was a factor there, too, and there were significant differences between Saxons and Thuringians in the south, Brandenburgers in the middle and Mecklenburgers and Pomeranians in the north, in addition to which there was a Slav minority, the Sorbs in the south-east. The replacement of the states by districts in the early 1950s had diluted this only slightly. More important than this, however, was a continuing sense of belonging to something greater than the GDR. GDR citizens watched West German TV and had contact with Western relatives. They shared a language with West Germans, read some of the same literature and looked with envy on the economic success of what, to them, was 'the other part of Germany'. By the 1980s there was evidence that many younger East Germans were beginning to accept the concept of GDR identity, but they were doing so without really surrendering a sense of Germanness.

Ultimately, relations between the two German states in this period are shot through with contradictions. West Germany claimed to retain a sense of a united Germany while it pursued a West European integrationist stance that took little account of the GDR. Its citizens came to regard such archetypal German cities as Dresden and Weimar as essentially foreign. A new, Federal German identity was created that was Western in outlook and, at times, extremely Americanised. Unification was, for the majority, at best a distant dream, so much so that, in 1987, ideology was quietly put to one side as Honecker was received on a 'working visit' to Bonn with all the pomp and ceremony normally reserved for foreign dignitaries. Even the GDR flag flew side by side with the West German one.

The GDR officially abandoned German unity, and in January 1989 Honecker admitted just how unrealistic he considered the prospect of a socialist transformation of West Germany when he said that the Wall would still exist in 100 years, a statement that eerily echoed Hitler's claims of a 'thousand-year Reich'. East German society, for all its political, economic and military links with the East, was much less Sovietised than West Germany was Americanised. GDR citizens looked west, not to America, but to their West German cousins and neighbours, and they retained a sense of identity that was German, but not 'Federal German'.

In the late 1980s it seemed that Brandt's Ostpolitik, subsequently adopted and continued by the CDU, had helped reinforce the division of Germany. There were even those in the West who had begun to accept the proposition that there were two nations in Germany. It is probably fair to say that by 1989 there was a sense that German unification was simply not an issue. The only repositories of a sense of Germanness that transcended the Berlin Wall were the West German constitution and the hearts and minds of most East German citizens.

6

UNIFICATION, 1989–90

Introduction

Until the late summer of 1989 there was little indication, from any quarter, of the radical, historic changes that were about to take place in Germany. The new US ambassador in Bonn, Vernon Walters, had claimed in the spring of 1989 that he would see Germany reunited during his period in office, but no one took him seriously. West Germans were not prepared for change, and East Germans could not see how they could possibly change their system. The fiercely anti-communist newspaper *Bild*, on 1 August 1989, signalled the extent to which even conservative and nationalist West Germans had come to terms with the continuing division of Germany by ceasing its practice of putting the letters 'DDR' in inverted commas. Those inverted commas, a blunt denial of the legitimacy of the GDR, disappeared four years after the death of Axel Springer himself.

When change came inside the GDR it happened in the context of developments outside the country which provoked a range of responses from East Germans. Events in the Soviet Union and Hungary, in particular, created a new atmosphere in Eastern Europe, but it was the response of the citizens and leadership of the GDR that ultimately made political change possible. The most memorable date in all these events was the day on which the Berlin Wall was opened, 9 November 1989. Yet historians agree that the most significant event, which opened the way to the radical reforms that ultimately led to German unification, was one month earlier, on 9 October 1989 in Leipzig. The result of that evening's events was that East Germany experienced a peaceful revolution in which not a single life was lost in anger. Less than a year later the two German states were united to create a new Federal Republic, a single Germany in Europe for only the second time in its history.

International Context

In April 1985 the countries that adhered to the Warsaw Pact, first signed in 1955, agreed to extend the validity of the treaty for a further 20 years. It seemed as if the political division of Europe would remain. However, just one month previously the Communist Party of the Soviet Union had elected a new, younger leader who was aware of the need for a reduction in arms spending, more consumer goods and more open relations with the West. Brezhnev had died in 1982, but there followed two ageing leaders, Andropov, who died in 1984, and Chernenko, who died in 1985, before a new, younger element in the leadership was able to gain control.

Two words from the Russian language have become Gorbachev's legacy to the English and German languages: *glasnost*, meaning openness, and *perestroika*, meaning reform/restructuring. The Soviet Union that Gorbachev attempted to create was new, more open and more responsive to its people's needs. It wished to move towards an economy that would be a mixture of capitalist enterprise and state control. Above all, it also ceased to claim a right to dominate Eastern Europe: the Brezhnev Doctrine was formally abandoned in favour of what is sometimes called the 'Sinatra Doctrine' ('I did it my way'). Of course, all of this happened gradually, but happen it did, and this new approach was the ultimate creator of the preconditions for change in Eastern Europe, despite a degree of opposition from within the Soviet Union (Young, 1996, pp. 225–33).

Glasnost had barely been introduced when it was put to the test by the nuclear explosion at Chernobyl in the Ukraine in April 1986. This event, and the investigations that followed, led to widespread criticism not only of circumstances in the Ukraine, but also of the privileges that the party leadership enjoyed. Soviet citizens became more questioning of those aspects of Soviet history that the leadership had attempted to cover up. One of the most famous incidents was the massacre of 14,000 Poles at Katyn in World War II, which the Soviets had always blamed on the Nazis. A series of discoveries in 1988–9 made it plain that this massacre had been committed not by the Nazis but by Soviet forces in March 1940, when the territory was under Soviet control (Pearson, 1998, pp. 118–19).

Reactions in and outside the Soviet Union to such discoveries and to *glasnost* and *perestroika* were mixed. Some countries, such as Hungary and Poland, were determined to make maximum use of their new freedom to manoeuvre. Some of the Soviet republics, especially the Baltic states of Lithuania, Latvia and Estonia, reacted by emphasising their individuality and their right to a separate identity and political independence. By contrast, many hardline communists simply rejected the evidence provided by the new openness, with Romania and the GDR the states that seemed most inclined to oppose Gorbachev's new approach.

In 1989 'it was in Hungary that the fuse was finally ignited' (Kettenacker, 1997, p. 186). The Hungarian leadership decided that the new Soviet attitude meant that it was free to open Hungary's borders with the West (i.e. Austria) and lift travel restrictions not only on its own citizens but on other East Europeans, too. That was in September 1989. The reaction in the GDR to the changed atmosphere emanating from the Soviet Union was somewhat different.

Forebodings of Change

The SED's reaction was one of outright rejection of *glasnost*. In April 1987 in an interview with the West German magazine *Stern*, the SED Politburo member Kurt Hager responded to a question about *glasnost* by asking whether, if your neighbour was redecorating, that meant that you had to as well. When the interview was also published in *Neues Deutschland* it provoked protests from SED branches throughout the GDR against this comment and in defence of *glasnost*. The protests were met with repression and expulsions from the party. In November 1988, when the German-language edition of the Soviet youth magazine *Sputnik* attacked Stalin for making a pact with Hitler in 1940, it was banned in the GDR. It was unprecedented for the GDR to ban a Soviet publication, and the move caused widespread protest. The present writer, who was teaching English at Rostock University at the time, sensed his students' feelings and spoke out in defence of *Sputnik* for which he was called to book by the SED branch secretary at the university, despite not being a Communist Party member. The students themselves passed resolutions condemning the ban, for which they received visits from high-ranking party officials from Berlin, who ordered them back into line under pain of expulsion from the university. Similar responses were reported all over the GDR.

More and more people were applying to leave the GDR. Citizens did not have the legal right to leave the country, whether on holiday or permanently: the SED leadership denied that the Helsinki Agreement accorded citizens the right to freely move from one state to another; instead, it engaged in repressive measures, including arrests, demotion and sacking of individuals, pressurising relatives, and threatening to remove children from their parents' care in order to force a retraction of an application to emigrate from the GDR. All this met with extremely limited success.

The numbers of applicants kept rising, and 1988 was no exception. At the end of 1988, 114,000 people had a current application to leave, in addition to some 40,000 East Germans who had left legally or illegally in that year.

Though the SED 'allowed and even officially accompanied a massive peace demonstration in September 1987' (Thomaneck and Niven, 2001, p. 58), it felt distinctly uneasy at the prospect of change. Demonstrators at the annual commemorative march for Rosa Luxemburg in January 1988 and January 1989 were arrested, while schoolboys who protested against military service were expelled from school and faced with the prospect of never being able to study. In May 1989 the authorities engaged in massive falsification of local election results, which led to citizens' groups lodging official protests. The SED's claim of a 98.84 per cent 'Yes' vote for the single list of candidates on a 98.77 per cent turnout (a typical result from the previous 40 years) was hotly disputed. In the midst of these events, the SED had shown itself unable to resist a sideswipe at the Federal Republic. In spring 1989, as a controversy raged in West Germany over the right of foreigners living there to vote in local elections, the GDR gave this right to all non-citizens who had been resident for at least six months. The absurdity of this was illustrated when some exchange students from the USA and Great Britain were invited to vote after eight months of a nine-month stay.

Though the SED tried to resist change, the pressure on it was becoming too great. Events both inside and outside the GDR brought matters to a head in the summer of 1989.

The long, hot summer of 1989

The pace of events in 1989 was simply breathtaking. No one knew what change might happen next. It is impossible to convey a feel for these developments without listing some of the most important. The two words most used in describing this period are 'protest' and 'demonstrate'.

New travel laws for GDR citizens that were introduced in November 1988 took effect on 1 January 1989. These increased travel opportunities to the West, including the possibility of obtaining a standing visa. In addition, the GDR parliament had decided that the administration should be answerable to the law: decisions on visa applications could be appealed in the courts from 1 July 1989. By the end of September, 161,000 people had applied to emigrate under these new laws, only 32,000 fewer than in the entire 17-year period from 1972 to 1988. In March in Leipzig around 600 people demonstrated for the right to emigrate.

In Hungary on 2 May 1989 the authorities began dismantling the secure border with Austria. Though the Hungarian army still patrolled the area, GDR citizens almost immediately began attempting to flee to the West. Some escaped, but many were caught, returned to Budapest and had their passport stamped. Returning to the GDR with such a stamp would have meant certain arrest. As a result, some East Germans fled into the West German embassy in Budapest. Others did so in East Berlin, Prague and Warsaw, often without first attempting to flee to the West. On 7 August, *Neues Deutschland* carried its first coded report on these actions. On 8 August, West Germany's diplomatic office in East Berlin had to be shut with 130 refugees inside. The Budapest embassy was shut on 13 August, followed by the one in Prague on 22 August. All were full of East Germans seeking permission to leave for the West.

On 19 August, 661 GDR citizens used the 'Pan-European Picnic' organised at Sopron on the Austrian–Hungarian border to flee to the West. In the same month Austria abolished the visa requirement for GDR citizens and Hungary allowed hundreds more to leave, despite protests from the GDR government. The total number of East Germans who fled through Hungary in August was probably 3000. This was the first mass exodus of East Germans since 1961.

On 31 August, Hungary informed the GDR government that it intended to recognise GDR citizens as refugees. From 11 September it formally allowed all GDR citizens to leave across any border they wished. It had thus suspended its treaties with the GDR. GDR citizens in Czechoslovakia made their way to Hungary and from there to the West. Within three days, 15,000 East Germans arrived in the Federal Republic. Berlin SED leader Günter Schabowski reacted on 25 August by blaming 'West German imperialism' for these developments, others in the leadership accused Hungary of 'betrayal' and *Neues Deutschland* carried at least one story claiming that GDR citizens were being kidnapped and brought to the West.

What was clear to all was that thousands of GDR citizens were attempting to leave. East Germans still in the GDR became more and more impatient with developments, which they were able to follow every day on West German television. The SED seemed to be burying its head in the sand and continuing with plans for the GDR's 40th birthday celebrations on 7 October, as if nothing had changed. On 2 September, the Protestant Church put the blame for the mass exodus on the SED's failure to change. New opposition groups began to form, including New Forum, Democratic Awakening, Democracy Now, the United Left and the re-launched Social Democrats, known initially as the SDP of the GDR. New Forum applied on 19 September for recognition as a political group, but was rejected as anti-constitutional within 48 hours. In the same month sections of the East German CDU and LDPD began to demand that their parties reject the leadership of the SED and adopt a more critical position.

On 4 September the so-called 'Monday Demonstrations' in Leipzig began to take on greater significance. On that evening around 1200 people protested outside St Nicholas's Church for the right to emigrate. Police and Stasi broke up demonstrations on the following two Mondays. On 25 September at the demonstration by around 5000 people a different slogan was heard. Instead of the cry 'We want out', which had dominated until then, 'We're staying here' was the call. The protesters wanted to reform the GDR, not simply flee. To the SED this was far more threatening. In the next few days it attempted to deal with the refugees by agreeing to a mass exodus in trains, which, for supposedly face-saving reasons, would travel back through the GDR. The first trains left on 1 October. Within three days, however, the West German embassy in Prague was again full. The second convoy, on 4 October, was met by demonstrators in Dresden who wished to board the trains. They fought a running battle with riot police. Meanwhile, Honecker had written in *Neues Deutschland* on 2 October that he would 'shed no tears' for those who had left. That night the Leipzig demonstration grew to 25,000.

9 October 1989

On 7 October the GDR celebrated its 40th birthday with parades, pomp and ceremony. Most of the SED leaders took the salute at the main parade in Berlin, where they were joined by Gorbachev. The situation was almost surreal. While Honecker was hosting a reception in the Palace of the Republic in Berlin thousands of citizens all over the GDR protested peacefully. Gorbachev, as guest of honour, warned his SED hosts of the dangers facing socialist countries. Specifically, he commented that 'those who arrive too late are punished by life itself'. The population itself barely took the birthday seriously, referring to it instead in humorous tones. One contemporary joke referred to the fact that retired people had always had the right to travel freely: Question: 'What will happen in 2009?' Answer: 'The GDR will be 60 and can travel to the West.' In fact, the GDR 'travelled to the West' just before its 41st birthday.

Allowing thousands of people to leave for the West was seen by some in the SED leadership as opening the pressure cooker to let some steam out. Far more serious was the threat posed by those who continued to demonstrate in the GDR with their slogan 'We're staying here'. Just two days after the birthday celebrations crowds again gathered in Leipzig, but the atmosphere was tense and full of fore-boding. It became clear that the SED was preparing to put a violent end to the demonstrations. Defence Minister Heinz Kessler had mobilised extra army units, including paratroop-ers, while the Stasi chief Erich Mielke had ordered all Stasi members to carry arms. On the ground, some soldiers on duty attempted to telephone relatives and friends to advise them to stay at home, hospital staff numbers were reinforced and extra blood supplies were brought to Leipzig. A bloody scenario was entirely plausible, since the SED had praised the Chinese Communist leadership for its massacre of stu-dents at Tiananmen Square in Beijing in June 1989. That afternoon Leipzig radio broadcast an appeal from three members of the local SED leadership and three prominent demonstrators, calling for a peaceful demonstration. The crowd, numbering 70,000, began chanting 'We are the people'. For reasons that have not yet been completely ex-plained, the security forces, who were armed and waiting in side streets, did not intervene. Some suggest that Honecker decided there should be no shooting, since he did not want to be responsible for causing civil war. Or perhaps an order from Berlin to intervene was disobeyed locally. The fact that the Soviets, unlike in 1953, would not become involved prob-ably also played a role. The SED certainly possessed the means to violently crush the demonstration, but it chose not to do so. The ideological structures that sustained SED rule were disintegrating. It is to the credit of the peaceful demonstrators and the SED alike that there was no bloodbath in Leipzig that day.

The demonstration on 9 October 1989 was a victory for two things: peace and change. That it was a victory for peace was in no small measure due to the influence of the Protest-ant Church. The Monday demonstrations were based around a Leipzig church, St Nicholas's, just as many of the oppositional movements in the 1980s had been loosely based in churches such as the Gethsemane and Zion churches in Berlin. Church leaders were clear that they wanted peace, that there should be no attempt to violently overthrow the government. 'Give us peace' had been the prayer of those assembled in St Nicholas's Church before the mass demonstration, and peace was what they got. The influence of the Protestant (Lutheran) Church in maintaining the peace can hardly be over-estimated, even though few of the demonstrators were churchgoers. What happened in the months that followed has often been called the 'soft' or 'gentle' revolution. It has also been called a 'Protestant revolution'.

Yet 9 October was also a victory for change, for if the SED was not prepared to use force to stop the demonstrations, then it could not resist the demand for change, which grew stronger by the day. On 16 October the number of demonstrators in Leipzig rose to 120,000, on 23 October 200,000, on 30 October more than 250,000, and on 6 November 'hundreds of thousands' in the largest demonstration to date. By this stage hundreds of thousands of people had demonstrated in all of the major cities. The largest gathering was at Alexanderplatz in Berlin on 4 November 1989. More than half a million people assembled to protest for democracy in the GDR. Writers such as Stefan Heym, Christa Wolf and Christoph Hein were among the speakers.

The SED's reaction was to engage in cosmetic changes while attempting to retain a degree of control. Letters were published in newspapers that were critical of aspects of the SED's policies, and the SED attempted to engage in dialogue with various groups. Behind the scenes a coup was planned against Honecker. On 18 October he was removed as General Secretary of the SED and replaced by Egon Krenz. It is a somewhat sad testament to Honecker's Marxist discipline that when he realised a majority of the Politburo was against him he also voted for his own removal, so that the decision would be, as usual, unanimous.

Krenz was never likely to be more than a temporary solution. He was intensely disliked in many quarters, not least because he was the Politburo member who had visited Beijing to congratulate the Chinese leadership on its actions at Tiananmen Square. Changes in government would be needed, too. Six days later Krenz was elected Chairman of the State Council in the Volkskammer, but 52 deputies either voted against him or abstained. On 26 October the SED admitted that dialogue was necessary. At regional level it was already taking place. Regional party secretaries were also being replaced. On 8 November the Politburo was radically overhauled and reduced in size. But it was on 9 November 1989 that the citizens of the GDR began to celebrate, and people throughout the world celebrated with them.

9 November 1989

No one, either in the GDR or in West Germany, was prepared for events as they unfolded on the evening of 9 November 1989. Helmut Kohl was on a trip to Poland at the time. Demonstrations continued in regional centres while West German politicians, including Johannes Rau, Minister President of North Rhine-Westphalia, visited the GDR. That evening, at a press conference called at the end of the two-day meeting of the Politburo, Günter Schabowski announced new travel regulations which would allow all GDR citizens, with few exceptions, to apply for and receive a visa for travel to the West. The full import of his words was not entirely clear. When asked when the new regulations would come into force, Schabowski shuffled his papers looking for a date. He seemed uncertain as he said 'immediately'.

Within a few short hours thousands of people had gathered at the various border crossings demanding to be allowed to go across to West Berlin. Eventually, the border guards simply opened the checkpoints, and tens of thousands of East Germans streamed into West Berlin. There were scenes of jubilation as they were greeted by West Berliners. People danced and sang, climbed the Wall, and started hacking pieces off it with hammers, unchallenged by GDR border guards. On 10 November Kohl, Genscher and Willy Brandt, who had been ruling mayor of West Berlin when the Wall was built, rushed to the scene to join the celebrations. Within four days 4.3 million visas were issued to GDR citizens, while many thousands more crossed without a visa. The events of that week were watched on television across the world. Yet perhaps one of the most exhilarating scenes was the long queues of GDR citizens waiting to return home a few days later. It is estimated that only around 1 per cent stayed in the West.

The most concrete symbol of the division of Germany, the Berlin Wall, was gone. By the end of November, fifty new crossings had been opened, both in Berlin and along the East–West German border. On 22 December Kohl and the new GDR Prime Minister, Hans Modrow, symbolically reopened the Brandenburg Gate. The physical manifestation of the division of Germany had been removed. There remained, however, two German states and a range of views about the way forward.

Reactions in Germany

No one knew where this massive change would lead. Kohl telephoned Krenz on 11 November and agreed to meet him in the GDR in the near future. On 13 November Hans Modrow, the popular SED regional secretary from Dresden, became the GDR's new Prime Minister. An opinion poll showed that half of the population had great hopes, while half had fears resulting from the changes. Around 90 per cent wanted a changed electoral system, while a similar number said they would definitely be staying in the GDR. On 17 November, Modrow presented a new cabinet in which almost half of the ministers (12 out of 28) were not from the SED. On the same day the Ministry of State Security (Stasi) was dissolved and replaced by an Office of National Security. Monday demonstrations continued, with more than 200,000 in Leipzig on 13 November and several hundred thousand all over the GDR on 20 November. More than 3 million East Germans visited West Germany on 17–19 November, the second weekend after the opening of the Wall. Organisations in all sections of East German life, from students to architects, from sporting organisations to trade unions, called for radical changes to the way their business and politics in the GDR as a whole were conducted. It was a time of enthusiasm for political involvement and for change. On 22 November the SED suggested a 'Round Table', at which representatives from all walks of life could consult with the government. Films that had been banned for years in the GDR were now premiered. Banned books could now be published. Few people, if anyone, had a clear idea of where the changes might end.

Thoughts inevitably began to turn to the question of sovereignty and the possibility of unification with West Germany. Many in the GDR did not want unification. Modrow's government wanted a better form of socialism. Many of those who had been most involved in the earlier movements wanted a reformed GDR. Some spoke of a 'Third Way' between the Marxism of the SED and the capitalism of West Germany. Christa Wolf, Stefan Heym and others published an appeal on 26 November 'For Our Country', calling for the GDR to become a democratic socialist alternative to the Federal Republic, but few were listening. The tone of the demonstrations had begun to change. Instead of 'We are the people' many had begun to chant 'We are one people'. In fact, forty years of division meant that the East and West Germans had become somewhat different peoples. When East Germans claimed 'We are one people', which in

German can also mean 'We are a people', many West Germans replied facetiously 'Yes, so are we!' Nevertheless, the clamour for unity increased daily.

It was Helmut Kohl who first spelt out a clear determination to achieve German unity. Despite clearly expressed reservations on the part of some Western Allies, and a reluctance to move too quickly on the part of the SPD leader Oskar Lafontaine, on 28 November 1989 Kohl published a 'ten-point plan' for overcoming the division of Germany. He envisaged a confederation between the two states, with increased co-operation firmly rooted in wider European structures, including disarmament. Kohl was trying to reassure the Allies that a united Germany would not simply 'go it alone'. His tenth point made it clear that unification was his final aim. He also expressed gratitude for the support for German unity received from both Nato and the European Community earlier in 1989.

Reactions Abroad

Supporting the concept of German unification in spring 1989, when it was on no political agenda, was one thing. Actually coming out in favour after the Wall had come down was an entirely different matter. Many in the West had been quite happy to pay lip service to the concept of German unity as long as there was no realistic possibility of it actually being achieved. But many also remembered the two World Wars that had been fought by Germany in the twentieth century, and were afraid that a reunited country would again try to dominate the continent. Indeed, the first unification of Germany had been created at war (with France), and it seemed to some that a unified Germany was inherently dangerous. It was just such fears that led the French writer François Mauriac to comment in the early 1960s that 'I like Germany so much that I am glad there are two of them' (Balfour, 1992, p. 156). In addition, by the late 1980s the European Community had four large member states that were approximately equal in size, with between 50 million and 60 million inhabitants each (France, West Germany, Great Britain and Italy). United Germany, with almost 80 million inhabitants, would be far larger than any other state.

France was initially opposed to the concept, but French President François Mitterand could not publicly say so. Privately he confided to Genscher that he saw unification as inevitable, but he irritated West Germany by paying a state visit to the GDR on 20 December, the first ever by a leader of the Western Allies, thus giving the impression that he 'wished to invigorate a dying body' (Kettenacker, 1997, p. 200). Throughout 1990 France supported Poland's demands for recognition of the Oder–Neisse border. It also attempted to counter the possibility that Germany might focus more on the East by obtaining greater commitment to European unity from Bonn. In this he had some success, though Kohl's commitment to unity remained paramount.

The USA came out in support of German unification at a relatively early stage, and Bush reminded other Allies of their long-standing support for unification (Pond, 1993, pp. 161–9). Though voices were raised against unification in sections of the US media (see James and Stone, 1992, pp. 165–217), the administration of George C. Bush saw unification as inevitable and was primarily concerned that the united country should be a member of Nato. Its position, which was also Bonn's, was that united Germany's choice of alliances was its own business as a sovereign country. Throughout 1990 the US government remained committed to the goal of Nato membership, which was achieved with only minor concessions to the Soviets.

The British government under Margaret Thatcher was hostile to unity from the outset, as were sections of the British media. The Irish politician and journalist, Conor Cruise O'Brien, a former editor of the liberal London *Observer*, even raised the spectre in October 1989 in the London

Times of a united Germany being a 'Fourth Reich' (James and Stone, 1992, pp. 221–3). At a meeting in Paris on 18 November, Thatcher argued that the Helsinki Final Act must apply, thereby ruling out any border changes. For her, reunification was not an option, though it soon became apparent that she was in no position to dictate the agenda. She advised Gorbachev that a rush to unity would threaten his position and thus European security. She has since written, about her position on the question of unification: 'the wishes and interests of Germany's neighbours and other powers must be fully taken into account' (Thatcher, 1995, p. 792). Nevertheless, when it became obvious that unification was unavoidable, she acquiesced. At a famous meeting in spring 1990 with expert advisers on Germany it was decided that 'we should be nice to the Germans' (James and Stone, 1992, p. 239).

The Soviet reaction was one of concern for its security. Of course, changes in Eastern Europe had made changes in the GDR possible. But the prospect of unification was entirely different, even if for most it was an obvious consequence of liberalisation. The Soviet leadership, and especially the Soviet military, could not countenance the advancement of Nato's borders up to the Oder–Neisse Line. The memory of World War II was much too vivid for most Russians to accept the possibility of a united Germany as a member of a military alliance that was hostile to the Soviet Union. Negotiations would be necessary before the Soviets would agree to a unified Germany in Nato. Indeed, in the autumn of 1989 it was not at all clear that Gorbachev could agree to this.

In Poland there was concern about the power of a united Germany, especially one which continued to claim the territories east of the Oder–Neisse Line. Though the Bundestag passed a resolution on 8 November 1989 assuring Poland that its right to live in secure borders would be threatened neither now nor in the future by territorial claims from Germany, the official position was that Germany in its 1937 borders continued to legally exist. Conservative politicians continued to claim that the border question was unresolved: CSU Chair Theo Waigel had done just that at the annual meeting of Silesian expellees in Hanover in July 1989, and was explicitly supported by his party for doing so. It was clear that the Oder–Neisse question would have to be addressed.

The other important reaction was the Israeli one. Israeli Prime Minister Yitzhak Shamir, an ultra-conservative politician, claimed on several occasions that a united Germany posed a 'deadly threat' to Jews, a claim that provoked protest from Chancellor Kohl in December 1989. The reactions in Israel were largely negative, with unification being described as a 'world disaster' by one commentator, while one politician described having to swallow German unification as equivalent to being forced to eat pork (James and Stone, 1992, pp. 287–306). The memory of the Holocaust was too strong, though some voices of reconciliation, such as the mayor of Jerusalem, Teddy Kollek, spoke in favour of unification.

Leaderships aside, a majority of the population in most countries was in favour of unification, with support ranging from 78 per cent in Italy to 68 per cent in France, 61 per cent in Great Britain and 51 per cent in Russia. Only in Poland (64 per cent) and Denmark (51 per cent) was there a majority against. Despite the sharp criticisms in Israel, most Israelis were indifferent.

As we shall see, most issues surrounding the status of a united Germany were resolved in 1990. In late 1989, the East Germans themselves were preoccupied with changing their own society.

The Path to Democracy

As it became obvious that the very existence of the GDR was threatened, the SED began to reorganise. Its members were leaving in their thousands. The entire Politburo had resigned on 3 December 1989. At a special conference on 8 December, Krenz was replaced as party leader by the young, charismatic Berlin lawyer, Gregor Gysi. One week later the party renamed itself the SED – Party of Democratic Social- ism (SED–PDS). The party organised a demonstration of 250,000 people on 3 January 1990 against the rise of Nazism in the GDR since the fall of the Wall. 'Stalinists' were ex- cluded from party membership, as were all former members of the Politburo. But there were also demonstrations against the SED–PDS. The first Monday demonstrations in 1990 were directed against the SED, and on 22 January there were anti-SED protests in several cities, with more than 100,000 people taking part in Leipzig. Calls for the party to dissolve were debated but rejected. Instead, the name 'SED' was dropped on 4 February 1990, and the party became simply the PDS. Though it handed much of its property to the state, it retained much more.

The powers of the Round Table, which continued to meet, strengthened in the winter of 1989–90, and it effect- ively came to have a veto over government decisions. Stasi headquarters in Lichtenberg in Berlin were stormed that month, and it now seems clear that secret services from both East and West used the occasion to steal documents. Government plans to establish a new secret police to replace the Stasi were shelved in response to Round Table pressure. A new cabinet was formed in East Berlin on 11 January, but the CDU left it within two weeks. Newspapers became much more critical, no longer simply repeating the government line. At the end of January free, multi-party elections planned for 6 May 1990 (this had been agreed by the Round Table in December) were brought forward to 18 March. On 5 February a government of national unity was created under Hans Modrow as Prime Minister.

During this period the former Block Parties realigned and reinvented themselves. The CDU elected a new chairman, Lothar de Maizière, and allied itself to Kohl's CDU in the West. The Farmers' party (DBD) joined them in the new

CDU. The National Democrats and Liberal Democrats formed an 'Alliance of Free Democrats' for the election, aligned to the West German FDP. A new party, the SDP of the GDR, changed its name to SPD in January 1990 and fought the election as a sister party to the West German SPD. The Bavarian CSU founded a sister party, the German Social Union (DSU). Some of the parties formed in the autumn, such as Democracy Now and New Forum, formed an electoral group called Alliance 90. And, of course, the SED had become the PDS.

Going into the election the SPD were favourites. Yet Kohl had come to be seen in many eyes as the Chancellor who would guarantee speedy unification. His ten-point plan for gradual unification had been overtaken by events almost within weeks. The masses were clamouring for unity sooner rather than later. Though Willy Brandt was extremely popular in the GDR, SPD leader Lafontaine's note of caution was unwelcome there. Also, Kohl was seen to have greater contemporary relevance than Brandt. Kohl had been greeted by wildly enthusiastic crowds on his first visit to the GDR when he met Modrow in Dresden on 19 December 1989. He had also promised comprehensive economic aid for the GDR at a meeting with Modrow in Switzerland on 3 February. Now, in March 1990, a vote for the GDR–CDU was seen as a proxy vote for Kohl and unification.

The CDU joined the DSU and Democratic Awakening in forming a pact, the 'Alliance for Germany', for the election. Just 0.25 per cent of the vote was needed to win one of the 400 seats. In the end, the CDU-led Alliance won a comfortable victory, taking 48 per cent of the vote and 192 seats. The SPD managed just 22 per cent and 88 seats, the PDS 16 per cent and 66 seats, the Free Democrats 5 per cent and 21 seats. The party that represented the true spirit of the previous autumn, Alliance 90, took just 3 per cent of the vote and 12 seats. Politics had moved on rapidly. Only 13 of the 400 candidates elected had been members of the old, communist-dominated parliament.

The result was a resounding victory for Kohl's policy of rapid unification. De Maizière became Prime Minister of a grand coalition of CDU, DSU, DA, Free Democrats and SPD. It was the first and last freely elected government in the history of the GDR. It's biggest challenge was to co-operate with the Bonn government to create the conditions in which unification could happen.

Economic Union

The national euphoria that was created in 1989–90 was coupled with a large degree of social fear (Jarausch, 1995, p. 171). The GDR had been in dire financial straits. A report by five leading GDR economists in October 1989 had shown that productivity in the GDR was 40 per cent lower than in West Germany. Imports had increased at a far greater rate than exports. Foreign debts of around US$26.5 billion meant that the country was threatened with insolvency in 1990. Industry had become antiquated, and the economy was no longer able to bear the high cost of the subsidies of basic foodstuffs, travel and housing. The experts proposed increased co-operation with the Federal Republic as a way out of the crisis.

Ordinary East Germans were concerned that their goods were simply not of the same high standard as most West German goods. They were also not in a position to buy many West German products because their own currency was almost worthless in the international money markets. One GDR Mark was worth anything between one-quarter and one-tenth of a DM. That was one reason for a continued exodus of East Germans from the GDR after 9 November 1989. By the end of 1989 more than 300,000 people had left for the West in that year alone. In the first six months of 1990 another 250,000 left for the West, equivalent to 4000 people a week. The population of the GDR was demanding economic union, and many of them voted for it with their feet. Some East Germans argued that if the DM would not come to them, then they would have to go to the DM. West German fears of massive unemployment being created by large-scale immigration from the GDR were raised.

In such circumstances there was little option but to aim for economic and currency union between the two states, and on 7 February 1990 the Bonn government declared its readiness to engage in discussions with a view to achieving just that. On 23 April, agreement was reached on the terms of an 'economic, currency and social union' with the GDR. Subsidies would be removed and industry would have to conform to Western standards. A trust, the *Treuhand,* was to be created to administer GDR companies in the hope that they would be bought and made profitable, but with the task of winding them down where this was not possible. Throughout this period it became clear that GDR industry was able to offer little competition to the West, and hundreds of companies closed, creating mass unemployment. GDR industry was ill prepared for this move, and it paid heavily in the early 1990s for the change.

For most of the population there were two issues: the introduction of the DM and the rate at which GDR Marks would be exchanged. The introduction of the DM was quickly agreed, but there was some dispute between the Bundesbank and Kohl over the exchange rate. The bankers, especially Bundesbank president Karl Otto Pöhl, argued for an exchange rate of 2:1. If more GDR Marks were needed to buy 1DM, then East German goods would be more competitive because of lower production costs, and lower East German spending power would reduce debts. On the other hand, exchanging at a rate of 1:1 would give East Germans more money to spend, more ability to buy Western goods, and would also make their salaries more valuable, since these were already barely half the West German level. The choice was between favouring production and favouring consumption.

On 23 April the West German cabinet approved a compromise. Salaries were converted at a rate of 1:1, as were savings up to DM4000. Savings over this amount and debts would be converted at a rate of 2:1, while pensions would be set at 70 per cent of average salary. Some modifications to this were made, favouring pensioners in particular, but the essentials remained. In addition, the Soviets intervened in the debate on economic and social union to ensure that all decisions about land ownership made during the occupation period of 1945–9 should be respected: many West Germans were already looking at property lost in the previous 45 years with a view to recovering it.

The local government elections of 6 May in the GDR turned into a vote on economic union. The CDU, SPD and PDS all lost some votes, but the CDU remained the strongest party overall, though the PDS dominated East Berlin and the SPD won in Leipzig. On 18 May 1990, the State Treaty on economic, currency and social union was signed in Bonn. It was ratified in both parliaments in June and took effect on 1 July 1990. With it the GDR surrendered its economic sovereignty. This was the decisive internal step on the road to German unity.

Obstacles to Unification

When the USA took the lead in supporting German unification the question was largely when, rather than if, the country would be unified, at least from a Western perspective. Nevertheless, there remained a powerful obstacle to be overcome. Soviet reservations remained and were supported by the SED–PDS leadership in the GDR. Largely these related to the question of neutrality versus Nato membership for the united Germany, and to Germany's territorial claims. By 1 February 1990 the SED–PDS Prime Minister, Hans Modrow, who had just returned from a visit to Moscow, was putting forward a plan for a united Germany that would be militarily neutral.

The turning point was 10 February 1990. On that day Kohl and Genscher met Gorbachev in Moscow and persuaded him to respect any decision by the Germans to unite. Gorbachev agreed with his guests that the German Question would be resolved in the context of developing East–West relations and would be part of an overall European settlement. Both sides thus got what they wanted. The Germans got a commitment of Soviet support for unification, while Gorbachev got a commitment that wider concerns would also be addressed.

Three days later in Ottawa, at a joint meeting of Nato and Warsaw Pact foreign ministers, the so-called 'two plus four' talks were agreed. The four victorious Allies of World War II, who still had certain rights in Germany and especially Berlin, would negotiate with both German states over sovereignty and the international dimensions of the unification process. Though smaller countries such as Poland were excluded, the Soviets made it plain that they would demand guarantees in respect of the Oder–Neisse Line. The West Germans were delighted with the formula, since it meant that the future of Germany would not be decided over their heads (Jarausch, 1995, p. 173).

Bush and Kohl made it plain that they were determined to see a united Germany in Nato. The Soviets, for their part, were persuaded to make concessions on this point by West German offers of financial aid. All sides were clear that these negotiations were equivalent to negotiations on the peace treaty that had never been signed after 1945. Negotiations continued over a period of seven months, with meetings in Bonn in May, Berlin in June and Paris in July. Poland participated in the Paris meeting. Finally, on 12 September 1990, a treaty was signed in Moscow.

The agreement recognised the territory and borders of united Germany as those of the two postwar German states plus all of Berlin. The Oder–Neisse Line would be confirmed as the legal border between Germany and Poland, while Germany renounced all territorial claims against any states. Germany agreed to live in peace and maintain military personnel numbering no more than 370,000 men. German troops would be stationed on the territory of the ex-GDR after unification, but they would not be integrated into Nato command structures until the departure of the Soviet troops, who would be withdrawn from Germany by 31 August 1994. Nuclear weapons would never be stationed on the territory of the ex-GDR. United Germany would have the right to enter any alliances it pleased. Allied rights in Germany that had existed since 1945 would cease on unification, so that Germany would from that day regain full sovereignty. The treaty was ratified by the united German parliament on 5 October 1990 and by the Allies in the months that followed. What had seemed utterly unrealistic in spring 1990, a united Germany in Nato with Soviet approval, was now reality. Economic conditions in the Soviet Union had left Gorbachev with little choice but to accept German credits and subsidies in return for this concession.

The path to German unity was now clear from an international perspective, but the Germans themselves argued about the form that unification should take. There were two options. One was that the GDR and the Federal Republic should both cease to exist, to be replaced by a new, united Germany that would draw on the traditions of both German states. This was the option favoured by many who felt that, for all its failings, the GDR and its people had a number of positive things to contribute to the new Germany. The second option was to use Article 23 of the Basic Law, by which states could simply 'accede' to the Federal Republic. This was the mode of accession that had been used by the Saarland in 1957. Critics of this option felt that rather than a true unification it would create an extended Federal Republic in which East Germans might feel that their experiences and hopes were devalued.

The arguments raged, but West Germany was in every respect the stronger of the two states. Most West Germans felt that the Bonn Republic had given them a degree of stability unknown in German history and they were reluctant to destroy that system. Constitutional lawyers were attracted by the simplicity of this latter solution, while many East Germans were attracted by it because it promised more rapid unification than perhaps lengthy negotiations over the creation of a new republic. In blunt terms, the West Germans liked what they'd already got and the East Germans wanted to join them almost at any price. De Maizière's government made it clear that it would press for accession under Article 23, which would necessitate re-creating the five states that had been abolished in 1952. This was proposed on 2 July; on 23 August the Volkskammer finally approved accession on those terms. The states would be re-created on the date of accession.

A Treaty of Unification was needed, and negotiations on this began on 6 July 1990. The Federal Republic was extended to include the territory of the old GDR and the whole of Berlin, which would now be united as a single state within the Federal Republic. A number of compromises on individual laws were reached, such as on abortion law, whereby East German law would be allowed to diverge from West German law only until 31 December 1992. Otherwise, the GDR disappeared from the map of Europe, its territory and people becoming part of an extended Federal Republic. The Treaty of Unification received the necessary two-thirds majority in the Bundestag and Volkskammer on 20 September 1990. The date for unification, set after much debate, was 3 October 1990.

Unification

On 3 October 1990 there were celebrations throughout Germany and amongst friends of Germany all over the world. At one minute past midnight the five reconstituted states formally joined the Federal Republic, and Berlin was also reunited as a single city. In the preceding weeks and months the two economies had been united, a single currency was used in the whole of Germany and the political parties in East and West had largely united to form all-German parties. It was, for many, the happiest year of their lives. At the beginning of 1989 the thought that Germany would soon be united was regarded by almost all observers as absurd. By the end of 1990 it had happened. The GDR was consigned to history that day. Helmut Kohl, whose single-mindedness had steered Germany towards this event, was fêted as the 'Chancellor of Unity'.

On 14 October he received his first reward, when four of the five new states returned CDU-led governments. In Saxony the CDU even won an outright majority. Only in Brandenburg did the SPD emerge as the largest party. However, the big test would be the federal election on 2 December, the first free, all-German election since 1932. Kohl was confident, and in the end his confidence was justified. Though the CDU achieved its worst result since 1949, 43.8 per cent, Kohl was the clear winner together with his coalition partners, the FDP, who scored 11 per cent, their best result since 1961. The SPD lost votes, taking 33.5 per cent, its worst result since the 1950s. The Greens managed just 5.2 per cent, while the PDS achieved 11 per cent in the East, which was just 2.4 per cent nationally. A court case had resulted in a judgement that the 5 per cent clause should be applied separately in the East and West, despite CDU attempts to impose a unified 5 per cent clause, with the result that the PDS won seats despite its low vote. On the same day the CDU emerged from the state election in reunited Berlin as the largest party there.

Together, the coalition parties had won 55 per cent of the vote in both East and West. Kohl was the undisputed leader of the new, united Germany. He had skilfully taken control of events in both parts of Germany over the preceding 13 months and shaped a united Germany that was an enlarged Federal Republic. The new Federal Republic was the achievement of something barely considered possible just 18 months previously. It was, for millions of Germans, the fulfilment of a dream. In the euphoria of the occasion it was easy to lose sight of the problems that accompanied the new state's birth.

7

UNITED GERMANY, 1990–2003

Introduction

United Germany was part of a new Europe that emerged in the early 1990s in the aftermath of the Cold War. The west was dominant, but the break-up of the east was often bloody. States had to adapt and Germany perhaps more than most had to find a new role in the new order. For long, West Germany had been economically strong but politically weak, afraid because of its Nazi legacy to adopt an active political role in international affairs. Its emergence as a strong political force in Europe was one of the major issues of the decade.

Germany has had to come to terms with the communist past of its eastern part, and this has caused deep resentment among many east Germans, while being seen as necessary by many others. Germany has also had to come to terms with a resurgent nationalism that has at times expressed itself in attacks on foreigners. United Germany has brought out a new sense of the nation and of nationalism in many Germans – one which with time has become less inhibited by the legacy of Nazism and the Holocaust. While neo-Nazi groups have had very limited regional and no national success in electoral terms, those who wish to 'move on' from the legacy of the 1940s have become more vocal. This remains a complex and controversial issue.

The country also faced a range of internal problems that needed to be addressed. Political unification did not unite the people of east and west overnight. This has proved a long and arduous task that is still far from complete. Indeed, politically the two halves of Germany have diverged somewhat since 1990, despite living in a single political entity. Economically and socially there remain divisions, though there is little doubt that in the long term these will be overcome. The economic cost has been enormous, far greater than anyone foresaw in 1990, and the greatest burden has been borne by the western states of the unified country. By contrast, for many in the west, daily life has barely changed. In social terms it is ordinary east Germans who have had to adapt to a new life.

The election of 2002 showed that even after twelve years of living in the same state Germans remain divided in their political loyalties. There are, effectively, two different but overlapping political systems in Germany, with a four-party system in the western states and a three-party system in the eastern ones and a hybrid of the two in Berlin. Only two parties, the CDU and SPD, are truly national. In social and party political terms the two halves of Germany are integrating very slowly indeed.

Politics and Political Parties

The Bundestag election of December 1990 was merely the end of the beginning. Kohl's CDU and its FDP allies had won a resounding victory nationally. The SPD and Greens were also strongly represented throughout Germany, having won seats in all or almost all state parliaments, though the Greens had suffered a national setback and now had only eastern representatives in the Bundestag. The ex-communists of the PDS had scored 11.1 per cent in the east and were represented in Bonn on a low national score only by virtue of the application of separate 5 per cent clauses in east and west (see Appendix 3). They were represented in all the east German state parliaments and Berlin (see Appendix 5a) but to most it seemed that, though they might survive a little longer as a regional party, they were ultimately destined to disappear. Unification was seen to have been achieved by the policies of the western parties, especially the CDU and FDP, and Kohl was seen by most as the 'Chancellor of Unity'.

Yet within a few short years this situation began to change. Eastern voters proved volatile, and there were none of the certainties that pertained to old West German politics, where winning power at national or state level usually meant retaining power for at least a decade, or in some cases, thirty years or more. East Germans wanted rapid improvements and they quickly became disillusioned with the slow pace of progress towards economic prosperity. West Germans also became resentful of the financial sacrifices they were expected to make for the sake of unity. In January 1991 the SPD regained control of Hesse, a state it had lost to the CDU in 1987 after 40 years in power. In April 1991, the CDU lost control of the state of Rhineland-Palatinate, a state it had governed since 1947. As a result the CDU-led government in Bonn lost its majority in the Bundesrat, just four months after its resounding victory in the Bundestag elections.

The population appeared to become bored with politics and distrustful of the perceived ability of politicians to feather their own nests. In 1992, Federal President Richard von Weizsäcker criticised politicians for having only one special talent: the ability to criticise others. Political parties receive funding from the government in Germany based on the number of votes they receive, but on occasion the level of support has been so high (DM5 per vote in 1984) that it has been declared unconstitutional. Politicians also receive high salaries and a range of non-taxable allowances and benefits for secretarial support, as well as free travel on the rail network. The extent of general disillusionment was such that a new word entered the German language at this time, *Politikverdrossenheit*, meaning 'disenchantment with politics'. In the newly democratised east, membership of political parties declined continuously (Parkes, 1997, pp. 54–8).

By 1994 Kohl was no longer an east German hero. We shall see that economic failures were the main reason for this, but east Germans also resented the way in which their past behaviour was being judged critically by westerners. Many also resented the fact that almost everything eastern, even down to the aesthetically more pleasing east German traffic lights, was being discarded in favour of western equivalents. Indeed, a campaign to save the east German traffic lights was launched, itself a testament to just how little the east Germans were able to save. In the middle of this take-over the PDS was reborn as the only party which represented specifically east German as opposed to all-German interests.

The 1994 election saw the CDU/CSU and FDP coalition retain power by the tiniest of margins, just 0.3 per cent of the vote over the combined opposition parties, though as a result of so-called 'overhanging seats' its majority increased from two to ten seats (see Appendix 1). For the first time in the history of the Federal Republic the combined centre–right vote was less than 50 per cent, while in eastern Germany the Kohl government won just 42 per cent of the vote, down almost 13 per cent on 1990 (see Appendix 3). The election was won in the west. When the Bundestag met, Kohl was re-elected as Chancellor with just one vote more than the minimum required.

The PDS almost doubled its national vote, while in the east it took almost 20 per cent and won four constituencies in east Berlin, thereby circumventing the 5 per cent barrier, which once again applied to the country as a whole. It entered the new parliament with 30 seats. Its success was partly due to its socialism and its representation of eastern interests, but it was also a response from east Germans to the so-called 'red socks' campaign launched by the CDU, which claimed that the SPD and PDS were both just variations on the same communist theme. The election saw the FDP wiped out in the east and the CDU drop 3 per cent, while the SPD and PDS each made significant gains.

By the mid-1990s the economic situation in the east was showing few signs of improvement, while unemployment was still high. The western parties had been demonising the PDS since unification, despite the fact that at local government level they had been co-operating since 1990. In state elections held throughout the east in 1994 the PDS increased its vote, while in all states but one the FDP and Greens were wiped out. The exception was Saxony-Anhalt, where an SPD–Green minority government was formed with tacit support from the PDS. The CDU consolidated its grip on Saxony under the westerner Kurt Biedenkopf, who was known to have less than friendly relations with Kohl, but it lost votes everywhere else. By 1995 the new SPD leader, Oskar Lafontaine, had decided that co-operation with the PDS might be possible after all.

With no economic improvement shown in the mid-1990s, the 1998 election brought about decisive change. For the first time in the history of the Federal Republic there was a complete change of government at an election rather than simply a reshuffling of coalition partners. The CDU/CSU slumped to 35.2 per cent, its worst result ever apart from 1949, while in the east it won just 27.3 per cent. The FDP and Greens both suffered minor losses, while the SPD and PDS again improved. The SPD was able to form a coalition with the Greens, which enjoyed a secure 21-seat majority. Gerhard Schröder was the new Chancellor, while a young radical environmentalist protester of the 1970s who had been the first Green minister at state level in the 1980s, Joschka Fischer, became Vice-Chancellor and Foreign Minister.

The ensuing four years saw a range of policy innovations, including attempts to eliminate nuclear power from Germany by setting a limit on the life span of existing plants and preventing the building of new ones. The SPD–Green coalition also brought in new laws on citizenship, and promoted environmental protection, legal reform, and the integration of foreigners. In 2001 a law was introduced creating what is in effect homosexual marriage ('Recorded

Life Partnerships'), and a constitutional appeal against this was rejected in the summer of 2002. However, economic difficulties remained the biggest problem, especially unemployment, and the government had little success in dealing with these. Unemployment remained high at over 4 million (9.7 per cent) in July 2002.

Those years also saw a range of revelations come to light about illegal financial payments dating back to the 1970s, some of them connected to the Flick scandal. The scandal began in Hesse but hit the CDU at national level too. Helmut Kohl found himself facing allegations of accepting illegal payments totalling over DM2 million, and the CDU was facing the most serious political crisis of its history. In 1999 Kohl admitted receiving the money and using it in secret accounts, but he refused to name the donors. A legal investigation into embezzlement by Kohl was stopped in June 2001 on payment by him of a fine of DM300,000. He resigned as Honorary Chairman of the CDU after being asked to step down temporarily by the party. Kohl also went to the Supreme Administrative Court to prevent Stasi files from being used in the case. It seems that the Stasi had known for years about illegal financial dealings by West German politicians. In July 2001 he won his case, and Federal Interior Minister Otto Schily (SPD) called for files on other prominent politicians to be similarly kept secret. Yet by the summer of 2002 the CDU had fully recovered from the scandal. The election, for the first time ever, of a woman as party chairperson to succeed Kohl, the east German Angela Merkel, had helped in this process. Despite this, her perceived weakness in the party as the financial scandals began to subside led to the CSU chairman and Minister President of Bavaria, Edmund Stoiber, being nominated as the CDU/CSU candidate for Chancellor in 2002.

The Bundestag election of 22 September 2002 saw the SPD–Green coalition retain power by the slenderest of margins, largely thanks to an improved performance by the Greens. Throughout the year, high unemployment and a worsening economic performance had made it seem likely that the CDU/CSU and FDP, led by Stoiber, would take power, but in the summer two main events contrived to rally support for the government. One was the massive flooding, that hit eastern Germany in particular. In times of catastrophe it pays to be in power: Schröder was able to divert government money for immediate practical relief, while Stoiber could only offer moral support. The second issue was the ongoing Iraq crisis. As US President George W. Bush made it clear that the 'war on terrorism' would now become a war against Saddam Hussein's regime in Iraq, Schröder and Fischer apparently spoke for a majority of Germans in opposing the idea of war, especially if, as threatened, the US went to war without a UN mandate. Stoiber and the CDU/CSU were at a loss to react and tried instead to present such a scenario as merely 'hypothetical'.

In the end, the SPD–Green coalition took 306 seats in the reduced 603-seat parliament, a majority of just nine. The SPD and CDU/CSU finished equal on 38.5 per cent of the vote, but the Greens maintained a 1.2 per cent lead over the FDP. Yet the vote once again showed a significant disparity between east and west. Whereas the CDU-led opposition had a 1 per cent lead over the SPD–Green coalition in the western states, the government easily defeated the liberal–conservative opposition in the east (44.4 to 34.7). The PDS dropped below the 5 per cent hurdle and thus won just two constituency seats in east Berlin: in reducing the size of the Bundestag the Berlin seats had been drawn specifically to reduce the PDS's grip on the east by amalgamating large areas of it with west Berlin districts where the party was much weaker. Yet the PDS remained a significant factor in the east, with 16.9 per cent of the vote there. Germany was set for a period of precarious government.

That government became even more precarious when, in February 2003, the SPD was resoundingly defeated in state elections in Hesse and Schröder's home state of Lower Saxony. The CDU won outright in Hesse, dispensing with its FDP coalition partner of the previous four years, while in Lower Saxony it joined with the FDP to take power from the SPD and Greens. As a result, in cases of dispute between the two houses of parliament in Berlin, the SPD–Green government no longer had a sufficient majority to over-rule CDU/CSU objections.

Foreign Policy and European Integration

After 1990 Germany began to assume a political role that was more in keeping with its economic strength. It was no longer an 'economic giant and political dwarf' (Parkes, 1997, p. 117). Germany's sense of being a large nation with a central role to play not just in the European Community but in Europe as a whole was reawakened. In addition, its Atlanticist policy deepened through its close relationship with the US and its more active role in Nato, it lost no time attempting to become a major European and world player.

In the early and mid-1990s Germany concluded a range of treaties with its eastern neighbours, including Poland and the Soviet Union in 1990 and 1991. In 1991 it also re-established diplomatic relations with the Baltic states of Lithuania, Latvia and Estonia, which had emerged from the ruins of the Soviet Union. When war began in Iraq in 1991, Germany gave political support to the US-led offensive, though there were large-scale demonstrations against the war in Germany and the left was distinctly uneasy. One anti-war slogan suggested that no blood should be shed for oil, a reference to the claim that the war was about protecting oil fields in Kuwait rather than any democratic ideals (Kuwait was, and is, not a democracy). It seemed only a matter of time before Germany's involvement would have to become more than just political.

The opportunity came in the first Balkan conflict in 1992. Some have argued that Germany helped provoke that conflict by leading the European Community into being among the first to recognise the breakaway Yugoslav republics of Slovenia and Croatia. In 1992, against opposition from the SPD, the Greens and the PDS, the coalition government sent a destroyer to the Adriatic to help patrol the economic sanctions against what was left of Yugoslavia. In 1993, German peacekeepers went to Bosnia and Somalia under UN auspices. In 1994, UN General Secretary Boutros Boutros Ghali asked Germany for soldiers to engage in standing UN peacekeeping duties, while US President Clinton supported an increased foreign policy role for Germany. In 1995, German soldiers were deployed outside Nato for the first time since 1945 when they were sent to Bosnia and Croatia to protect Nato missions there. In 1996, a large majority in the Bundestag supported German military participation in the SFOR mission to help restore normality to Bosnia, while in 1999 Germany also agreed to send soldiers to Kosovo as part of the KFOR mission there. In March of that year, in an action which highlighted just how sensitive German military activity could be given Germany's recent past, four German jets took part in the bombing of Yugoslavia that was designed to end the conflict in Kosovo. In 2001, Germany renewed its support for military deployment in Kosovo and also supported peacekeeping activity in Macedonia. The SPD's opposition to such activity in the early 1990s had modified as events in former Yugoslavia unfolded and reports of mass murders committed there became known, so that when an SPD-led government took power in 1998 there was no fundamental change in this policy. By the summer of 2002, German soldiers were also engaged in military activity in Afghanistan.

Germany developed its role in international affairs by concluding more treaties and trade agreements with other powers and by becoming more vocal. It attempted, without success, to obtain a permanent seat on the UN Security Council. The 1989 massacre at Tiananmen Square was quietly forgotten when Germany concluded trade agreements with China in 1993, though Chinese Premier Li Peng put an early end to his 1994 visit to Bonn when demonstrators confronted him. In June 1996 there was something of a falling out with China when the Dalai Lama was welcomed to Bonn and China's continued occupation of Tibet was criticised in a Bundestag resolution, but Foreign Minister Kinkel and President Herzog visited China later that year to smooth things over. A 1996 treaty with the Czech Republic in which the Czechs expressed regret for the expulsion of the country's German-speaking population after 1945 was approved in both parliaments in 1997, despite opposition from expellee groups. In February 2000, the German government criticised in unusually forthright terms the participation in government in Austria of the far-right Freedom Party, showing once again that it was prepared to flex its new-found political muscle.

Relations with the US were generally cordial, and Germans were united in their sympathy for the US after the terrorist attacks on 9 September 2001. However, this did not translate into uncritical support for US reactions to those events, and there remained a degree of scepticism, in Germany as in most of Europe on a popular level, towards plans to invade Iraq. Similarly, Germany was with the rest of Europe in its exasperation at US refusal to sign the Kyoto Agreement on the environment, and Chancellor Gerhard Schröder publicly disagreed with President George W. Bush on this subject at a meeting in Washington in March 2001. On the Israeli–Palestinian conflict Germany is somewhat less critical of Israel's continued occupation of the Palestinian Territories than other European countries such as France.

Europe has remained a constant priority for German governments of all hues since 1949 and this has not changed since unification. As Chancellor, Helmut Kohl was a consistent supporter of the process of European integration. Germany participated in the Schengen Agreement of 1990, in force from 1992, which created a common travel area with France and the Benelux countries. At the end of 1991 he enthusiastically supported the Maastricht Agreement by which the European Community became the European Union. Similarly, Kohl's government followed its predecessors' support for the various currency agreements by supporting the establishment of the Exchange Rate Mechanism (ERM) in 1991 and the creation of the Euro in 1999, which became the daily currency in twelve states in 2002. Though the German population as a whole was divided on the loss of the DM, which most West Germans associated with their relative economic prosperity since 1945, Kohl enthusiastically championed the new single European currency (H. J. Michelmann, in Zimmer, 1997, pp. 26–7), despite fears that Germany would be unable to meet the convergence criteria. In the end, these criteria were somewhat elastic. Once again there was no change of policy under the SPD–Green coalition after 1998.

Germany had complaints similar to Britain's over the financing of the EU. In 1993 it contributed 29.8 per cent of the EU budget while receiving only 11.3 per cent of EU expenditure. Yet this has not provoked anything like the degree of euroscepticism that exists in British politics. Germany has also supported the cause of EU expansion into eastern Europe, though in 1997 it rejected Turkish membership while human rights violations persisted there, especially those directed at the Kurdish minority. Turkey reacted to this snub by referring to EU expansion as *Lebensraum*, a word used by the Nazis for their policy of forcibly removing native populations in conquered territories to make room for Germans.

Though this was a brutal charge, it contained a core of truth in the fear that the EU is dominated by Germany and that German industry and capital are moving into eastern Europe to fill the void left by the departure of the Soviets. This charge is dismissed by Germany and most of its western neighbours (Parkes, 1997, pp. 123–4). Certainly the vast bulk of Germany's trade is with western and not eastern Europe. Yet there is little doubt that Germany is an economic giant in Europe. Unification left it significantly larger than three countries, Britain, France and Italy, that had populations approximately equal to that of old West Germany.

Whatever Germany's intentions in eastern Europe may be, it is clear that it has adopted a new and much more pro-active role in world politics since 1990. It is no longer content simply to be an economic success (though the word 'success' has not been entirely appropriate since the early 1990s). The lobbying for a permanent German seat on the UN Security Council which Kohl's government carried out in the early 1990s (albeit without success) was a testament to Germany's new active role. Germany has 'moved from the submissiveness of 1949–87 to active and vigorous participation' in Nato, the EU and the UN (W. Thomas, in James, 1998, p. 211). Though Germany's behaviour towards its neighbours has been consistently peaceful since 1949, the early 1940s are still within living memory for many people in Europe. Germany has remained for many a 'mistrusted giant' (Geiss, 1997, p. 120).

On no issue was this more ably demonstrated than on the question of war with Iraq, which dominated world politics in 2002–3. Germany, France and a number of other countries were fundamentally opposed to George W. Bush's plan to go to war, if necessary without a UN mandate. The verbal exchanges between members of the US administration on the one hand, especially Donald Rumsfeld and Colin Powell, and French and German leaders on the other, are quite without parallel in the history of US–European relations when one considers that these countries are supposed to be allies. The massive demonstrations that took place across the world in February 2003, and opinion polls in almost every country in Europe, suggested that the population there was solidly anti-war and that European governments that supported the US stance were out of touch with their people. Yet Bush was determined to effect 'regime change' in Iraq and used US economic muscle to 'persuade' weaker states. European critics of this attitude wanted to give weapons inspectors more time and suspected that Bush's real agenda was not democratisation of Iraq but gaining access to its oil resources.

Industry and Finance – West

The cost of German unification spiralled, and reached sums that no one imagined or could have foreseen in 1990. Though the east Germans have borne most of the social burden of unification, the west Germans have been its pay-masters. Financial sacrifices have been made continuously since 1990 to help rebuild the eastern states, and more than a decade later there still seemed to be no end in sight.

In 1990 Kohl had insisted that no additional taxes would be needed to pay for unification, yet within nine months of unification a so-called 'solidarity supplement' of 7.5 per cent was put on income tax, initially for one year. On 1 January 1995 it was reintroduced and was still in place in 2002, though at the reduced level of 5.5 per cent. Cutbacks in other areas became necessary, with the result that in 1992 Germany stopped financing the development of its own fighter plane, the Jäger 90, in favour of the Eurofighter in collaboration with Britain, Italy and Spain. In 1993 the car manufacturer Volkswagen was compelled to introduce a four-day working week. The German economy experienced negative growth in that year (−1.2 per cent) for the first time in ten years and only the fourth time since 1950. Annual growth has not risen above 3 per cent since then, though it has usually been much lower. By 1994 the scale of the economic recession was such that 4 million people were unemployed. This represented 10 per cent of the working population, and this figure had even increased by early 2003. However, unemployment in 1994 stood at only 7.9 per cent in the western states, compared to 16 per cent in the eastern states (C. Flockton, in Larres, 2001, p. 79).

The economic failures of the early 1990s undoubtedly contributed to the decline in the popularity of Kohl's government in the west, though in 1994 it still obtained 3.4 per cent more there than the combined opposition in the Bundestag. By the mid-1990s there was growing optimism in some quarters that the worst of the recession might be over, but this proved not to be the case (C. Flockton, in Larres, 2001, p. 63). The car manufacturer Daimler-Benz made record losses in 1995 and within three years it had merged with the US automobile giant Chrysler. State money was misused in 1996 to save jobs at the Vulkan Shipyard in Bremen (Baumann, 2001, p. 1013). Benefits for the long-term unemployed were reduced in that same year, while a government savings package which reduced health benefits, raised the retirement age and reduced employee rights proved extremely unpopular. Some of it was vetoed in the Bundesrat. In 1997 an attempted reform of the tax system away from income tax and towards VAT was decisively rejected by the SPD and the Bundesrat and had to be abandoned. By contrast, the government was able to reduce the level of pensions using a law that did not require approval from the Bundesrat. It also agreed with the Bundesbank a revaluation upwards of the country's gold reserves, a step dismissed by many as 'creative accounting'.

Few of these measures proved popular, and there was still no prospect of an end to the need for financial transfers to the east. By the same token, economic support for the east was not improving the situation at a rate that satisfied east Germans. By the time of the 1998 Bundestag election the coalition government had been able to satisfy no one in Germany that it was getting on top of the economic recession. As a result, its vote slumped to 41.4 per cent (44 per cent in the west but just 30.6 per cent in the east).

The new SPD-led government after 1998 had little success in mastering the economic situation. It introduced its own savings package in 1999 and also revised the tax system to benefit lower earners while simultaneously introducing an 'eco-tax' on environmental pollutants such as petrol, gas and heating oil. A reform of the tax system, with a significant lowering of the levels of income tax, was approved in the summer of 2000 with the support of the Bundesrat after concessions to states in which the CDU governed. In 2001, child benefits and support for students were also increased.

Yet none of this seemed to make much of an impression on the unemployment figures or the rate of economic growth. Economic growth in 2001 was just 0.6 per cent, having hit a post-unification high of 3 per cent in 2000. In 2001, unemployment stood at 9.4 per cent, or just under 4 million. It had decreased slightly under the SPD and Greens, but the decrease was entirely in the west. Unemployment there had dropped from 8.8 per cent in 1999 to 7.4 per cent in 2001. In the east in the same period it had gone from 17.6 per cent to 17.5 per cent. By the summer of 2002, unemployment was increasing again. Unemployment in the western states was comparable to the EU average. In the east it was $2\frac{1}{2}$ times that average. There was widespread discontent at the government's performance on this front.

There were some notable economic successes in recent years, such as the Volkswagen take-over of Rolls Royce (though the brand name was subsequently sold to BMW), and the Internet server *t-online*, which became the second largest in the world after AOL when it went onto the market in 2000. Nevertheless, the overall economic outlook improved little, and after the election of September 2002 it got worse. Unemployment again rose and taxes had to be increased. Though daily life may have changed little since 1990 for the vast majority of west Germans who do not live close to the east, there is a large degree of resentment at the economic sacrifices that have been made. The new Germany is seen by many to have taken away the economic stability and the certainties of the old Federal Republic and replaced them with ongoing recession. 'D-Mark nationalism' was the pejorative name given to the old attitude, but it was a comfortable, fairly certain existence that is now gone. When, in January 2002, the D-Mark was replaced by the Euro, this merely confirmed the sense of lost security.

Industry and Finance – East

If many people in the west have lost a sense of security, many in the east have had to face a loss of identity. Most of this loss was in political and cultural terms, but east Germans also had to confront a very real sense of material uncertainty. Even as they appeared to become wealthier with the introduction of the DM many were losing their jobs. Many of these, especially women, never returned to work. After the security of full employment in the GDR this was a shock: 16 per cent official unemployment in 1993–4 did not include the fact that many more were in part-time jobs or on shorter working hours. Of social significance was that the number of east German women in work dropped from 90 per cent to 73 per cent by 1993, and to 70 per cent by 2000 (Parkes, 1997, p. 95; and Harenberg, 2002, p. 51).

East German industry was simply uncompetitive by western standards. Its goods were of a lower quality, and productivity was significantly lower than in the west. In addition, the currency conversion rate of 1990, which had proved popular with voters, had lumbered industry with debts it found almost impossible to pay. Since most industry had belonged to the state there were two options available from 1990 onwards. One was for the German state to assume control of this industry and attempt to make it profitable, the other was privatisation. Privatisation was the option chosen in the last days of the GDR, when the *Treuhand* ('Trust') institution was created.

The *Treuhand* began privatising with alacrity. Within two months, in August 1990, it had sold a 60 per cent share in east German electricity to three west German companies. By June 1991 it had sold 2583 firms into private ownership

(Baumann, 2001, p. 950). East German car manufacture ceased in 1991, with one of the plants taken over by Volkswagen. Other companies, such as the publisher Reclam and the camera and optics company Carl Zeiss Jena, were taken over by western companies of the same name that had been founded after 1945 when the parent company in the east was under Soviet control. By the time the *Treuhand* finished its job at the end of 1994 it had privatised around 15,000 companies and shut down 3600. The new investors had officially brought more than DM200 billion in investment and secured 1.5 million jobs. The *Treuhand* had made an operating loss of over DM250 billion.

The *Treuhand's* activity was controversial. There were widespread accusations that western companies, which frequently bought east German companies for a symbolic DM1 while promising to revitalise them, in fact stripped many of them of their best assets and personnel and then simply closed them down or gave them a minimal role in the new company. It was felt that the *Treuhand* condoned this practice (Geiss, 1997, pp. 109–10). This was seen as particularly true in the few cases where an eastern company's goods could potentially compete with western ones.

East Germans also had to cope with lower wages, higher rents and higher costs in general for most products. In 1991 there were widespread strikes in the east, caused by dissatisfaction at the economic misery. In Leipzig in March, some 800,000 attended the largest Monday demonstration since unification. However, eighteen months after the original Monday demonstrations their actions now changed little. In 1991, rents in the east were reduced, but civil servants, including teachers, were paid only 60 per cent of the salaries their western counterparts received. By 1993 this had risen to 80 per cent. By 2002 the figure varied from state to state, with east Berliners receiving the same as their western counterparts, while Brandenburg teachers were paid 86 per cent of western salaries. In Mecklenburg, teachers had lost their status as civil servants.

By 1997 the west had subsidised the reconstruction of the east in the amount of more than DM1 trillion (1 thousand billion). The subsidies continued after that. In 1997 the western states and the federal government agreed to pay off the debts inherited from GDR times by the local government districts in the east. Another form of subsidy was the financial redistribution scheme known as the 'States' Finance Equalisation', which was in place long before unification and which helps ensure that the financial gap between richer and poorer federal states does not become too great. In 2001 five states, all of them western, were net contributors, while eleven states, including all five eastern states and Berlin, were net beneficiaries. The five eastern states received a total of DM7.3 billion in 2001, while Berlin received DM5.5 billion, much of it going to the east of the city.

Despite these subsidies, the economic situation in the east remained dire. Economic and social weakness contributed to a degree of political volatility in the east, epitomised by state elections in Saxony-Anhalt, the eastern state with the highest rate of unemployment. In 1990 it returned a CDU–FDP coalition. In 1994, an SPD–Green minority coalition was formed, tolerated by the PDS, while the FDP fell below 5 per cent. In 1998, the neo-Nazi DVU won almost 13 per cent, but a minority Social Democratic government was formed, again tolerated by the PDS, after the Greens dropped below 5 per cent. In 2002, the neo-Nazis lost out, while the FDP returned to form a coalition with the Christian Democrats, putting the SPD and PDS into opposition. This is the most extreme example of rapid political change in the east. In most of the other eastern states, voters since 1994 have been more likely to switch freely between the three large parties, the CDU, SPD and PDS, though the DVU won 5.3 per cent in Brandenburg in 1999. The PDS and other protest votes are probably a reflection of the fact that east Germans are less likely than their western counterparts to express faith in the political system of the Federal

Republic. In 1997, only 31 per cent of east Germans regarded this system as the best, compared with 80 per cent of west Germans (Thumfahrt, 2002, p. 815).

It would be fair to say that most east Germans are economically better off now than they were in the GDR. True, there is a lesser sense of social security than before, but most have benefited from unification. Even those who are unemployed are generally in possession of more material goods than they were in the GDR. Nevertheless, there is a sense among east Germans that they have been taken over by a big brother who brought liberty and a degree of wealth, but whose help does nothing for their self-confidence (Geiss, 1997, p. 111). East Germans were like children, in 1990, who did not understand the extent to which Kohl's demand for a 1:1 exchange rate was a populist move aimed at winning votes, rather than sound financial management. Both they and the west Germans have been paying for that folly ever since. In 1990, east Germans had expected a new economic miracle to match the West German one of the 1950s. Instead, 'they got the joys and miseries of transformation' (D. Haselbach, in Zimmer, 1997, p. 179).

Social Integration of the East

Integrating the two parts of Germany also meant confronting those areas of society where laws and institutions differed. The reconstituted east German states acceded to the Federal Republic in October 1990, and this meant that there was no longer a need for some separate institutions. Thus the GDR's soccer team played its last international on 12 September 1990, beating Belgium 2–0. In 1991 the Protestant Churches were reunited under the EKD umbrella after just over twenty years of division. Soviet troops left the east by 1994, while German troops were stationed there from 1990 on. In addition, after forty years of paying lip service to Berlin as the true capital of Germany, a vote in parliament in

1991 only just favoured Berlin over Bonn (338 to 320), though the government did not move there until 1999. This step was essential if east Germans were to feel part of the newly united country.

Other issues proved more difficult to resolve, in particular the long battle for a unified abortion law. Since the early 1970s, GDR women had been used to abortion on demand in the first twelve weeks of pregnancy. By contrast, in the West it had been available since 1975 only in certain circumstances, such as physical or mental health problems in the mother or child, in cases of rape, or where the mother's social and economic status was difficult. The Unification Treaty had given the government until the end of 1992 to produce a unified law. A new law passed by the government in 1992, allowing for abortion after twelve weeks on condition that the pregnant woman seek medical advice (which she could choose to reject), was thrown out by the Federal Constitutional Court (BVG) in 1993. It was not until 1995 that the Court accepted a compromise law, which allowed women to have an abortion on grounds based on a mixture of social and medical indicators within a fixed time scale and requiring medical consultation. An attempt by the Free State of Bavaria to introduce its own, tighter law on the subject was annulled by the BVG in 1997. The Catholic Church responded to the new law when the Pope issued an instruction to bishops and priests not to provide the required advice service, since this advice could be rejected.

In the course of forty years living under communist rule, most East Germans had given up religion. A majority had never been baptised, though most of the GDR had been Protestant in 1950. In Brandenburg the state parliament introduced a school subject in 1996 called LER (Shaping Life – Ethics – Religious Knowledge) in place of religious instruction along confessional lines, which exists in most other states. At present only around 25 per cent of Brandenburgers belong to any religion, so that separate religious instruction seemed to make no sense. LER was a specifically eastern, post-GDR response to the requirement to adapt to the western education system, which included religious instruction, and it stands in stark contrast to the attempt in Bavaria to make a crucifix mandatory in all classrooms, a move declared unconstitutional in 1995. A constitutional appeal against the teaching of LER was rejected in July 2002.

Two further aspects of integration have been the attempt to fuse the states of Berlin and Brandenburg, and the reorganisation of local government within Berlin. All of the political parties except the PDS favoured the unification of Brandenburg with Berlin, which it completely surrounds. Historically they have always had close ties, with Berlin only being separated administratively in 1881, while 'Greater Berlin' in its present boundaries was created as late as 1920. However, many easterners were not ready to accept unification with a city that they saw as dominated by west Berliners. Though both parliaments approved the move, by the required majorities, the referenda on unification in May 1996 saw 63 per cent of Brandenburgers reject the move, while 53 per cent of Berliners (mostly west Berliners) were in favour. Co-operation between the two states continues, and politicians have still not given up hopes for fusion in the long term.

In Berlin there were until the end of 2000, 23 local government districts, 12 in the west and 11 in the east. This was considered by many to be excessive, and a proposal to reduce this number to 12, with effect from January 2001, was approved by the Berlin city government in 1998. However, many suspected that the real reason behind this reform was western objections to the dominance of the PDS in the central district of Mitte, which became the location of most government ministries in 1999. It is noticeable that Mitte has been amalgamated with two western districts, thereby significantly reducing the influence of the PDS. Apart from neighbouring Friedrichshain, it was the only eastern district to suffer this fate.

Integration has not always been easy, and the western-dominated authorities have been wary of both the PDS and what they perceive to be east German, post-GDR particularism. Nowhere has western determination to eliminate the influence and legacy of the GDR been more obvious than in the handling of Stasi files and the treatment of those considered to have worked for the Stasi or to have been overly sympathetic to the GDR system and government.

The GDR Past

The Unification Treaty of 1990 provided for the dismissal of those with Stasi links or who had been engaged in human rights abuses so as to make them unsuitable for public service (McAdams, 2001, p. 2). Simply put, the west Germans and many east German civil rights activists considered that there should be no role in teaching, the civil service or any aspect of public life in a democratic society for those who had helped maintain the 'totalitarian' system of the GDR. They considered that a process similar to denazification would be needed. Since east Germans had lived under various 'totalitarian' systems continuously since 1933, west Germans would have to take the lead in introducing democracy.

This attitude was in certain respects simplistic. For all its failings, the GDR cannot simply be lumped together with Nazi Germany as 'totalitarian'. First, the GDR never produced anything even close to Auschwitz. Secondly, if, as one commentator has put it, the GDR had far more spies than Nazi Germany, it was because the fear of retribution was much less: GDR citizens were not executed for telling jokes about Honecker as Germans were for jokes about Hitler. Finally, though it is hypothetical, there can be little doubt that the SS and Gestapo would have arrested and/or shot the Monday demonstrators in Leipzig. They certainly would not have negotiated with them. The GDR's 'totalitarianism', if such it was, was benign compared with Nazism.

Nevertheless, crimes were committed in the name of the GDR state that could not be defended. Among these were the shooting dead of persons who attempted to flee across the border. It is estimated that 239 were shot dead at the Berlin Wall alone (Sikorski and Laabs, 1998, p. 116). Political opponents were often imprisoned. Election results were falsified. Also, what are considered in the West to be basic civil rights and freedoms, such as the right to criticise and the right to travel, were denied by the state.

From 1990 on, anyone who was found to have spied for the Stasi, or who was even suspected of doing so, lost his or her job in the civil service or was forced to resign from politics. Various charges were laid against SED leaders, including political responsibility for the deaths at the Wall. Honecker was arrested in 1992 when he returned to Germany from Moscow. In court he accepted responsibility for building the Wall and for the deaths at it but rejected any sense of political or moral guilt. The trial was stopped in 1993 due to illness and he died in exile in Chile in 1994. In 1993, 86-year-old Erich Mielke, head of the Stasi from 1957 until 1989, who had been in court on a range of similar charges, was finally convicted of the murder of two policemen in Berlin in 1931 and sentenced to six years imprisonment. He was released in 1995 and died in Berlin in 2000. In the so-called Politburo Trial, Honecker's successor Egon Krenz was sentenced in 1997 with other leading SED members such as Günter Schabowski, for their political responsibility for the shootings at the Wall. Having exhausted the appeals procedure, Krenz began serving time in January 2000.

These sentences are illustrative of the treatment of the GDR leadership after unification. Yet the first trials, which started in 1991, were aimed at much smaller fish, namely the border guards themselves. In January 1992 a former GDR border guard was sentenced to $3\frac{1}{2}$ years in jail for the killing of 20-year-old Chris Gueffroy at the Wall in February 1989. More convictions followed. By the end of 1995 the authorities had initiated criminal investigations against 15,000 east Germans, of which 8000 were ongoing (Baumann, 2001, p. 1014).

The difficulty initially had been in defining the nature of the crimes committed. Much as some west Germans liked the idea of doing so, it would have been impossible legally and politically to apply west German law retrospectively to actions committed under GDR law. It seemed obvious to all, that those who shot civilians at the Berlin Wall had participated in an unjust order, but the final test would have to be one of legality. In the end, individuals could only be accused of breaching GDR law. That is the procedure that was adopted. The killings at the Wall had been illegal even under GDR law (McAdams, 2001, p. 33).

Some areas proved problematic, especially the issue of spying and its consequences after unification. Though there is little love among ordinary east Germans for Stasi operatives, the case of Markus Wolf was one that provoked resentment at perceived double standards. Wolf was a son of the writer Friedrich Wolf and a committed communist, who had spent his childhood in Russian exile from the Nazis. From 1956 to 1986 he was in charge of Stasi espionage in the West, especially West Germany. He ran countless agents and inflicted some of the greatest espionage defeats on the West in his time. Perversely, his greatest success, the penetration of the West German Chancellor's Office in the early 1970s, led to an event that was undesirable in the GDR, the fall of Willy Brandt (Wolf, 1998, pp. 151–73). After leaving the Stasi in 1986 he became a writer and also supported demands for reform in 1989. In 1993 he was sentenced by a federal court to six years in prison for treason, a charge he denounced as absurd, since he had never been a West German citizen and therefore could not have been a traitor to the Federal Republic while working for the Stasi. In 1995 the BVG upheld this view, making it impossible to convict GDR spies who had only operated in the GDR. Wolf was released, but in 1997 he was sentenced to $3\frac{1}{2}$ years for the false imprisonment of others. It is rather ironic that Wolf could have escaped prosecution by betraying his former colleagues: the US offered to protect him after 1990 in return for just such information, an offer he consistently refused to accept. It is a telling fact, one that adds to the accusation of Western hypocrisy, that no Western spies have been sentenced since unification. Many east Germans simply regard the whole process as victor's justice rather than true justice (McAdams, 2001, p. 7).

Spying on other East Germans was something that tens of thousands of GDR citizens were engaged in. The varied reasons for this have been discussed in Chapter 5. After 1990, Stasi files revealed the names of thousands of those who had spied on friends, neighbours, families and even spouses. One particularly poignant case was that of the civil rights activist Vera Wollenberger, whose husband Knud had reported on her to the Stasi for years. An early activist in the SPD, Ibrahim Böhme, was forced to resign when such information became public. Even some writers, such as Sascha Anderson, who were considered part of the alternative scene in Prenzlauer Berg, a bohemian district of East Berlin, were later revealed to have been Stasi spies. School teachers and other civil servants found to have worked for the Stasi were dismissed.

Yet the cases were not always clear cut. The eminent GDR writer Christa Wolf published a short story in 1990 entitled 'What Remains'. In it a writer, identifiable with Wolf herself, is under surveillance by the Stasi. Wolf was attacked as an opportunist for publishing the text now rather than in GDR times, and matters were subsequently complicated by the revelation that Wolf had herself spied for the Stasi for a brief period around 1960 (G. Carr and G. Paul, in Burns, 1995, p. 339). Yet such criticisms ignored the fact that Wolf had been a progressive writer who had herself been the subject of censorship in the GDR and had also been widely praised for her writing in the West. Until 1990 she, Stefan Heym and others had been praised in the West for their oppositional stance, opposing, for example, the expulsion of Biermann in 1976. The attacks on Wolf were part of a 'widespread tendency to belittle the achievements of writers, film-makers and artists associated with the German Democratic Republic' (A. Goodbody, D. Tate and I. Wallace, in Burns 1995, p. 147). Heym, some of whose novels never appeared in the GDR and whose articles critical of the SED were frequently published in the West before 1990, was ostracised after November 1989 because of his initial support, as a socialist, for the continued existence of the GDR, albeit a radically reformed one.

Another extremely ambiguous case is that of Manfred Stolpe. Stolpe was a member of the Protestant Church of Berlin–Brandenburg who had frequent contacts with the state and the Stasi. In 1990 he joined the SPD and was elected Minister President of Brandenburg after the state elections (it was the only eastern state won by the SPD in 1990). From 1970 to 1989, Stolpe had been regarded by the Stasi as a contact person, an informal collaborator (IM) with the code name 'Secretary'. He vehemently denied that he had worked for the Stasi, claiming that his contacts were entirely in the interests of the Church and had been sanctioned at the highest level. The Church's delicate position in the 1970s and 1980s, when it wished to co-exist with the communist state but was also serving in a protective function towards a range of oppositional groups, made such contacts unavoidable. An investigation by the Brandenburg state parliament in 1992 proved inconclusive. Another case was that of CDU politician Lothar de Maizière, the last Prime Minister of the GDR. In December 1990 he was forced to resign as CDU deputy chairman when accusations were made that he had collaborated with the Stasi. The report, issued in February 1991, showed that he probably was not aware that the Stasi regarded him as an IM. He resigned from politics in September 1991.

The voters of Brandenburg gave their verdict on the Stolpe and related issues when, in 1994, the SPD, led by him, won 54 per cent of the vote in the state election, an increase of 16 per cent. In 1996, state prosecutors finally dropped their investigation against him for lack of evidence.

Many east Germans felt that west Germans were sitting in judgement of them without really understanding the nature of GDR society. There were, it was felt, unrealistic expectations that everyone in the GDR should have been engaged in active opposition to the state, with the result that anyone who had not been was now under suspicion. In addition, as the case of de Maizière illustrated, Stasi files were such that anyone who held regular conversations with another individual could be regarded as an IM without even knowing that their conversation partner was a Stasi operative. Spying, whether on neighbouring states or on neighbours in apartment blocks, was a murky business that could not simply be cleared up on the basis of files. The authorities had set up the 'Gauck Authority' (named after its head, Joachim Gauck) in 1990 in order to allow individuals access to Stasi files held on them, but it seemed that these files were being used to impose a collective air of guilt around all east Germans.

Yet if GDR leaders and those who collaborated with the system were guilty of maintaining an unjust regime and persecuting its citizens, were West German leaders not guilty of complicity in this through their ongoing contacts with, co-operation with and subsidising of the GDR? Should East Germans really carry all the blame for the Cold War and its results? Also, did not West Germany also persecute some of its citizens, for example through the banning and arrests of communists in the 1950s or the employment ban of the 1970s? Why should east Germans have to answer for injustice but not west Germans? (Thomaneck and Niven, 2001, p. 88).

Most westerners were not interested in such considerations. In June 1990 the Kohl government had destroyed 1000 metres of Stasi documents on western politicians and institutions without reviewing their contents. When, in 2000, Gauck offered to turn over 170 metres of files on financial dealings to the inquiry into illegal political payments, Kohl insisted that one should not use documentation from 'that criminal regime' and threatened to go to the BVG to stop their publication (McAdams, 2001, pp. 181–2). Interestingly, some SPD politicians supported him. Kohl had quite happily used documents from the same source to discredit east Germans in the 1990s, but it seemed that what was sauce for the east German goose should not now also be sauce for the west German gander. East Germans allowed themselves a wry smile at the hypocrisy of this attitude.

Similarly, a parliamentary committee investigation in the early 1990s into the GDR Commercial Co-ordination (KoKo) group and its leader, Alexander Schalck-Golodkowski, suggested that Western politicians and industry may have helped Schalck-Golodkowski in his frequently shady transactions aimed at securing hard currency and technology for the GDR. Indeed, it was claimed that the West German Interior Minister, Wolfgang Schäuble, had even illegally offered him some protection from prosecution when he fled the GDR in December 1989. The Committee's final report in 1994 played down suggestions of Western collusion, though the one Green member of the committee submitted a minority report that ruthlessly exposed Western collaboration with KoKo. The federal government promptly put a thirty-year ban on its publication (Thomaneck and Niven, 2001, p. 89). The GDR's past, it seemed, must be dealt with, while West Germany's past needed protecting.

There were ambiguities and inconsistencies aplenty in the attempts to come to terms with the GDR past in the 1990s. For many east Germans the whole process was divisive and hindered their integration into the new Germany. Some have reacted to it by engaging in 'Ostalgie', a nostalgic re-engagement with the securities and memories of their GDR youth. Others have reinforced their sense of east German identity and expressed this politically by voting for the PDS. Nevertheless, many regard the process as having been a necessary reckoning with an undemocratic past that could not have been allowed to simply pass uncriticised into the new Germany. More than ten years after unification, 'participants and observers alike remain divided over the wisdom and efficacy of Bonn's reckoning with the GDR' (McAdams, 2001, p. 6).

Foreigners, Refugees, Asylum Seekers and Ethnic Germans

In 1990 there were 5 million foreigners in West Germany, representing 8 per cent of the population. By 2002, united Germany had almost 8 million non-nationals, or 10 per cent of its population. Throughout the decade the non-German population had increased through the arrival of refugees and asylum seekers, while some came to work. Foreign families also had a higher birth rate than Germans. Turks are the biggest ethnic minority, accounting for 28 per cent of the total.

In the 1990s there was ongoing debate about the role of foreigners in Germany. Partly this was about restricting the numbers of asylum seekers, many of whom were regarded as 'economic migrants', i.e. seeking a better standard of living rather than fleeing persecution. In 1993 the country's asylum laws were tightened, and 1994 saw an immediate 66 per cent drop in the number of asylum seekers. This measure did not end the problem, however.

Some who went to Germany were seen as genuine refugees, for example from the various conflicts in the Balkans, and Germany responded to this by taking in more refugees than any other European country. More than 340,000 people from former Yugoslavia found a temporary home in Germany in the 1990s, compared with just 15,000 in France and 13,000 in Great Britain. These refugees were accepted on a temporary basis only, and after 1994 repatriation of the Croatians began, with a lull in 1995 after renewed fighting there. From 1996 the Bosnians were repatriated. In a similar spirit of humanitarianism a large number of asylum seekers were accepted from Kosovo in 1998. On another issue, agreement was reached in 1995 with the Vietnamese government to repatriate the 40,000 Vietnamese, mostly former contract workers in the GDR, who were still living illegally in Germany. Financial subsidies to Vietnam eased the negotiations.

One other set of immigrants to Germany were the ethnic German resettlers. Since 1913, German nationality law had been based on blood line rather than place of birth. Thus, German citizenship could be claimed by those of ethnic German origin whose ancestors had gone to Transylvania, the Volga region of Russia or any one of numerous places in eastern Europe many centuries before. In the 1990s hundreds of thousands of these 'Germans' applied to migrate to Germany. Frequently they spoke only Russian, since the German connection in the family was tenuous to say the least. Nevertheless, the German authorities welcomed them with open arms and spent vast sums of money integrating them into life in Germany.

By contrast, the German-born children of foreign workers did not receive automatic citizenship. Though a child might have been born in Munich and lived there all its life, even speaking fluent Bavarian dialect, if its parents were Turkish (or Italian, Greek or whatever) then it, too, was regarded by the German authorities as foreign. This was an ongoing subject for debate, with the Greens, the PDS and sections of the SPD and FDP favouring dual citizenship, something vehemently opposed by the CDU and especially the CSU. It was an emotive issue for many, illustrated not least by the campaign to collect signatures against dual citizenship in Hesse, launched by the CDU before the state election in February 1995. The resulting vote swing was just enough to oust the SPD–Green coalition in favour of a CDU–FDP coalition, as a consequence of which the SPD–Green national government also lost its majority in the Bundesrat.

An attempt to change the law was rejected by the Bundestag in March 1998, while Kohl was still Chancellor. In 1999, the new SPD-led government made a second attempt to change the law and, with the help of the FDP, was successful. The law is a compromise, with the German-born children of foreigners now receiving German citizenship at birth if at least one parent has lived in Germany for eight years or has held an unlimited residence permit for at least three years. The child must then choose either German or his/her parents' citizenship before its 23rd birthday.

Nevertheless, the law remains controversial, and a range of measures aimed at reducing the 'foreign' population have been introduced. One prominent case was that of a 14-year-old German-born child of Turkish parents, known as 'Mehmet', who was a repeated offender, with some 61 convictions to his name. The Munich authorities decided that the appropriate punishment was to expel Mehmet and his family to Turkey. They felt that this might have the added benefit of reducing the number of crimes committed by foreigners. The Bavarian Administrative Court declared the expulsion of his parents to be illegal, so when Mehmet committed his 62nd crime he was expelled, as a 14-year-old, to Turkey without his parents. The Federal Supreme Administrative Court finally declared this action illegal in July 2002.

The Nazi Past and Neo-Nazis

Attempts by conservative politicians to prevent the integration of foreigners and to limit their numbers in Germany are one aspect of attitudes to the question of nationality. Another more disturbing aspect has been the rise in violence by neo-Nazis in the 1990s and their re-emergence in regional politics. Racially motivated attacks have been a prominent feature of German political life in the 1990s. Though there have been many large demonstrations against racism, the problem remains, both on the streets and in electoral terms.

After the defeat of the NPD at federal level in 1969 and the subsequent disappearance of the party at state level, neo-Nazis enjoyed no electoral success at state or federal level until 1987. In that year the German People's Union (DVU) took a seat in Bremerhaven in the Bremen state election. In early 1989, the Republikaner took 7.5 per cent in West Berlin state elections and 7.1 per cent in West German elections to the European Parliament in Strasbourg. More success followed through the 1990s, but it has been sporadic, inconsistent and divided between two main parties (see Appendix 4). There has been no pattern of steady success, and certainly nothing comparable to the success enjoyed by populist neo-fascist parties in France, Italy, Belgium and Austria.

More troubling is the level of racist violence that has been perpetrated in Germany since unification. Attacks on foreigners and on refugee hostels have been commonplace and have cost a number of lives. In September 1991, in Hoyerswerda in Saxony, young skinheads attacked refugee hostels for almost a week and were often applauded by the residents for doing so. In the same week a hostel for asylum seekers in Saarlouis on the French border was burned down, killing one Ghanaian and injuring two Nigerians. In August 1992, young neo-Nazis attacked a refugee hostel in Rostock in Mecklenburg and fought running battles with the police while also being applauded by German residents. A Jewish barracks in the Sachsenhausen concentration camp north of Berlin was burned down in September 1992. In November 1992 in Mölln, Schleswig-Holstein, two houses inhabited by Turks were burned and three people killed. The authorities reacted by banning a number of neo-Nazi organisations. The population reacted with protests against the attacks on foreigners. On 8 November, 300,000 people demonstrated in Berlin and there were further protests in a number of German cities in the run-up to Christmas 1992.

Attacks of this nature continued throughout the 1990s, though the number of attacks steadily decreased before rising again in 1998. In 2000 there was a 59 per cent increase in the number of racially motivated attacks, including a 69 per cent increase in the number of anti-Semitic attacks, which made up 9 per cent of the total. Most notable had been the arson attacks on the Lübeck synagogue in 1994 and

1995 and a bomb attack in July 2000 in Düsseldorf, which injured ten, mostly Jewish immigrants from eastern Europe. Again, the authorities reacted with more bans, and called on the courts to consider banning the NPD. There have also been arrests and convictions for murder, inciting racial hatred, and membership of illegal organisations. The population reacted with more demonstrations against racism, notably 200,000 people in Berlin on 9 November 2000, the anniversary of the Nazi *Kristallnacht* pogroms in 1938.

A report on the violence in 1991 showed that two-thirds of the perpetrators were under twenty years of age while only 3 per cent were over thirty (P. Panayi, in Larres, 2001, p. 139). It is also the case that whole areas in the suburbs of east Berlin and provincial east German towns are dominated by neo-Nazi skinheads. Yet electoral success for neo-Nazis has been sparse in the east, and opinion polls consistently show a lower level of anti-Semitism there than in the west, with only slightly higher xenophobia. The success of neo-Nazism in attracting young people in the eastern states is in large part a response to the high rate of unemployment and lack of social facilities to be found there. A lack of information on anti-Semitism and the failure to integrate foreigners in the GDR also contributed in the early 1990s, but this can hardly apply to young people today, who were small children when the Wall fell. Though the actions of neo-Nazis are at times murderous, there appears to be little real ideological underpinning for most young east Germans. The remedy clearly lies in social and economic measures for the east.

It was not just the GDR's past that Germany was forced to confront in the 1990s. Politicians have on occasion made anti-Semitic statements or shown something less than sensitivity towards the Nazi past. In the midst of the CDU financial scandal, which had started with revelations from Hesse, it transpired that two leading CDU politicians there had been illegally transferring money out of Germany to Switzerland and then bringing it back as supposed donations from grateful but anonymous Jewish survivors of Nazism. In 1998 the writer Martin Walser complained that the Holocaust was being instrumentalised to make Germans feel guilty about the past. Making it plain that he regarded it as impossible that any sane person could deny the existence of Auschwitz, he also felt that commemorations had become an almost daily routine, which caused people to switch off, and that this did justice neither to the victims nor to the Germans. The chairman of the Central Council of Jews in Germany, Ignatz Bubis, responded by accusing Walser of 'intellectual arson' and 'latent anti-Semitism', though he withdrew these accusations after the two men met in December 1998. In the summer of 2002, Walser caused another controversy with the publication of a novel, *Death of a Critic*, which included references to the high priest of German literary criticism, Marcel Reich-Ranicki, who is Jewish, that were thought by some to be anti-Semitic. This controversy became linked to a statement by a leading FDP politician, Jürgen Möllemann, who accused the Deputy Chair of the Central Council of Jews, Michel Friedman, of provoking anti-Semitism through his 'arrogant and hateful' manner. The FDP also appeared to be flirting with populist right-wing sentiments by praising Jörg Haider, the former leader of the Austrian Freedom Party, which many regard as a neo-Nazi party.

Daniel Goldhagen's book *Hitler's Willing Executioners* caused major public debate even before the German translation was published in August 1996. Historians of both right and left were critical of many of the book's central tenets, not least the theory that the Holocaust had been the logical conclusion of an exceptionally virulent strain of anti-Semitism inherent in the German people since the Middle Ages but which somehow disappeared in West Germany after 1945 (Niven, 2002, p. 122). Despite the criticisms, the book struck a chord with the German public, showing that many Germans were thinking critically about their past. By contrast, an exhibition on the crimes of the Wehrmacht (German Army) in 1941–4, which toured Germany and Austria between 1995 and 1999, divided the German public as no exhibition had done previously. It challenged the generally accepted truth that the Wehrmacht had simply conducted a military war while the murderous crimes of World War II had been committed by the SS and its adjuncts, by documenting Wehrmacht participation in some of those crimes. Greens, the SPD, the PDS and most of the FDP supported the exhibition, but CDU and especially CSU opposition was so vehement that even some neo-Nazis felt emboldened enough to organise protests. Some sections of the German public were obviously not yet ready to break that particular taboo (Niven, 2002, pp. 143–74).

By contrast, official Germany continued to make amends for the past. In 1998 Volkswagen, Siemens and other companies set up private compensation funds for the forced labourers, mostly from eastern Europe, who had worked for them under the Nazis. In 2000, the federal government created a public fund for this and reached agreement on a total of DM10 billion to be raised, with 50 per cent each from the government and industry. The first payments were made in June 2001. In 2000, Federal President Johannes Rau became the first German president to speak to the Israeli parliament, the Knesset. In his speech, made in German, he asked the Jewish people and Israel to forgive the Germans for the injustices done by them to Jews. As a practical measure, throughout the 1990s Germany gave residence to Jewish Soviet citizens who wished to leave former Soviet republics, whether their ancestry was part-German or not.

The Nazi past remains a difficult subject for Germans. In the GDR a brief period of denazification was followed by concentration, in the classroom, in historiography and in writing, on resistance to Nazism rather than on its passive victims. As a result, most GDR citizens were more aware of heroic communists than of Jews who had suffered. There were few Jews left in the GDR, the GDR refused to pay reparations to Israel or Jewish organisations, and there was little sense of an historic obligation to the Jews.

West Germany had been making restitution since the early 1950s, and united Germany has continued this tradition. Yet financial dealings are just one part of the equation. Another is the attempt to establish normal relations between Israel and Germany on the one hand, and the attempt to have a relationship of equals between Germans and Jews on the other. There are those in both Germany and Israel who do not want the former. Some argue that the magnitude of the Holocaust was such that a 'normal' relationship will never be possible. Nevertheless, many are striving for just that. Such a relationship would include not just the right to support Israel, but also the right to criticise it, as some have done since September 2000 and the latest flaring up of its conflict with the Palestinians. Yet such criticism is rarely seen in Israel in the context of Germany's overall support, both moral and material, for that country.

Similarly, in Germany most wish for a normal relationship with their Jewish neighbours. Sometimes this desire is put rather abruptly and insensitively, as in one letter to *Der Spiegel* in the wake of the Walser and Möllemann controversies in June 2002. The author wrote that when he met a Jewish person he wished to feel that a greeting rather than an apology was expected. Others work in a spirit of co-operation to negotiate both an awareness of the past and an acceptance of the need to live side by side and share the present. They work actively to combat anti-Semitism. Nevertheless, the German–Jewish relationship is one that remains fraught.

Conclusion

Election results are just one reflection of the fact that Germany remains, in many ways, a society divided along east–west lines (see Appendix 5b). The success of the PDS and failures of the Greens and FDP illustrate the political sense of *east* Germanness that persists. 'The PDS has defined itself both as an Eastern party with national aspirations and as a socialist party with some communist membership' (G. R. Kleinfeld, in Merkl, 1999, p. 168). The national aspiration is there, and the PDS now organises throughout Germany, though with very limited success outside the east (it crossed the 5 per cent barrier in west Berlin in the state election of 2001, its first major success in the west). And its socialism, despite the existence of a minority 'Communist Platform' pressure group in the party, is nebulous and probably defined only as radical because the SPD, in common with other social democratic and labour parties in Europe, has shifted firmly to the centre and even to the right. In the east the PDS has become more populist than socialist.

That said, it represents a set of core values that are different from those which developed in western Germany after 1945. There is a greater sense of equality and solidarity with the underdog in the east than in the west. Even those who did not join the SED shared a sense of solidarity with Cuba, Chile, Vietnam and other places that divided opinion in West German society. At home, east Germans have had to cope with higher unemployment and lower wages than in the west continuously since 1990. The mood in 1996 has been described as one of 'post-natal depression' (Kettenacker, 1997, p. 213). By 2003 the mood had hardly changed. Some east Germans, having been liberated from communism, felt as if they had been re-colonised (Geiss, 1997, p. 109). Many still resent what they see as western arrogance towards them, while west Germans retort that east Germans are ungrateful for the vast subsidies that they have received since 1990. Two new terms have passed into the German language as a result: *Besser-Wessis*, which means 'better westerners' but is a play on the word *Besserwisser*, meaning 'know-all', and *Jammer-Ossis*, which means 'complaining easterners'. There is little mutual understanding expressed in these concepts.

One east German response has been 'Ostalgie', a nostalgic attitude to the old GDR. Thus, more than three-quarters of east Germans have come to regard socialism as a good idea that was badly practised in the GDR, a view that would not be shared in most of west Germany (Kettenacker, 1997, p. 221). They have put this into practice by buying memorabilia, organising events and social evenings with GDR music and film, and engaging in campaigns to save what few remnants of GDR life remained after 1990. As one commentator has written, such an attitude would have been unthinkable in respect of Nazism (Allinson, 2002, p. 174). Certainly, such an attitude towards the Third Reich would brand one a Nazi, whereas those who engage in 'Ostalgie' are not necessarily all communists. One celebrated case already referred to was the campaign to save the GDR traffic lights. It is a testament to the lack of real power that east Germans enjoyed after unification that such an inconsequential part of their daily lives should have been the subject of such a campaign.

It is also a testament to the fact that unification was a western take-over rather than a symbiosis that the authorities tried to standardise something as insignificant as traffic lights. To many west Germans unification was not really unification. Rather, it was absorption and assimilation of their eastern countrymen who had been treading the 'wrong' path for forty years. It is telling that even an informed west German commentator can claim that the burden of unifying Germany was 'not just a matter of economic but also of cultural and psychological assimilation' (Kettenacker, 1997, p. 213). Yet many east Germans simply did not wish to be 'assimilated'. Which takes us back to *Besser-Wessis* and *Jammer-Ossis*.

West Germans certainly have longer democratic traditions and a more successful economy than ever existed in the GDR. Most east Germans are happy to accept these benefits. But east Germans brought forty years of very different experiences and values into united Germany in 1990. Theirs has been the greater adaptation, even if west Germany's has been the greater overall financial sacrifice. The two sides are still becoming familiar with each other. On the one hand they now cheer the same national football team and the same athletes, they serve in the same army and navy, and they deal as one nation with Brussels, Washington and the world in general. They have problems with racism in east and west alike, they face similar economic problems, albeit on a greater scale in the east, and they have normal disagreements on education, foreigners and other political issues. Their voting patterns in east and west may show little evidence of converging (W. M. Chandler, in Larres, 2001, pp. 88–106) and they certainly maintain their regional differences, but they are slowly learning to speak the same language again. For all the difficulties that have been confronted and the many which remain, it seems apposite to recall Willy Brandt's words in 1989 and declare that what belongs together is, indeed, growing together.

CONCLUSION:
A NATION ONCE AGAIN?

Germany has always occupied a unique position in Europe, placed as it is between east and west. Until the mid-nineteenth century 'Germany' was still a very loosely defined and uncertain concept. Its name in French until 1871 was *les Allemagnes*, 'the Germanies', reflecting its political division into many states. Long before the partition of Germany in 1949, the Rhineland and most of western Germany had looked to western Europe for cultural ties, while the political capitals to the east, Vienna and Berlin, had looked west for culture but east for land and power. In the nineteenth century, united Germany with Prussia at its head was very much a central rather than a west European power. It saw enemies on all sides, and in 1914 it went to war with them.

By 1945 Germany's *Sonderweg* (special path) had led it to Nazism, World War II and the Holocaust, in that order. Nazism looked neither westwards nor eastwards but inwards for its cultural inspiration. The Germans and other Germanic peoples such as the Scandinavians, the Dutch and the English were seen by Hitler and his followers as a 'master race' that needed to expand eastwards to survive. They also supposedly needed to be 'cleansed' of 'racial impurities', which led ultimately to the building of gas chambers at Auschwitz and the murder of Jews as 'non-Aryans'. Roma and Sinti, gays, Poles, Russians and others also fell victim to this ideology. Germany's murderous narcissism under Nazism led to its defeat by, and ostracisation from, the community of nations.

Its punishment, inflicted almost by chance rather than design, was political division. West Germany was able to pursue a western-orientated policy of building democracy and political ties with France, Great Britain and the new western superpower of the twentieth century, the USA. It established a successful liberal democracy that was never really threatened by extremism, despite the best attempts of neo-Nazis in the 1960s and establishment over-reaction to left-wing terrorism in the 1970s. It gave most of its citizens a high standard of living. In foreign policy it pursued rapprochement and, ultimately, integration with its western neighbours. It co-operated fully as a member of the US-led military alliance, Nato, while also conscious that, because of its recent past, it should not be seen to exercise its full political potential. And, crucially, it attempted to make reparation to the victims of the murderous policies of Nazi Germany. But it was only half a country.

East Germany pursued a very different path. Its integration into the Soviet-led military and economic blocs was completed fairly rapidly in the 1950s. It rejected responsibility for Nazism and refused to pay reparations to the victims of Nazi crimes. Its political system was a nominal multi-party state that was in practice dominated by one party, the communist SED. Economically it was the most successful state in eastern Europe, with the highest standard of living, though this was threatened in the 1980s. Yet its economic successes paled when set beside West Germany's. The common language and family ties meant that, unfortunately for the SED, West Germany rather than eastern Europe was most citizens' ultimate yardstick of economic success. The GDR tried to be a whole country and failed.

The end of the division of Germany created a new set of problems, not least of which was the need to find a new, common identity, both internally and externally. One of the most quoted slogans of 1990 was *Wir sind wieder wer* ('We are somebody again'). Many Germans who had repressed their nationalist feelings while their country was divided now felt that Germany should be less inhibited in the sphere of foreign policy. Others began to challenge what they perceived as Germany's constant need to recall the Holocaust and felt that it was time for Germany to be 'like any other state', something that had not been possible while the country was divided. For some, this undoubtedly meant simply forgetting the Holocaust. For others it means not allowing the past to overshadow everything that is done in the present. It is a difficult problem for Germany, one which successive governments have attempted to approach with sensitivity.

The problem is encapsulated in the desire of many to be less repressed about their Germanness, to once again be a nation. For many, the German 'nation' had never ceased to exist, even when the country was divided. Unification was always the aim of nationalists, who were never content with the slogan 'Two states, one nation'. In its extreme form, this feeling has been expressed in neo-Nazism and xenophobia. Others simply desire to have the same kind of pride in their nationality that their neighbours have. Dissenting voices, such as that of Günter Grass, spoke of a cultural nation that they considered unfit for political unification. Despite such minority views, Germany has been finding its nationalist voice again since unification.

Nevertheless, the events of 1990 brought social disunity in their wake. East Germans did not envisage the attempted assimilation that was to follow. Most did not want simply to become west Germans, though some have tried to do so. They have different memories, a different past, and often different values. Similarly, though they may live in one state, east and west Germans have different voting patterns and different economic circumstances. Easterners are more than 2.5 times as likely to be unemployed as westerners. Even when they have employment they often earn less than their western counterparts. Their young people have fewer job prospects than in the west. Though their average standard of living and material wealth have increased since 1990, east

Germans remain the poor relations in Germany, with a distinctive east German identity. Social unity between east and west is still a long way off.

This has created its own problems, one of which is the massive presence of neo-Nazism and xenophobia in the east, especially among the young. Although this is an all-German problem, and racist attacks are by no means confined to the east, the west has few areas of social deprivation where neo-Nazis and skinheads dominate not just youth clubs but whole residential districts, in the way that they do in the east. Paradoxically, most of the limited electoral success enjoyed by neo-Nazis during the 1990s was in the west.

An east–west divide remains in Germany, some twelve years after unification. The Bundestag election result of 2002 confirmed this, with the PDS again polling well in the east while its electoral support in the west was almost non-existent. Unemployment in Germany as a whole remains high, though the bulk of this burden is borne by the east. And opinion polls consistently show less commitment to and belief in liberal democracy in the east than among west Germans.

Less difficult has been united Germany's attempt to find an international role. Put simply, it has jumped in feet first and made something of a splash. The Bundeswehr was intended to be a purely defensive army for deployment within Nato, but after unification Kohl moved quickly to approve so-called 'out of area deployment', and the BVG approved this in 1994. German troops are now involved in military missions the world over, while Germany took a leading role in promoting political changes such as the break-up of Yugoslavia. In 2002–3 it was every bit as vociferous as France in opposing the US government's desire for war in Iraq. It has also openly criticised its neighbours as never before, as when the Austrian Freedom Party entered government there in 2000. Not all Germans are happy with these developments, since they look to history and fear a united Germany that exercises military muscle. Defenders of the new policy point out, however, that in no instance has Germany acted alone militarily: on Iraq it consistently argued that a UN mandate was required.

Moreover, Germany has continued to pursue a policy of closer European integration, even sacrificing its much beloved DM in January 2002 in favour of the Euro. It also supports EU expansion eastwards. There is little doubt that its motivation lies now, as in the 1950s, at least partly in the desire to promote peace between European nations, though economic interests are undoubtedly also a factor.

Despite the fact that the pre-1990 West German institutions were carried forward almost unchanged into united Germany, the Berlin Republic, as united Germany has been called, is a political institution very different from the Bonn Republic. It is clearly the most populous state in Europe after Russia. It has adopted a new foreign policy that gives it a greater presence in the world as a whole, not just in Europe. Its political centre of gravity has moved away from the sleepy, westward-looking town on the Rhine that is Bonn, towards Berlin, a multi-cultural city of millions that is just forty miles from the Polish border. The children and grandchildren of the Deutschmark and the economic miracle have been joined by 16 million Germans from a very different background. Politics have become more fluid. In 1972 less than 10 per cent of the entire adult population did not vote for the three main parties, CDU/CSU, SPD and FDP, most of that 10 per cent choosing to abstain. In the 1990s and again in 2002 one-third of the population consistently either abstained or voted for other parties (see Appendix 1). The old certainties that were an integral part of life in the 'economic giant but political dwarf' no longer applied.

Is Germany once again going its own way in history, adopting a new *Sonderweg* that could lead ultimately to isolation and perhaps even conflict with its neighbours? This is unlikely. United for only the second time in history, Germany arose from the ruins of two failed political experiments on its soil in the twentieth century. It will probably be many more years before the internal differences and contradictions that derive from the unification process are resolved. But it has become a state that is at peace with its neighbours. Unilateral military action by Germany is unthinkable and does not appear to be on the agenda of any political party other than a few electorally insignificant neo-Nazis. Germans retain a desire, developed after 1945, to be liked by their neighbours, at least in political terms. To paraphrase Margaret Thatcher, they want their neighbours to 'be nice' to them. Germany is once again in the middle of Europe, but not sandwiched between enemies. Rather, it has become a bridgehead for EU expansion to the east in the greatest single attempt at uniting Europe that history has seen. For all its contradictions, united Germany is firmly embedded in the new European order. And for all their problems, the Germans are in the process of becoming a nation once again, united now in peace, not war.

Appendix 1 Federal election results, 1949–2002

Elections to the Bundestag, West Germany, 1949–87; United Germany 1990–2002

Year	CDU/CSU %	Seats	SPD %	Seats	FDP %	Seats	Greens %	Seats	KPD/PDS* %	Seats	Others %	Seats	Total Seats	Turnout %	Cons. 1† %	Cons. 2† %
1949	31.0	139	29.2	131	11.9	52	–	–	5.7	15	22.2	65[1]	402	78.5	72.1	56.6
1953	45.2	243	28.8	151	9.5	48	–	–	2.2	0	14.3	45[2]	487	85.5	83.5	71.4
1957	50.2	270	31.8	169	7.7	41	–	–	–	–	10.3	17[3]	497	87.8	89.7	78.8
1961	45.3	242	36.2	190	12.8	67	–	–	–	–	5.7	0	499	87.7	94.3	82.7
1965	47.6	245	39.3	202	9.5	49	–	–	–	–	3.6	0	496	86.8	96.4	83.7
1969	46.1	242	42.7	224	5.8	30	–	–	–	–	5.4	0	496	86.7	94.6	82.0
1972	44.9	225	45.8	230	8.4	41	–	–	–	–	0.9	0	496	91.1	99.1	90.3
1976	48.6	243	42.6	214	7.9	39	–	–	–	–	0.9	0	496	90.7	99.1	89.9
1980	44.5	226	42.9	218	10.6	53	1.5	0	–	–	0.5	0	497	88.6	98.0	86.8
1983	48.8	244	38.2	193	7.0	34	5.6	27	–	–	0.4	0	498	89.1	94.0	83.8
1987	44.3	223	37.0	186	9.1	46	8.3	42	–	–	1.3	0	497	84.3	90.4	76.2

1990	43.8	319	33.5	239	11.0	79	5.1	8	2.4	17	4.2	0	662	77.8	88.3	68.7
1994	41.5	294	36.4	252	6.9	47	7.3	49	4.4	30	3.5	0	672	79.1	84.8	67.1
1998	35.2	245	40.9	298	6.2	43	6.7	47	5.1	36	5.9	0	669	82.2	82.3	67.7
2002	38.5	248	38.5	251	7.4	47	8.6	55	4.0	2	3.0	0	603	79.1	84.4	66.8

Cons. 1   This is the total for the three parties that have been represented continuously in the Bundestag since 1949, the CDU/CSU, the FDP and the SPD.
Cons. 2   This column is the percentage of the total electorate that voted for the CDU/CSU, SPD and FDP combined at each election. It is obtained by multiplying the turnout and the percentage of the vote obtained by the three parties.

†'Cons.' is short for consolidation of the vote.

*KPD in 1949 and 1953; PDS from 1990.

[1] Including German Party 17, German Reich Party 5, Centre Party 10, Bavarian Party 17, Economic Reconstruction Union 12, and others 4.

[2] Including German Party 15, League of Expellees 27, Centre Party 3.

[3] German Party 17.

Appendix 2 Leading political office-holders, 1949–2002

Governments and heads of state in the Federal Republic, 1949–90, and the GDR, 1949–90

(a) Governments in the Federal Republic (West Germany), 1949–90

Period	Governing Parties	Chancellor	Vice-Chancellor	Foreign Minister
1949–1953	CDU/CSU, FDP, DP	Adenauer (CDU)	Blücher (FDP)	–
1953–1955	CDU/CSU, FDP, DP	Adenauer (CDU)	Blücher (FDP)	Adenauer (CDU)
1955–1957	CDU/CSU, FDP, DP	Adenauer (CDU)	Blücher (FDP)	Brentano (CDU)
1957–1959	CDU/CSU, DP	Adenauer (CDU)	Erhard (CDU)	Brentano (CDU)
1959–1961	CDU/CSU	Adenauer (CDU)	Erhard (CDU)	Brentano (CDU)
1961–1963	CDU/CSU, FDP	Adenauer (CDU)	Erhard (CDU)	Schröder (CDU)
1963–1966	CDU/CSU, FDP	Erhard (CDU)	Mende (FDP)	Schröder (CDU)
1966–1969	CDU/CSU, SPD	Kiesinger (CDU)	Brandt (SPD)	Brandt (SPD)
1969–1974	SPD, FDP	Brandt (SPD)	Scheel (FDP)	Scheel (FDP)
1974–1982	SPD, FDP	Schmidt (SPD)	Genscher (FDP)	Genscher (FDP)
1982–1990	CDU/CSU, FDP	Kohl (CDU)	Genscher (FDP)	Genscher (FDP)

(b) Governments in the Federal Republic (United Germany), 1990–2002

Period	Governing Parties	Chancellor	Vice-Chancellor	Foreign Minister
1990–1992	CDU/CSU, FDP	Kohl (CDU)	Genscher (FDP)	Genscher (FDP)
1992–1993	CDU/CSU, FDP	Kohl (CDU)	Möllemann (FDP)	Kinkel (FDP)
1993–1998	CDU/CSU, FDP	Kohl (CDU)	Kinkel (FDP)	Kinkel (FDP)
1998–	SPD, Greens	Schröder (SPD)	Fischer (Green)	Fischer (Green)

(c) Presidents of the Federal Republic, 1949–2002

1949–1959	Theodor Heuss (FDP)	1979–1984	Karl Carstens (CDU)
1959–1969	Heinrich Lübke (CDU)	1984–1994	Richard von Weizsäcker (CDU)
1969–1974	Gustav Heinemann (SPD)	1994–1999	Roman Herzog (CSU)
1974–1979	Walter Scheel (FDP)	1999–	Johannes Rau (SPD)

(d) Governments of the GDR, 1949–1990

Period	Head of State[1]	Prime Minister[2]	SED General Secretary[3]
1949–1960	Wilhelm Pieck (SED)	Otto Grotewohl (SED)	Walter Ulbricht (SED)
1960–1964	Walter Ulbricht (SED)	Otto Grotewohl (SED)	Walter Ulbricht (SED)
1964–1971	Walter Ulbricht (SED)	Willi Stoph (SED)	Walter Ulbricht (SED)
1971–1973	Walter Ulbricht (SED)	Willi Stoph (SED)	Erich Honecker (SED)
1973–1976	Willi Stoph (SED)	Horst Sindermann (SED)	Erich Honecker (SED)
1976–1989	Erich Honecker (SED)	Willi Stoph (SED)	Erich Honecker (SED)
Autumn 1989	Egon Krenz (SED)	Hans Modrow (SED)	Egon Krenz (SED)
1989–1990	Manfred Gerlach (LDPD)	Hans Modrow (SED–PDS)	–
After 18 March 1990	–	Lothar de Mazière (CDU)	–

[1] From 1949 to 1960 this post was called President. From 1960 to 1990 the post was 'Chairman of the State Council'.

[2] Officially known as 'Chairman of the Council of Ministers'.

[3] From 1954 to 1976 the post was known as 'First Secretary' rather than 'General Secretary'. In December 1990 the party was replaced by the SED–PDS, which later dropped the SED title completely. The post was abolished and replaced by that of 'Chairperson'. This new post had no role in the government of the GDR.

Appendix 3   Federal elections, 1990–2002: East–West comparison

%	1990	1994	1998	2002
Federal Republic				
Turnout	77.8	79.1	82.2	79.1
CDU/CSU	43.8	41.5	35.2	38.5
SPD	33.5	36.4	40.9	38.5
FDP	11.0	6.9	6.2	7.4
B90/Green	5.1	7.3	6.7	8.6
PDS	2.4	4.4	5.1	4.0
Others	4.2	3.5	5.9	3.0
Western Germany				
%	1990	1994	1998	2002
Turnout	78.4	80.7	82.8	80.7
CDU/CSU	44.3	42.1	37.0	40.8
SPD	35.7	37.5	42.3	38.3
FDP	10.6	7.7	7.0	7.6
B90/Green	4.8	7.9	7.3	9.4
PDS	0.3	1.0	1.2	1.1
Others	4.3	3.8	5.2	2.8
Eastern Germany				
%	1990	1994	1998	2002
Turnout	75.5	73.4	80.0	72.9
CDU/CSU	41.8	38.5	27.3	28.3
SPD	24.3	31.5	35.1	39.7
FDP	12.9	3.5	3.3	6.4
B90/Green	6.1	4.3	4.1	4.7
PDS	11.1	19.8	21.6	16.9
Others	3.8	2.4	8.6	4.0

Source: Statistics for 1990 from Grosser et al. 1996, p. 402. My calculations for 1994–2002 are based on statistics provided by Federal Electoral Commission at www.bundeswahlleiter.de. These figures are based on the borders that existed until 3 October 1990. Statistics frequently given by other sources, such as 9.9% for the PDS in the East in 1990, are mistakenly based on results from the 'five new eastern states' without East Berlin. In 2002, because two Berlin constituencies (out of 299 in the whole country) straddled the old east–west divide, I have estimated percentages based on 1998 results and 2002 changes elsewhere. I estimate that my calculations are correct to within 0.1%.

Appendix 4   Neo-Nazi electoral successes since 1945

Neo-Nazi successes (where seats were won) at state and European elections since 1945

Year	State	Party	%
1945–1968			
1951	Lower Saxony	Socialist Reich Party	11.0
1951	Lower Saxony	German Reich Party	2.2[*]
1951	Bremen	Socialist Reich Party	7.7
1955	Lower Saxony	German Reich Party	3.8[*]
1959	Rhineland-Palatinate	German Reich Party	5.1
1963	Bremen	German Party[**]	5.2
1966	Hesse	NPD	7.9
1966	Bavaria	NPD	7.4
1967	Rhineland-Palatinate	NPD	6.9
1967	Schleswig-Holstein	NPD	5.8
1967	Lower Saxony	NPD	7.0
1967	Bremen	NPD	8.8
1968	Baden-Württemberg	NPD	9.8
1987–2003			
1987	Bremen	DVU	3.4[***]
1989	West Berlin	Republikaner	7.5
1989	European Parliament	Republikaner	7.1
1991	Bremen	DVU	6.2
1992	Baden-Württemberg	Republikaner	10.9
1992	Schleswig-Holstein	DVU	6.3
1996	Baden-Württemberg	Republikaner	9.1
1998	Saxony-Anhalt	DVU	12.9
1999	Bremen	DVU	3.0[***]
1999	Brandenburg	DVU	5.3
2003	Bremen	DVU	2.3[***]

[*] The 5% threshold did not apply in this election.

[**] The German Party that re-formed in 1962 was a neo-Nazi party that became part of the NPD. The party that dissolved in 1959 had been a conservative nationalist party in coalition with the CDU. For that reason the successes of the 1950s are not included in this table.

[***] The 5% threshold is applied separately to the cities of Bremen and Bremerhaven, which together constitute the state of Bremen. In 1987, 1999 and 2003 the DVU crossed the threshold in Bremerhaven but not Bremen.

Appendix 5 Party success at state level

(a) State election results, 1989–92

State/year	Year	CDU	SPD	FDP	Gr.	PDS	Other	Government
Western states								
Baden-Württemberg	1992	x	x	x	x		x[1]	CDU/SPD
Bavaria	1990	x	x	x	x			CSU
Bremen	1991	x	x	x	x		x[2]	SPD/FDP/Gr
Hamburg	1991	x	x	x	x			SPD
Hesse	1991	x	x	x	x			SPD/Green
Lower Saxony	1990	x	x	x	x			SPD/Green
North Rhine-Westphalia	1990	x	x	x	x			SPD
Rhineland-Palatinate	1991	x	x	x	x			SPD/FDP
Saarland	1990	x	x	x				SPD
Schleswig-Holstein	1992	x	x	x			x[2] x[3]	SPD
West Berlin	1989	x	x		x		x[1]	SPD/AL
Berlin	1990	x	x	x	x	x		CDU/SPD
Eastern states								
Brandenburg	1990	x	x	x	x	x		SPD/FDP/Gr
Mecklenburg-West Pomer.	1990	x	x	x		x		CDU/FDP
Saxony	1990	x	x	x	x	x		CDU
Saxony-Anhalt	1990	x	x	x	x	x		CDU/FDP
Thuringia	1990	x	x	x	x	x		CDU/FDP

[1] Republikaner.

[2] DVU (German People's Union).

[3] SSW (Party of the South Schleswig Danish Minority).

Appendix

(b)   State election results, 1999–May 2003

State/year	Year	CDU	SPD	FDP	Gr.	PDS	Other	Government
Western States								
Baden-Württemberg	2001	x	x	x	x			CDU/FDP
Bavaria	1999	x	x		x			CSU
Bremen	2003	x	x	x	x		x[1]	SPD/CDU
Hamburg	2001	x	x	x	x		x[2]	CDU/PRO/FDP
Hesse	2003	x	x	x	x			CDU
Lower Saxony	2003	x	x	x	x			CDU/FDP
North Rhine-Westphalia	2000	x	x	x	x			SPD/Green
Rhineland-Palatinate	2001	x	x	x	x			SPD/FDP
Saarland	1999	x	x					CDU
Schleswig-Holstein	2000	x	x	x	x		x[3]	SPD/Green
Berlin	2001	x	x	x	x	x		SPD/PDS
Eastern States								
Brandenburg	1999	x	x			x	x[1]	SPD/CDU
Mecklenburg-W. Pomer.	2002	x	x			x		SPD/PDS
Saxony	1999	x	x			x		CDU
Saxony-Anhalt	2002	x	x	x		x		CDU/FDP
Thuringia	1999	x	x			x		CDU

[1]   DVU (German People's Union).

[2]   Schill Party (Party of Law and Order).

[3]   SSW (Party of the South Schleswig Danish Minority).

Notes

In Bavaria the CSU operates in place of the CDU.

In Berlin, Bremen and Hamburg the Greens were formerly called the 'Alternative List' (AL) or 'Green Alternative List' (GAL).

BIBLIOGRAPHY

Alcock, Antony, *A Short History of Europe* (Basingstoke, 1998).

Allinson, Mark, *Politics and Popular Opinion in East Germany, 1945–1968* (Manchester, 2000).

Allinson, Mark, *Germany and Austria, 1814–2000* (London and New York, 2002).

Alter, Peter, *The German Question and Europe: A History* (London, 2000).

Alter, Reinhard and Peter Monteath (eds), *Rewriting the German Past: History and Identity in the New Germany* (Atlantic Highlands, NJ, 1997).

Anderson, Jeffrey, *German Unification and the Union of Europe* (Cambridge, 1999).

Ardagh, John, *Germany and the Germans* (Harmondsworth, 1995).

Arendt, Hannah, *Eichmann in Jerusalem: A Report on the Banality of Evil* (Harmondsworth, 1994).

Bahro, Rudolf, *The Alternative in Eastern Europe* (London, 1978).

Balfour, Michael, *Germany: The Tides of Power* (London, 1992).

Baring, Arnulf (ed.), *Germany's New Position in Europe* (Oxford and Providence, NJ, 1994).

Barker, Peter (ed.), *The GDR and its History: Rückblick und Revision* (Amsterdam and Atlanta, GA, 2000).

Baumann, Wolf-Rüdiger et al., *Fischer Chronik Deutschland* (Frankfurt/Main, 2001).

Bedürftig, Friedemann, *Taschenlexikon Deutschland nach 1945* (Munich, Zurich, 1998).

Berghahn, V. R., *Modern Germany* (Cambridge, 1982).

Bibliography

Boa, Elizabeth and Rachel Palfreyman, *Heimat, A German Dream: Regional Loyalties and National Identity in German Culture, 1890–1990* (Oxford, 2000).

Brandt, Willy, *A Peace Policy for Europe* (London, 1969).

Brentano, Heinrich von, *Germany and Europe* (London, 1964).

Burns, Rob (ed.), *German Cultural Studies: An Introduction* (Oxford, 1995).

Childs, David, *The GDR: Moscow's German Ally* (London, 1983).

Costabile-Heming, Carol Anne, Rachel J. Halverson and Kristie A. Foell (eds), *Textual Responses to German Unification* (Berlin and New York, 2001).

Crawley, Aidan, *The Rise of Western Germany, 1945–1972* (London, 1973).

Dalton, Russell J., *The New Germany Votes* (Oxford, 1993).

Dedman, Martin J., *The Origins and Development of the European Union, 1945–95* (London and New York, 1996).

Dennis, Mike, *German Democratic Republic* (London and New York, 1988).

Dennis, Mike, *The Rise and Fall of the German Democratic Republic, 1945–1990* (Harlow, 2000).

Deutscher, Isaac, *Stalin* (Harmondsworth, 1979).

Deutschkron, Inge, *Israel und die Deutschen* (Cologne, 1991).

Durrani, Osman, Colin Good and Kevin Hilliard (eds), *The New Germany: Literature and Society after Unification* (Sheffield, 1995).

Ermarth, Michael (ed.), *America and the Shaping of German Society, 1945–1955* (Oxford and Providence, NJ, 1993).

Evans, Richard J., *In Hitler's Shadow: West German Historians and the Attempt to Escape from the Nazi Past* (London and New York, 1989).

Frank, Mario, *Walter Ulbricht. Eine deutsche Biografie* (Berlin, 2001).

Fraser, T. G., *The Arab–Israeli Conflict* (Basingstoke, 1995).

Fritsch-Bournazel, Renata, *Confronting the German Question: Germans on the East–West Divide* (Oxford, 1988).

Fritsch-Bournazel, Renata, *Europe and German Unification* (New York and Oxford, 1992).

Fulbrook, Mary, *Germany, 1918–1990: The Divided Nation* (London, 1991).

Fulbrook, Mary, *The Two Germanies, 1945–1990: Problems of Interpretation* (Basingstoke, 1992).

Fulbrook, Mary, *Anatomy of a Dictatorship: Inside the GDR, 1949–1989* (Oxford, 1995).

Fulbrook, Mary, *German National Identity after the Holocaust* (Cambridge, 1999).

Garton Ash, Timothy, *We Are the People* (London, 1990).

Garton Ash, Timothy, *In Europe's Name: Germany and the Divided Continent* (London, 1994).

Gaus, Günter, *Wo Deutschland liegt* (Hamburg, 1983).

Geiss, Immanuel, *The Question of German Unification, 1806–1996* (London and New York, 1997).

Glaessner, Gert-Joachim, *The Unification Process in Germany: From Dictatorship to Democracy* (London, 1992).

Glaessner, Gert-Joachim (ed.), *Germany after Unification* (Amsterdam and Atlanta, GA, 1996).

Glees, Anthony, *Reinventing Germany: German Political Developments since 1945* (Oxford, 1996).

Görtemaker, Manfred, *Unifying Germany, 1989–1990* (Basingstoke, 1994).

Grass, Günter, *Two States – One Nation? The Case against German Reunification* (London, 1990).

Grieder, Peter, *The East German Leadership, 1946–1973* (Manchester, 1999).

Grosser, Alfred, *Germany in Our Time* (Harmondsworth, 1974).

Grosser, Dieter et al. (eds), *Bundesrepublik und DDR, 1969–1990* (Stuttgart, 1996).

Hahn, H.-J. (ed.), *Germany in the 1990s* (Amsterdam and Atlanta, GA, 1995).

Hahn, H.-J., *Education and Society in Germany* (Oxford and New York, 1998).

Harenberg, Bodo (ed.), *Aktuell 2003* (Dortmund, Harenberg, 2002).

Herf, Jeffrey, *Divided Memory: The Nazi Past in the Two Germanys* (Cambridge, MA, 1997).

Hilton, Christopher, *The Wall: The People's Story* (Stroud, 2002).

Hobsbawm, E. J., *Nations and Nationalism since 1780* (Cambridge, 1991).

Hobsbawm, E. J., *Age of Extremes: The Short Twentieth Century, 1914–1991* (London, 1995).

Hobsbawm, E. J., *On History* (London, 1998).

Ignatieff, Michael, 'Germany', in Michael Ignatieff, *Blood and Belonging: Journeys into the New Nationalism* (London, 1993).

James, Harold and Marla Stone (eds), *When the Wall Came Down: Reactions to German Unification* (London and New York, 1992).

Bibliography

James, Peter (ed.), *Modern Germany* (London, 1998).

Jarausch, Konrad H., *The Rush to German Unity* (Oxford, 1994).

Jarausch, Konrad H., *Die unverhoffte Einheit 1989–1990* (Frankfurt/ Main, 1995).

Jarausch, Konrad H. (ed.), *After Unity: Reconfiguring German Identities* (Providence, NJ, and Oxford, 1997).

Jarausch, Konrad H. and Volker Gransow (eds), *Uniting Germany: Documents and Debates, 1944–1993* (Providence, NJ, and Oxford, 1994).

Jones, Alun, *The New Germany* (Chichester, 1995).

Joppke, Christian, *East German Dissidents and the Revolution of 1989* (Basingstoke, 1995).

Keithly, David M., *The Collapse of East German Communism* (Westport, CT, and London, 1992).

Kettenacker, Lothar, *Germany since 1945* (Oxford, 1997).

Kolinsky, Eva, *Women in 20th-century Germany: A Reader* (Manchester, 1995).

Kolinsky, Eva and Wilfried van der Will (eds), *Modern German Culture* (Cambridge, 1998).

Kramer, A., *The West German Economy* (Oxford, 1991).

Krisch, Henry, *German Politics under Soviet Occupation* (New York, 1974).

Lappin, Elena (ed.), *Jewish Voices, German Words: Growing Up Jewish in Postwar Germany and Austria* (North Haven, CT, 1994).

Larres, Klaus, 'A Widow's Revenge: Willy Brandt's Ostpolitik, Neo-Conservatism and the German Federal Election of 1994', *German Politics*, 4 (1995), vol. 1, pp. 42–63.

Larres, Klaus (ed.), *Germany since Unification: The Development of the Berlin Republic* (Basingstoke, 2001).

Lee, Stephen J., *The Weimar Republic* (London and New York, 1998).

Lewis, Derek and John R. P. McKenzie (eds), *The New Germany* (Exeter, 1995).

Lewis, Rand C., *A Nazi Legacy: Right-Wing Extremism in Postwar Germany* (New York, 1991).

Maier, Charles S., *Dissolution: The Crisis of Communism and the End of East Germany* (Princeton, NJ, 1997).

Major, Patrick and Jonathan Osmond (eds), *The Workers' and Peasants' State: Communism and Society in East Germany under Ulbricht, 1945–71* (Manchester, 2002).

Marsh, David, *Germany and Europe: The Crisis of Unity* (London, 1994).

Bibliography

Marshall, Barbara, *Willy Brandt* (London, 1990).

McAdams, A. James, *Germany Divided: From the Wall to Unification* (Princeton, NJ, 1993).

McAdams, A. James, *Judging the Past in Unified Germany* (Cambridge, 2001).

McFalls, Laurence and Lothar Probst (eds), *After the GDR: New Perspectives on the Old GDR and the Young Länder* (Amsterdam and Atlanta, NJ, 2001).

Merkl, Peter H. (ed.), *The Federal Republic of Germany at Fifty: The End of a Century of Turmoil* (Basingstoke, 1999).

Milfull, John (ed.), *Why Germany?* (Oxford, 1993).

Mommsen, Hans, *The Legacy of the Holocaust and German National Identity* (New York, 1999).

Neven-du Mont, Jürgen, *After Hitler: Report from a West German City* (Harmondsworth, 1974).

Nicholls, A. J., *The Bonn Republic: West German Democracy, 1945–1990* (Harlow, 1997).

Nickel, Erich, *Die BRD. Ein historischer berblick* (Berlin, 1989).

Niehuss, Merith and Ulrike Lindner (eds), *Deutsche Geschichte in Quellen und Darstellung*, vol. 10 (Stuttgart, 1998).

Niven, Bill, *Facing the Nazi Past: United Germany and the Legacy of the Third Reich* (London, 2002).

O'Doherty, Paul, 'The GDR and its Jewish Citizens', in Paul O'Doherty, *The Portrayal of Jews in GDR Prose Fiction* (Amsterdam and Atlanta, GA, 1997), pp. 23–74.

Oppen, Karoline von, *The Role of the Writer in the Unification of Germany, 1989–1990* (New York, 2000).

Ostermann, Christian F., *Uprising in East Germany, 1953* (Budapest, 2001).

Ostow, Robin, *Jews in Contemporary East Germany* (Basingstoke, 1989).

Parkes, Stuart, *Understanding Contemporary Germany* (London and New York, 1997).

Paterson, William E. and David Southern, *Governing Germany* (Oxford, 1992).

Pearson, Raymond, *The Rise and Fall of the Soviet Empire* (Basingstoke, 1998).

Peterson, Edward N., *The Secret Police and the Revolution: The Fall of the German Democratic Republic* (Westport, CT, 2002).

Pittman, Avril, *From Ostpolitik to Reunification: West German–Soviet Political Relations since 1974* (Cambridge, 1992).

Bibliography

Pond, Elizabeth, *Beyond the Wall: Germany's Road to Reunification* (Washington, DC, 1993).

Pritchard, Gareth, *The Making of the GDR, 1945–53: From Antifascism to Stalinism* (Manchester, 2000).

Radice, Giles, *The New Germans* (London, 1995).

Rapaport, Lynn, *Jews in Germany after the Holocaust* (Cambridge, 1997).

Reading, Brian, *The Fourth Reich* (London, 1995).

Reid, J. H., *Writing without Taboos* (Oxford, 1990).

Sandford, Gregory W., *From Hitler to Ulbricht: The Communist Reconstruction of East Germany, 1945–46* (Manchester, 2000).

Schoenbaum, David and Elizabeth Pond, *The German Question and Other German Questions* (Basingstoke, 1996).

Schwarz, Hans-Peter, *Konrad Adenauer*, vol. 1 (Providence, NJ, and Oxford, 1995).

Schwarz, Hans-Peter, *Konrad Adenauer*, vol. 2 (Providence, NJ, and Oxford, 1997).

Schweitzer, Carl Christoph, *Politics and Government in the Federal Republic of Germany* (Leamington Spa, 1994).

Sereny, Gitta, *The German Trauma: Experiences and Reflections, 1938–2000* (Harmondsworth, 2000).

Shirer, William L., *Berlin Diary* (New York, 1995).

Sikorski, Werner and Rainer Laabs, *Checkpoint Charlie and the Wall: A Divided People Rebel* (Berlin, 1998).

Simmons, Michael, *The Unloved Country: A Portrait of East Germany Today* (London, 1989).

Smith, Dennis B., *Japan since 1945* (Basingstoke, 1995).

Smith, Eric Owen, *The German Economy* (London and New York, 1994).

Staab, Andreas, *National Identity in Eastern Germany* (Westport, CT, 1998).

Staritz, Dietrich, *Geschichte der DDR* (Frankfurt/Main, 1996).

Steele, Jonathan, *Socialism with a German Face* (London, 1977).

Stratenschulte, Eckart D., *Kleine Geschichte Berlins* (Munich, 1997).

Taylor, A. J. P., *The Course of German History* (London, 1945).

Thatcher, Margaret, *The Downing Street Years* (London, 1995).

The Judgement of Nuremberg (London, 1999).

Thierse, Wolfgang, Spittmann-Rühle, Ilse, and Kuppe, Johannes L. (eds), *Zehn Jahre Deutsche Einheit. Eine Bilanz* (Opladen, 2000).

Bibliography

Thomaneck, J. K. A. and Bill Niven, *Dividing and Uniting Germany* (London, 2001).

Thränhardt, Dietrich, *Geschichte der Bundesrepublik Deutschland* (Frankfurt, 1996).

Thumfahrt, Alexander, *Die politische Integration Ostdeutschlands* (Frankfurt, 2002).

Uexküll, Gösta von, *Adenauer*, 8th edn (Reinbek, 1998).

Verheyen, Dirk, *The German Question* (Boulder, CO, 1991).

Wallace, Ian (ed.), *The GDR in the 1980s* (Dundee, 1984).

Wasserstein, Bernard, 'Three Germanies and the Jews', in Bernard Wasserstein, *Vanishing Diaspora* (Harmondsworth, 1997).

Watson, Alan, *The Germans* (London, 1995).

Watts, Meredith W., *Xenophobia in United Germany* (Basingstoke, 1997).

Webb, Adrian, *The Longman Companion to Germany since 1945* (London, 1998).

Weber, Hermann, *DDR. Grundriss der Geschichte 1945–1990* (Hanover, 1991).

Wehling, Hans-Georg (ed.), *Die deutschen Länder* (Opladen, 2002).

Williamson, D. G., *Germany from Defeat to Partition, 1945–1963* (Harlow, 2001).

Wolf, Markus, *Memoirs of a Spymaster* (London, 1998).

Young, John W., *Cold War Europe, 1945–1991* (London, 1996).

Zimmer, Matthias (ed.), *Germany: Phoenix in Trouble?* (Edmonton, 1997).

Internet Sources

American Institute for Contemporary German Studies: www.aicgs.org

Conference of University Teachers of German in Great Britain and Ireland: www.cutg.ac.uk (contains hundreds of links)

East German Studies Association: www.calvin.edu/cas/egsg/

Federal Statistics Agency: www.destatis.de

German History Society: members.lycos.co.uk/GHS/

The Bundesrat: www.bundesrat.de

The Bundestag: www.bundestag.de (including links to political parties)

The Federal Government: www.bundesregierung.de

INDEX

Index

Balkans, 212, 233
Baltic, 23, 180, 212
Bank of German States (BDL),
　30–1, 42
Barschel, Uwe, 156
Barthel, Kurt, 47
Barzel, Rainer, 115–16
Basic Law, 33, 70, 106, 201–2
Basic Treaty, 113–14, 116–19
Bavaria, 1, 7, 9–10, 28, 51, 70,
　84, 93, 173–4, 196, 210,
　224–5, 234–5
Bavarian Administrative Court,
　235
Bavarian People's Party, 9
Becker, Jurek, 134, 167–8
Beijing, 186
Belgium, 2, 25, 140, 223, 236
Belsen, 159
Ben Gurion, David, 55 6
Benelux, 29, 57–9, 214
Berg, Hermann von, 167
Berlin, 1, 5–10, 15, 31–3, 37, 41,
　46–7, 49–51, 64–8, 70,
　72–4, 82–4, 88, 95–9,
　107–8, 110, 113–14, 118,
　125, 127–8, 134–5, 138,
　145, 153, 161, 165, 167,
　169–70, 176–8, 181, 183–7,
　189–90, 199–201, 203, 206,
　208, 211, 221–5, 227–30,
　236–7, 241, 244, 248
　Alexanderplatz, 187
　Allied Kommandatura, 6
　Berlin Blockade, 30–2, 65
　Berlin Ultimatum, 66
　Berlin Wall, 37, 64–7, 73–4,
　　82, 125, 138, 177–8,
　　189–91, 227–8, 237
　Brandenburg Gate, 189

Free University, 95–6
Friedrichshain, 225
Gethsemane Church, 187
Humboldt University, 49, 166
Mitte, 225
Prenzlauer Berg, 229
Zion Church, 170, 187
Berufsverbot see Employment Ban
Bevin, Ernest, 22
Bible, the, 169
Biedenkopf, Kurt, 209
Biermann, Wolf, 86, 88, 133–4,
　166–7, 229
Bild (newspaper), 98, 178
Bismarck, Otto von, 2
Black September, 122, 127
Bloch, Ernst, 49, 97
Blüm, Norbert, 115, 150
BMW, 219
BND *see* Federal Intelligence
　Service
Böhme, Ibrahim, 229
Böll, Heinrich, 42, 97, 128
Bolsheviks, 7, 18, 24, 160
Bonn, 57, 61, 69, 79, 114, 118,
　128, 140–1, 144, 147, 153,
　176–7, 192, 197–200, 202,
　224, 248
Bormann, Martin, 11
Bosnia, 213, 233
Boutros Ghali, Boutros, 213
Brandeis University, 97
Brandenburg, 1, 13, 174, 176,
　203, 221–2, 224–5, 230
Brandt, Willy, 66, 68, 73–4, 78,
　83–5, 91–2, 101–7, 112–18,
　120, 122–3, 126, 130–5,
　147–9, 153, 155, 174, 177,
　189, 196, 228, 243
Brauchitsch, Eberhard von, 156

Index

Index

Index